P9-DMP-828

Breathing under Water

Breathing under Water

and Other East European Essays

STANISLAW BARANCZAK

HARVARD UNIVERSITY PRESS
Cambridge, Massachusetts, and London, England   1990

This book is printed on acid-free paper, and its binding
materials have been chosen for strength and durability.

Library of Congress Cataloging-in-Publication Data

Baranczak, Stanisław.
   Breathing under water and other East European essays / Stanisław
Baranczak.
      p.   cm.
   ISBN 0–674–08125–0 (alk. paper)
      1. Europe, Eastern—Intellectual life—20th century.
   2. Politics and literature—Europe, Eastern.
   3. Europe, Eastern—Politics and government—1945–
   4. East European literature—20th century—History and criticism.
   I. Title.
DJK50.B36   1990
947–dc20   89–49648
                                                                    CIP

Pages 253–254 constitute an extension of the copyright page.

Designed by Gwen Frankfeldt

Contents

Despair and Order

Fiction and Action

Rhyme and Time

Distance and Dialogue

Breathing under Water

Breathing under Water

If time extends into the future, then perhaps it would be logical to have not only "time capsules" preserving the past but also "future capsules" revealing what lies ahead. Instead of putting a copy of yesterday's newspaper in a watertight container for the benefit of our descendants (who otherwise might not believe that mankind could have been so foolish), we ourselves could receive from time to time a similar container with a newspaper that *will* be printed years from now, on some especially interesting day in the future. I wonder, for example, what my reaction would have been had I picked up today's newspaper, dated August 25, 1989, from my doorstep seven years ago, just months after the imposition of martial law in Poland and more than a year after my arrival in this country. What would I have made of the news about a million people forming a human chain in Lithuania, Latvia, and Estonia to demand independence for their Soviet-annexed countries? About thousands of East Germans fleeing to the West across Hungary's newly opened frontier with Austria? About Hungary's own dismantling of the Communist monopoly of power? About unsubdued demonstrations on the streets of Prague? About something called *perestroika* apparently under way in the Soviet Union itself, with Andrei Sakharov serving as a parliamentary deputy, Alexander Solzhenitsyn's *The Gulag Archipelago* being printed in a literary journal, and Soviet miners going on strike? And above all, about the election of a Solidarity activist as prime minister and the formation of Poland's first non-Communist government since World War Two?

What would I have said then, in 1982, when Poland's—and Eastern Europe's—hopes seemed to be crushed once again by brutal suppression, the only product of Communism that appeared never affected by mismanagement and always available in abundance? What would I have done with this foreknowledge one morning in May 1982, as I was preparing to give a speech on Poland at a Boston "conference of Soviet and Eastern European dissidents" called "Writers in Exile"?

There may be only one answer: I would never have believed that these developments could happen. At least not in such a not-so-distant future. I would have suspected some crude hoax, or a clumsy gesture of support on the part of a naïve well-wisher: after all, this is a free country, and anyone can conceive and print a fake issue of a newspaper if he so pleases. Yet had I believed or not, I would certainly have proceeded with my speech without changing a single word in it. This is what I said on that occasion, in May 1982.[1]

"In the 1950s Stanislaw Lem, a prominent Polish writer, wrote a grotesque science fiction story set on a certain distant planet. Its inhabitants, otherwise completely humanlike creatures, conformed to a social system that forced everyone to live his life in water—preferably under water. Bubbling sounds were the only acceptable means of communication, the official propaganda emphasized the advantages of being wet, and occasional breathing above water was considered almost a political offense— although everyone had to do it from time to time. And of course, the whole population suffered from rheumatism and dreamed all the time about some dry place to live. But the propaganda still maintained that the fishlike way of life, especially breathing under water, was the highest ideal toward which every citizen should strive.

"I can't help recalling that short story whenever I heard the word 'dissident.' Does someone who simply wants a breath of fresh air really deserve to be called a dissident? Should someone who simply can't live under water, his human lungs not allowing him to do so, necessarily be described that way?

"And let's consider another possible situation. Suppose that one day the whole population of that fictional planet decided to live on dry ground, and only the rulers, the propaganda people, and the police still preferred to stay in water and to bubble their absurd slogans. Who would be a dissident then? As everybody knows, the word 'dissident' comes from the Latin *dissidere*, which means to sit apart. This has at least two

2

connotations: someone who sits apart behaves abnormally, opposes the behavior considered typical and normal; or he and other people like him constitute a minority who sit apart from a supposedly much larger group. If we accept these two implied meanings, it becomes quite obvious that at least one of them cannot be applied to the so-called dissident in totalitarian countries. As many Eastern European writers have pointed out (I have especially in mind Václav Havel from Czechoslovakia), the so-called dissidents in such countries may of course constitute a minority, and they usually do; but on the other hand, they are the only normal people around. To put it more precisely, against the background of the rest of society, they seem to be the only human beings who want to live like human beings. The simplest definition, then, of a dissident writer is a writer who wants to practice his profession in a normal way—that is, without submitting his work to any control or interference. The simplest definition of a dissident scholar is a scholar who puts truth above propaganda—that is, who behaves normally, as every scholar actually should.

"When I look back on my last decade spent in Poland, I can describe the atmosphere only as a gradual return of the society to some priceless normality. I had a chance to participate in that process; and my literary experiences during that period, which consisted of contributing to the creation of the independent publishing movement, seemed to me first of all a defense of normal, human behavior against the faceless absurdity of state censorship. The point was that a word was to be a word and a value a value; that nothing was to be deformed, concealed, or falsified. It wasn't a matter of some lofty principles. It was, quite simply, a matter of its being physically impossible to breathe under water.

"I think the same can be said about everything else that has happened in Poland since the mid-seventies. At the beginning, the situation was quite typical of all totalitarian countries: a small group of normal people—so-called dissidents—surrounded by the majority of others who still preferred a way of life contrary to the human condition. Later, in 1980, something extremely atypical happened: the birth of a ten-million-strong phenomenon called Solidarity meant in practical terms that the word 'dissident' ceased to make any sense at all. In other words, not only the first but also the second connotation of that term was no longer valid. What happened in August 1980 consisted of a massive return of the whole society to normality. In that sense, all attempts to interpret the phenomenon according to traditional categories have been inaccurate and incomplete. Solidarity is not—or not only—a form of class struggle, as Western leftists would like it to be. And it's not only a form of antitotalitarian protest, as liberals would interpret it. And it's not only a national and religious revival, as right-wing conservatives would prefer to have it. It's all that together, or, to put it more simply, it's a way from absurdity to normality—the struggle for a life in which a butcher shop would sell real meat and not garbage, in which teachers would teach the real history of Poland and not lies, and in which writers would write real books and not pieces of propaganda. What happens today, and what is evolving into an amazing resistance against machine guns, water cannons, and loyalty oaths, is merely a result of the fact that it's impossible for people to go back under water once they have tasted the fresh air of freedom and truth.

"It's extremely important that the West should finally understand what has really been happening in Poland between 1980 and today. Because the West, in my opinion, still doesn't understand: we continue to hear about the supposed romanticism of Solidarity and the realism of the generals—as if there were anything irrational about Solidarity's vision of a rationally functioning society; as if it weren't those very generals who chose the path of sheer political lunacy, who waged war against the entire nation without any positive program. The same thing can be said about the question still raised by Western political observers: Didn't Solidarity go too far? Didn't Solidarity bring defeat upon itself?

"It would be too easy to dismiss these questions as a sign of hypocrisy, as an excuse for a lack of sympathy with Solidarity. In fact, the problem posed by these questions is important, and it demands some serious explanations and answers. However, let's notice one highly symptomatic thing: everybody in the West asks whether Solidarity went too far; nobody asks whether General Jaruzelski went too far. Despite all its sympathy and compassion, the West seems to accept silently the basic assumption of Eastern propaganda: that the Communist authorities are always right when they're defending their monopoly of power. *They* never go too far, even when they declare a state of war against their own people. It's the people who go too far and who quite necessarily bring defeat upon themselves each time they demand some clean air to breathe—some of those basic liberties the West enjoys.

"But as I stated before, I don't think that the very fact of asking that question is only and always a symptom of hypocrisy and, in an indirect way, of admitting that the world *is* divided into two spheres, only one of which has a right to enjoy freedom and democracy. The problem is more serious. The question of whether Solidarity went too far reflects a very basic difference between Western and Eastern ways of political thinking. Assuming that it was possible to stop halfway, the West simply doesn't understand that there was *no* halfway—there was no established point prior to which the process of liberation was safe and beyond which it was dangerous. In other words, the very fact of Solidarity's coming into existence was unacceptable to the Communist rulers. And from this point of view, everything Solidarity did afterward had almost no significance whatsoever.

"Here, of course, another question arises: Was the creation of Solidarity necessary? Perhaps it would have been better for Poland to reconcile itself to its totalitarian destiny? My answer to these questions is very simple. Yes, the creation of Solidarity *was* necessary. To be more exact, it was at the same time necessary and impossible, as one of Solidarity's leaders put it. Everyone in Poland, despite some superficial optimism, was aware of the risk involved. But everyone was likewise aware that people couldn't live under water any longer, that something had to be done in order to reverse Poland's trend toward catastrophe. Whoever asks whether it was really necessary to create Solidarity should realize that without Solidarity, Poland today would be a completely Sovietized country, ruled by corrupt and incompetent officials and inhabited by thoughtless slaves. And its hopes for the future, including an economic recovery, wouldn't be any better than they are now.

"As it is, Poland is a country under occupation, but it's a country of free people who know exactly what they want and who most certainly will continue their struggle to achieve it. It's a country in which, paradoxically, the only people who sit apart and still try to breathe under water, the only people who still behave abnormally and who constitute the minority—in other words, the only real dissidents in today's Poland—are its Communist rulers."

It would be tempting on this late August day in 1989 to gloat over my own farsightedness and take pride in the fact that I can still subscribe to what I said seven years ago; moreover, that what I said then has been

largely confirmed by the dizzying sequence of events taking place in Eastern Europe during the past year (including the Communists' devastating
defeat at the polls in Poland's first partly free parliamentary election in
June 1989, which proved their status as the political "minority" more
convincingly than any words). My English vocabulary has grown more
diversified since 1982, and I would no longer use a strong word such as
"hypocrisy" to describe the West's reaction to the 1981 suppression of
freedom in Poland, especially since very soon Western opinion became
much more unequivocal in condemning it and in defending the oppressed. Apart from that, however, I must admit it gives me satisfaction
today to remember that in the gloomy days of 1982, after yet another
desperate move toward freedom in Eastern Europe had suffered yet another crushing blow, I was not among those who put the disaster off
with a collective shrug ("What did they expect, anyway?") but among
those who persisted in calling the move "necessary."

"Necessary and impossible," to be exact. For, again, if back in 1982
someone had sent me a time capsule containing a paper printed in August 1989, I would not have believed this glimpse of the future. Or,
more precisely, I would have known better than to put any hope in it.
Good things such as the collapse of Communism were not supposed to
happen in our lifetime. As an Eastern European born in a totalitarian
country, I was well trained for two things, and by two very different
coaches. The Immovable History of my nation taught me that in my part
of the world nothing ever changes, and that it's safer not to harbor any
hope. The Recalcitrant Literature of my nation taught me that having
no hope does not preclude demanding change and, more generally, be-
having as a human being should. The unlikelihood of victory does not
render such behavior senseless; on the contrary, coming up for air is all
the more necessary when our heads are constantly forced under water.

This book, written by an Eastern European literary critic who did not
know that he lived at the end of a historic era, is about these two things:
trying to breathe under water and coming up for air.

Under Eastern Eyes

E.E.: The Extraterritorial

First, there is the optical shock. When the average Eastern European (E.E., for short) steps off a plane on his first visit to the New World, he is immediately struck by the orgy of colors. Of course, he had known something about America before; he used to contemplate postcards, listen to travelers' tales, watch American movies. But the reality is much more intensely colorful than Technicolor. E.E. never expected houses to be painted so brightly purple or blue, schoolbuses to be so warmly yellow, street signs to be so invitingly green. The way America is painted seems to him shockingly but pleasantly different from the drab colorlessness that envelops everything—streets, cars, housing projects, peoples' complexions—in his own country. The color of Eastern Europe is gray (with occasional flashes of red on national holidays). America has no single color; it is brilliantly multicolored, pluralistic, and bold even in the first visual impression it makes.

The very next thing E.E. notices is the size of everything. Besides being gaudier, the components of American reality are also bigger. I don't mean the obvious things like skyscrapers, cars, the Grand Canyon, or Kareem Abdul-Jabbar. But even the gulls at the beach seem to be somewhat oversized here, as if they had been fed all their lives with some especially nutritious gull food, sold in easy-to-open cans. Speaking of body size, the fat people in Eastern Europe are likewise no match for those in America. There are a lot of potbellies there, but their fat is the fat that results from sloppiness, bad food, and lack of time for exercise. Compared to this, the typical American fatty seems rather to be a kind of competitor who has deliberately set about breaking the world record for body weight. He, or she, somehow blends in harmoniously with the Rocky Mountains, the Sears Tower, and Buick station wagons.

One hour on American soil is enough for E.E. to sustain a cultural shock in addition to the optical one. Unlike his own country, the United States strikes him as a place where everything is in working order—well, most of the time. A bus may be late, but it finally does arrive. A book may be sold out, but you can find a copy in the library or ask the bookstore to reorder. The toilet may not flush, but here comes a superintendent and repairs it (at least until the next breakdown). This notion goes far beyond the mere availability of consumer goods and services. It represents a philosophical difference between two visions of Fate. E.E. typically needs a few months to get rid of his Eastern European fatalism, bred in him by the countless hours he has spent in his country hopelessly waiting at a bus stop, hunting for a sold-out book, begging a plumber to pay a visit. In Eastern Europe, one always expects the worst. Nothing is guaranteed or even predictable; everything—from the meat supply to the course of your own career—is subject to the mysterious whims of "them," meaning those who hold power at all levels (even the plumber is one of "them"—his power derives from his being in constant demand). In America, "them" seems to be replaced by "me": everything—and this is truly a new experience for E.E.—can be worked out, if one tries hard enough. Or at least so it seems to E.E., until the first time he gets into trouble with the I.R.S. or is caught speeding.

Acceptance of the idea that everything in America works or can be worked out, whether this idea is true or not, is perhaps the watershed moment for someone who has recently arrived from Eastern Europe. Having gotten used to this, he becomes a new man. That is, to a certain extent; there are still some vestiges of his old mentality which simply cannot be eradicated. In spite of all his euphoria, the New World sometimes also provokes feelings of cultural alienation, incomprehension, or disgust. Here is a partial list of things American which E.E. will never be able to come to terms with:

1. Barbara Walters
2. Wonder Bread
3. Stand-up parties

4. Baseball
5. Small talk
6. Dental bills
7. Muzak
8. Decaffeinated coffee
9. Catfood commercials
10. Being addressed on a first-name basis by strangers.

The list could easily be extended, but I hope its point is clear. Mind you, not all of the things listed above are perceived by E.E. as alien—though this is certainly the case with baseball, which seems to him to have brutally usurped the place of soccer, that one truly noble and intelligent game. Some other things seem illogical rather than alien. What's the point of standing at parties and wearing out your legs? What's the sense in drinking coffee that's not coffee at all? Still others remain alien, but on second thought E.E. grudgingly admits their logicality: the cost of filling a cavity is outrageous, but the operation is painless and well done, which cannot usually be said, after all, about dental care in his own country. On the other hand, Barbara Walters provokes in E.E. some definitely bad vibrations, precisely because she reminds him so much of the superficiality and pretentious blah-blah of Eastern Europe's own TV anchors; and certain TV commercials (those of the "no-more-ring-around-the-collar" or "you'll-never-go-back-to-thick" variety), though basically unknown as a genre in the Communist bloc, have much in common with the general mindlessness and bad taste of what serves as mass culture there.

America is indeed a land of opportunity, at least in the sense that here you always have the opportunity to escape from what you hate or to balance it with what you like. If you can't stand standing at parties, you can always sit down, even on the floor. If you hate Johnny Carson, you can watch Ted Koppel. It doesn't mean, though, that the cultural differences can be smoothed over easily. If E.E. happens to be a translator of literature, as I am, he cannot help thinking about this dilemma as a problem of translation from one language into another. There would be no problem at all—and the translator's profession would not exist—if every word or expression in a given language had an exact equivalent in another language. But sometimes a word has several different equivalents, or a group of synonymous words has only a single equivalent. It can also happen that there is no equivalent at all, since the thing noted by a word simply doesn't exist in another environment or culture. And finally there are also situations—the most difficult ones for the translator—in which there *seems* to exist a pair of exact equivalents, but in fact each of them means something quite different in its respective language, or their meanings overlap only partially.

What I mean by "language" here can be broadly understood as any established cultural system, but in the particular situation of E.E. in America the problem is most nagging, naturally, within language in its narrow sense. A visitor or immigrant in a foreign country is sensitive, as a rule, to the pitfalls of semantics; the necessity of communicating in a language that is not his own makes him painfully aware of the constant danger of being misunderstood due to his linguistic imprecision or erratic usage. But sometimes it is not his poor vocabulary that is to blame—it is, rather, this or that built-in incompatibility of two languages. And such instances make him think, in turn, of all the potential and actual misunderstandings on a more universal level—in the communication that goes on between nations, cultures, and political blocs.

Take the word "happy," perhaps one of the most frequently used words in Basic American. It's easy to open an English-Polish or English-Russian dictionary and find an equivalent adjective. In fact, however, it will not be equivalent. The Polish word for "happy" (and I believe this also holds for other Slavic languages) has a much more restricted meaning; it is generally reserved for rare states of profound bliss, or total satisfaction with serious things such as love, family, the meaning of life, and so on. Accordingly, it is not used as often as "happy" is in American common parlance. The question one hears at (stand-up) parties—"Is everybody happy?"—if translated literally into Polish, would seem to come from a metaphysical treatise or a political utopia rather than from social chitchat. Incidentally, it is also interesting that Slavic languages don't have an exact equivalent for the verb "to enjoy." I don't mean to say that Americans are a nation of superficial, backslapping enjoyers and happy-makers, as opposed to our suffering Slavic souls. What I'm trying to point out is only one example of the semantic incompatibilities which are so firmly ingrained in languages and cultures that they sometimes make mutual communication impossible—or, rather, they turn it into a ritual exchange of meaningless grunts and purrs. "Are you happy?" E.E. is asked by his cordial host. "Yes, I am." "Are you enjoying yourself?" "Sure I am." What else can be said? What would be the point in trying to explain that his Eastern European mind does not necessarily mean what his American vocabulary communicates?

But this is just an innocent example from the field of private emotions and the level of individual dialogue. The weight of the problem increases markedly whenever E.E. has to resort to the vocabulary of what really matters on the nation-to-nation plane—to the vocabulary of history, politics, and ideology. Take another word: "liberal." In my part of Europe this single word has several meanings at least. As an adjective qualifying the word for this or that political tendency, for instance, it means that someone belongs, within his own political camp, to the doves rather than to the hawks. Thus, a "liberal Communist" is the kind of Communist who would like to send only some of his country's dissidents to psychiatric hospitals. This is, however, a secondary and frequently ironic usage. In its primary sense, the word "liberal" denotes in Eastern Europe, just as it does traditionally in all of Europe, someone who is located rather toward the center of the political spectrum and who opposes, most of all, those ideological premises of both the left and the right which in his view threaten the principle of individual freedom. Now, what is an Eastern European liberal supposed to say when he is asked by an American acquaintance about his political orientation? To answer "I'm a liberal" would mean to risk a fundamental misunderstanding. The answer "I'm a neoconservative" would more or less transfer the desired meaning to the American ears, but E.E. cannot force his lips to pronounce that; "conservative" sounds like the opposite of what he has always considered himself. After all, in his own country he never wanted to "conserve" the status quo—on the contrary, as a dissident, defender of human rights, or just a thinking individual he was definitely "progressive" as opposed to the "conservative" powers-that-be. The translation from the language EE (Eastern European) into the language AA (Authentic American) is, at least in this particular case, virtually impossible. Even though the word "liberal" has the same Latin root as its Slavic cousins, and a similar sound

13

here and there, its actual meanings within different political systems, societies, and historical traditions are far from close.

This is precisely what I would call the continental drift of meanings. The word "liberal," to which other words such as "democratic" and "nationalistic" could be added, is just one of the more glaring examples of this phenomenon. In fact, the most basic premises of life in Eastern Europe are so different from those of the American way of life (whatever that means) that any attempt by individuals to communicate their personal experience is bound to wind up in semantic conundrums and misinterpretations. This wouldn't be surprising if we dealt with an Eastern European apparatchik coming to America on an official visit. To be sure, in his peculiar newspeak, words like "democracy" and "justice" have rather different connotations from the ones they have in the Declaration of Independence. But an Eastern European dissident usually believes that, given a chance, he would be able to communicate with the heirs of Thomas Jefferson without lapsing into semantic confusion. The reality, as a rule, thwarts his expectations; despite all the mutual sympathy on both sides of the Atlantic Ocean, the continental drift in semantics seems to be unstoppable. Nothing could be a better example of this than the American media's coverage of events in Poland over the past four years. Their attempts to "translate" the idiomatically Polish set of political and social meanings into a language comprehensible to the American audience ended up, for the most part, in a failure to communicate anything essential. The gulf between two social systems, two historical traditions, and two collective mentalities proved to be too wide to be bridged by sympathy alone.

Still, just as the differences between two ethnic languages create the need for translators, so all the incompatibilities between the Eastern European and American mentalities only make every form of semantic mediation all the more desirable. Personally, I believe in culture as a possible go-between. A single novel by, say, Milan Kundera or Tadeusz Konwicki, when translated into English, tells the American audience more about Czechoslovakia or Poland than ten years of *Newsweek* coverage. A single film by Andrzej Wajda is an incomparably better source of information about Eastern Europe than a thousand interviews with General Jaruzelski by Barbara Walters. A general can lie and be believed; in a work of art, we cannot fail to discover a false note because it simply hurts our ears. If you want to know why ten million unarmed people in an Eastern European country risked being crushed by Soviet tanks four years ago, don't ask party secretaries. Ask poets and artists.

In fact, to an ever greater extent Americans are doing just that, but a lot remains to be done. It's characteristic that in a country like Poland, despite all the officially sponsored propaganda against the United States, the people have always had a strong interest in American culture, and as a consequence they are amazingly familiar with it. If America wishes to understand better what's going on in today's world, it's time for the country to abandon the idea of cultural self-sufficiency and to reach deeper into other nations' minds. The widening gulf between collective mentalities has more than once been crossed in the past and it still can be bridged by the kind of insight that culture provides. The continental drift can be stopped.

[1984]

From Russia with Love

Is there any truth, after all, in the perverse paradox which holds that creativity can flourish only in the foul air of oppression, whereas a breeze of freedom makes it wither? Being an émigré myself, I'd rather dismiss it as a bogus generalization. As much as I hate to admit it, however, the career of Alexander Zinoviev is a case in point: since his expulsion from the Soviet Union in 1978 he has not written a single book that can stand comparison with his earlier satirical masterpieces, *The Yawning Heights* and *The Radiant Future*. For an admirer of these two works, to read *Homo Sovieticus*[1] is an embarrassing experience. Though it employs the same kind of eclectic technique, this book has nothing in common with the ironic ambiguity and comic force of Zinoviev's first novels.

The book is "disquieting," as its publisher claims, not in what it says but in its predictability, monotony, and flatness. If it's supposed to be a satire, it is an odd kind of satire, completely devoid of humor. If it's supposed to be a political analysis, it lacks convincing argumentation. If it's supposed to be a self-portrait of the title creature, it is a portrait painted without the necessary distance. The first-person narrator is, in fact, doing his best to repel us by his constant bumptiousness, the product of his unshaken belief in his own intellectual superiority. At the same time, his half-baked opinions and sweeping generalizations leave us no doubt that he hardly has the right to claim superiority in anything intellectual. Let us listen to the characteristic ring of his crude sarcasm mixed with categorical self-assertion.

> In the West clever and educated people call us *Homo Sovieticus*. They are proud to have discovered the existence of this type of man and thought up

such a beautiful name for him. Moreover they use this term in what is for us a derogatory and contemptuous sense. It has never occurred to them that we have actually done something, more than simply finding a name for ourselves, that we were the first to develop this type of man, while it took the West 50 years after this to invent a new little term for it; and the West reckons that its contribution to history was infinitely greater than ours. The conceit of the West deserves our mockery.

After a couple of statements like this, even the most patient reader begins to yawn.

The feeble outlines of Zinoviev's plot, and its sketchy characters, are these: First, the narrator is a specimen of Homo Sovieticus. Second, Homo Sovieticus is a "new type of man" created by the powerful, attractive force of an ideology that satisfies his desire to be part of "the collective" and thus be relieved of individual responsibility. Third, this "new type of man" is an indestructible and unchangeable phenomenon that will not only survive but prove victorious. Fourth, this means that the Soviet system will ultimately conquer the earth, especially since the West is weak, divided, naïve, shortsighted, and gutless. Fifth, the inevitability of the future triumph of Communism casts a new light on contemporary issues and makes us assume that virtually everything that is going on in the world—from the demonstrations of Western pacifists to the hunger strikes of Soviet dissidents—is just a component of a "Great Attack on the West," cleverly orchestrated by the KGB. In the final analysis, there is no such thing as spontaneous and sincere defense of freedom, justice, and human dignity, since even the force-fed dissidents and expelled émigrés are, either actually or "objectively," Soviet agents. (According to the narrator, "A man can be an ASS [Agent of the Soviet State] without knowing that he is one.")

There is something utterly boring in the narrator's personality, in his combination of primitiveness and presumptuousness, with added touches of paranoia, chauvinism, intolerance, and other equally attractive features. What develops before us is the self-portrait of a mind with restricted horizons and unrestricted arrogance. Since the action involves Soviet émigrés in Germany, let's use a German and a Soviet term: his mentality is that of a typical *Besserwisser* from the *nomenklatura*.

Not a nice person to be with, that's for sure. But let's give Zinoviev

17

the benefit of the doubt. Maybe this was exactly his intent. After all, the book is supposed to be a clinical study of Homo Sovieticus, "the product of human adaptation to certain social conditions." Therefore, the first-person narration could be considered a device that serves to present this type of human being from within, by means of self-portrayal. As in every dramatic monologue, this sort of presentation gives the author a chance to distance himself from the speaker, to make the narrator unwittingly unmask and compromise himself and thus turn self-portrayal into ironic self-betrayal. There are, to repeat, some reasons to suspect that this was indeed Zinoviev's intent. In his foreword he says: "This book is about Soviet Man. He is a new type of man, *Homo Sovieticus*. We will shorten him to Homosos. I have a dual relationship with this new being: I love him and at the same time I hate him; I respect him and I despise him. I am delighted with him and I am appalled by him. I myself am a Homosos. Therefore I am merciless and cruel when I describe him. Judge us, because you yourselves will be judged by us."

"Merciless and cruel"? Come on. To my taste, there is far more love than hate in this relationship. There is, in other words, not enough ironic distance between the author and his narrator. At the very least, there is no evidence in the text of the author's "despising" the narrator or being "appalled" by him. What was most striking in Zinoviev's early books was precisely his ability to multiply ironic mirrors, to play upon varying degrees of identification and distance between the author and his characters. In *Homo Sovieticus* the distance has all but disappeared. "I myself am a Homosos."

This entails, by the way, some cognitive paradoxes reminiscent of the parable about a Cretan who said all Cretans were liars. Since one of the chief characteristics of Homo Sovieticus is his indifference to the distinction between truth and lie, is a Homo Sovieticus who confesses such indifference lying or telling the truth? In the final analysis, the first-person monologue of an exemplary Homosos totally misses the mark as a rhetorical device: we have no reason to trust a single word of his, including his self-description.

Apart from self-description, however, there is also a great deal of indirect self-presentation in the narrator's monologue. In fact, only these indirect clues provide any reliable material for speculation on the nature of Homosos. One crucial clue of this sort is the dictatorial, manipulative dominance of the narrator over the reality represented. His plot and his characters are really no more than a chessboard and a set of pawns (black only) for the narrator's own game of self-affirmation. The rules are simple and consistent, as in every case of megalomania cum paranoia.

It's not difficult to penetrate the layers of the narrator's beliefs and detect the totalitarian mentality beneath them. Its chief ingredients, as they reveal themselves in the course of the narrator's monologue, are the cult of strength and brute force; the division of the world into "us" and "them"; contempt for the individual and idolatry of "the collective"; and immorality and relativism—that is to say, a deliberate blurring of the boundaries between good and evil and between truth and lie.

This understood, one cannot really wonder why Zinoviev's narrator so condescendingly ridicules the West, the system of parliamentary democracy, the individualistic and humanitarian set of values that molds the mentality of a typical Westerner. He simply hates and despises Homo Occidentalis as the exact opposite of Homo Sovieticus, that is, himself—an opposite that seems to him infinitely weaker and ultimately doomed. Even taking into account Zinoviev's love-hate relationship with his hero, it is obvious that at least at this point the perspectives of the author and his narrator do converge: this utter contempt for the decayed West is also the attitude of the writer himself. Whatever his credibility as Homo Sovieticus, his hatred of Homo Occidentalis is beyond any doubt.

It would be interesting to compare Zinoviev's views with those of some of the harshest critics of Western passivity in the face of the totalitarian threat, such as Solzhenitsyn or Jean-François Revel. Revel is clearly aware that the democracies *can* perish, but he writes in order to ward off the disaster; though critical, he still speaks on behalf of the West and the Western system of values. Solzhenitsyn (in his 1978 Harvard speech, for instance) goes a step further and finds the main source of the democracies' weaknesses in the essence of democracy itself. Yet even this ambiguous argument still results from his desire to stave off the totalitarian monster.

For Zinoviev, however, the monster has a human face—the face of Homo Sovieticus, the inevitable conqueror of the Western world. He "loves and hates" him, "respects and despises" him. But there is no shred of evidence in his book that he has anything except hate and contempt for the Western democracies. If we were to heed his advice, the only means of putting up successful resistance would be for the West to produce its own version of Homosos. I don't know about the rest of the West, but so far as I'm concerned, no thanks.

Besides, I could be convinced of the superiority of Homo Sovieticus only if I were sure of his existence. It's amusing that the structure of Zinoviev's reasoning resembles the structure of Communist ideology. It seems to be a charmingly logical system, but only if we forget the fact that its fundamental premise is wrong. What's wrong in Zinoviev is his basic assumption that political systems can be described in terms of the uniform and stable "new types of men" they produce. To speak of an unchangeable, exceptionless, absolute "type" of Homo Sovieticus is just as gross an oversimplification as to say that all Irishmen are red-haired. It's even more wrong than that, in fact, because an actual red-haired Irishman cannot change his hair color naturally, whereas an actual Homo Sovieticus can change his ideological coloring. Witness, for example, the "thaw" of 1956: after many years during which people's souls seemed totally devastated, even a minimal political relaxation was enough for hope of freedom and justice to resurface. Most of the people who heeded the voice of that hope in subsequent years (those who survived, that is) are now either in exile or in labor camps. I wonder how an inmate of a Siberian camp might feel when told by Zinoviev that objectively he is a Homo Sovieticus, too.

Zinoviev is far more of an expert on the reality of the Soviet Union than most of his readers, this reader included. But I dare say most of his readers can claim greater insight into the reality of a human soul, since Zinoviev apparently doesn't know much about it. At least he doesn't seem to realize that his theory of Homosos is every bit as false as any absolute generalization superimposed on the natural diversity and dynamics of the human world. A little common sense and a little knowledge of history are enough to convince one that all proclamations of the arrival of "a new type of man," whether their tone is triumphant or menacing, are just simplistic fallacies.

Obviously I do not mean to deny the existence of fundamental differences between political systems, societies, and systems of values. Nor am I trying to belittle the extent of the spiritual desolation of which Soviet totalitarianism is guilty. The views of a New England pacifist, who, after a brief visit to Moscow and a conversation with a KGB informer disguised as a physician, becomes convinced that the Soviet people are exactly like us, are just as wrong as Zinoviev's insistence that Homo Sovieticus has nothing in common whatsoever with Western man. In the end, the truth must lie somewhere in between Dr. Alexander Zinoviev and Dr. Bernard Lown.

[1986]

The New Alrightniks

Every Nabokov fan remembers the scene in *Pnin* in which the hero, an émigré Russian scholar who has lived for years on an American college campus, attempts to purchase some sports equipment:

> Pnin entered a sport shop in Waindell's Main Street and asked for a football. The request was unseasonable but he was offered one.
> "No, no," said Pnin, "I do not wish an egg or, for example, a torpedo. I want a simple football ball. Round!"
> And with wrists and palms he outlined a portable world. It was the same gesture he used in class when speaking of the "harmonical wholeness" of Pushkin.
> The salesman lifted a finger and silently fetched a soccer ball.
> "Yes, this I will buy," said Pnin with dignified satisfaction.

This captures perfectly the Eastern European's experience in the United States. We come here with our portable worlds sharply outlined. The years of living *there,* the cultural stereotypes we have inherited, the semantic distinctions that our native tongues imply—all have created in each of us a repertory of mental mannerisms that we, in our naïveté, take as a reflection of reality. One has only to pass through the now-symbolic Ellis Island for this illusion to burst with a bang. It's not only that the New World turns out to be actually new and surprising at every step. What throws an Eastern European émigré off balance even more is that his semantic system itself seems not to correspond to American reality. A word that in his system of thinking referred to a nicely rounded object denotes here something like "an egg or, for example, a torpedo."

There are two ways of dealing with this problem. One is Pninification:

the émigré sticks to his old mental habits and semantic categories, and gradually encloses himself in the cocoon of his Old World personality. (And he is at liberty to do so: this is, after all, a free country.) The other is the method adopted by the hero of Paul Mazursky's *Moscow on the Hudson,* who insists on playing his tenor saxophone like Lester Young and Coleman Hawkins. He may be different but he wants to join in, which is the only way (not always satisfactory, to be sure) of understanding the nature of the difference.

Vassily Aksyonov has chosen to join in. Written for an American audience, *In Search of Melancholy Baby* is a book-length autobiographical essay (whose chapters are interspersed with "Sketches for a Novel to Be") on a Soviet émigré's perception of America.[1] (Aksyonov has lived in the United States since 1980.) The book illustrates two sides of the émigré's problem simultaneously. In the spirit of a rich literary tradition dating back to Montesquieu's *Persian Letters,* it tries to reveal some truths about a country that only a visitor from a different part of the world can discern. At the same time, the encounter with America serves as a way of revealing truths about the Soviet mentality, and the Soviet reality of which it is a product. It's as if Montesquieu's device were being used to say as much about Persia as about France.

Both of Aksyonov's inquiries spring from the overwhelming sensation of cultural difference that is the lot of every newcomer from behind the Iron Curtain. From smells to intellectual discoveries, from food and cars to natural landscapes and urban planning (or the lack thereof), from taxes and finances to interracial relations or sexual mores, from sports and cocktail parties to the literary scene and the political system—everything is new. Some of the contrasts to the émigré's experience are almost distressingly symmetrical; but founded as they are on the author's empirical observation of both worlds, they serve to convince us that the American and Soviet ways of life indeed differ in every essential aspect:

> America's prosperity becomes apparent the moment you leave her large cities. In Russia the opposite is the case. What remains after the military has drained off most of the resources goes toward maintaining a minimal level of decency in the cities; the countryside and villages are left to rot.

> Among the even more striking differences is the difference in the way people learn about what goes on in the economy. The citizen of a society

with a "planned economy" has no way of assessing his country's coffers (*Pravda*'s daily hip-hip-hoorays to economic growth and prosperity notwithstanding); the citizen of a free market society has a never-ending stream of hard figures to go by. The Soviet feels he is astride a gigantic inert mass; the American enjoys the sensation of rising and falling; of pulsating activity; it may look chaotic but it is very much alive.

From such observations a highly favorable image of America arises— the image of a society based on what Aksyonov calls "beneficent inequality" or "economic inequality in a framework of human dignity," a society "freer of xenophobia than any other nation," a society that sincerely sets itself the task of resolving all its inner conflicts. Aksyonov places himself unabashedly among the "Soviet Americanophiles," and he goes to such extremes in his enthusiasm for the United States that he begins to sound decidedly conservative by American standards. Though he declares his support for "liberalism," he means only (with a characteristically Eastern European twist) that in the age-old struggle between the principle of liberty and the principle of equality, he is on the side of liberty. His Soviet experience has taught him to distrust "the utopias of equality," which never work out anyway, and to place the highest value on freedom, in spite of the social or economic strings attached to it.

The political orientation of Aksyonov's readers will, I think, largely determine the way his portrayal of America is received. Liberals (this time in the American sense) will probably excoriate him for having painted too rosy a picture. The charge is false. From his vantage point, Aksyonov can see the South Bronx as well as Beverly Hills. His account devotes a great deal of attention not only to "American fascinations" but also to "American frustrations." Aksyonov's most surprising discovery, among these frustrations, was not the existence of enclaves of destitution or racial tension (he found the reality itself much less shocking than its inflated image in Soviet propaganda), but what he calls "American provinciality":

In the Soviet Union we pictured Americans as "citizens of the world," cosmopolitans; here we find them to be detached, withdrawn, sequestered in their American planet . . . In a closed society like the Soviet Union, public interest . . . is directed outward, while in open, democratic America it is almost wholly inner directed. The outside world interests Americans much less . . . Despite the iron curtain the Soviet Union is in many ways closer to Europe than Europe's closest political and economic partner, America.

Provinciality and isolation also mark contemporary American literature, he claims. Both these features, along with the pressures of the commercial market, have caused it to "simply take its place in the ranks of Western literature as a whole. Now the aura of the hazardous undertaking belongs to the oppositional literatures of Eastern Europe and the Soviet Union."

Now and again, amid the oppositions, Aksyonov points out disquieting analogies—the *paperscape* produced by both countries' bureaucracies, for instance, and the fact that "while the U.S.S.R. inches toward capitalism, capitalism [in the United States] is undergoing a Socialist warp of apathy, poor service, and hackwork." Still, the most revealing parts of the book are those in which Aksyonov portrays not America but popular Soviet misconceptions about America. These come in many shapes and sizes, from propaganda's outright lies (according to which America is a land of universal misery, oppression, and injustice) to the illusions of the "Soviet Americanophiles": "Soviet propaganda has piled up so many lies in its lifetime that it now gives reverse results: a certain brand of 'critically thinking' Soviet citizen—and most of the new émigrés fall into the pattern—no longer believes a word of it; the critically thinking Soviet rejects both the lies of propaganda and the scraps of truth the propaganda machine needs to make the lies appear true."

But beyond the fabrications of propaganda and the fantasies of the pro-Western intelligentsia, we find yet another Soviet vision of the United States. This is the body of genuine beliefs shared by party apparatchiks and their hired intellectuals, most especially the so-called National Bolsheviks. Akysonov meticulously analyzes their writings on America. Theirs is a vision marked by utter "disdain for the strength of America and the West in general" and "contempt for America's lack of unity," which in the Soviet strongmen's minds can be identified only with decadence and degeneration.

Aksyonov argues exactly the opposite. For him, "If America was unified along Soviet or Iranian lines, it would no longer be America. It must therefore instill in its population a passionate desire to defends it multiplicity, its ferment, its intellectual and aesthetic waverings." He doesn't mince words in his conclusion: "Let me call a spade a spade: the anti-Americans of this world—Gabriel García Márquez included—are enemies of freedom and friends of a global concentration camp. The paradox of it all is that to remain what it is America must defend even its own anti-Americans."

Another "paradox of it all" (I would add) is that the first of the sentences quoted above has a rather right-wingish ring to it, while the second would probably be criticized as too liberal, if not leftist, by a good half of Aksyonov's fellow Eastern European exiles. His defense of America's inner multiplicity as the source of its outer strength places him decidedly beyond the pale of prevailing émigré opinions. Aksyonov's book should be compared with Solzhenitsyn's famous Harvard speech, or with Zinoviev's *Homo Sovieticus*. Their differences aside, Solzhenitsyn and Zinoviev share the notion that the very premises of democracy are the cause of its ultimate weakness, its ineffectuality in the struggle against totalitarianism. Aksyonov, by contrast, represents a position far more akin to Western values, far more supportive of them.

Which comes as no surprise, if you consider his background. His youthful fascination with America in the Moscow of the 1950s—when, as he notes, jazz was America's secret weapon, and the pro-Western *stateniks* emerged as the first Soviet dissidents—seems to lead directly into his present situation as a Russian writer who makes his home in Washington, D.C. To return to *Pnin*, there is a scene in which the hero says in his funny accent: "In two-three years I will also be taken for an American," and every American present roars with laughter. When Aksyonov declares in his final chapter: "Now I am . . . almost an American myself," we are compelled to take his words, accent or no accent, at face value—and, at the same time, to hope that he will never give up that "almost," which, for both the writer and his readers, makes all the difference.

[1987]

Pontiffs and Repairmen

The Cardinal and Communism

Polish wits like to tell the story of a mediocre painter who was commissioned to paint the image of God the Father. Thrilled by the greatness of his subject, he vowed to do all his painting on his knees. After a few days of such work, God suddenly appeared to him in person and thundered impatiently, "My son, you are not supposed to paint me on your knees. You are supposed to paint me well."

Andrzej Micewski's biography of the late Cardinal Stefan Wyszynski, Primate of Poland,[1] is a book by someone who never really gets up off his knees. A respected Catholic journalist and historian, Micewski bases his work on solid research, including previously unknown documents and his own conversations with the Primate. On the factual level, the book is indeed informative and cogent. Every detail of the portrayal of Wyszynski, however, is steeped *in odore sanctitatis*. We read about the "supernatural radiance" of his personality and "an interaction of the human and the divine in the way he fulfilled [his] role," even though the biography ostensibly focuses on "the temporal, sociopolitical role of the Primate of Poland." The cardinal's theological, ecclesiastical, political, and social decisions and undertakings are presented as infallible and ultimately triumphant; his stances on various issues are uniformly defended and praised. In other words, we are dealing with hagiography, not biography.

This can only be regretted, especially since Micewski's book is the most ambitious attempt to date to present the cardinal's extraordinary role as *interrex* of People's Poland, the most powerful moral authority to serve as a substitute for the absent authority of the country's political rulers. To be sure, Wyszynski was a truly great man, and I cannot imagine the skeptic who could deny his historic role. I find no difficulty in agreeing with Micewski when he describes Wyszynski as Poland's "only postwar statesman," who "in fact performed the function of national leader"—even though the clergyman became a statesman "against his own will," under the pressure of historical circumstances. We must realize that Wyszynski had been a bishop since 1946 and was Primate of Poland from 1948 until his death in 1981. His *interregnum*, then, coincides almost exactly with the history of Church-State relations in Communist Poland.

Besides occasional moments of glory, such as the Primate's release from prison in 1956, the triumphant celebration of Poland's millennium of Christianity in 1966, and the 1978 election of the Polish pope, Wyszynski's tenure consisted of years of bitter struggle with the regime. It is a regime that has always been bent on the elimination, or at least the forcible restriction, of the Church's spiritual influence; it has resorted to an enormous range of vicious tricks in order to achieve this, from creation of fake movements of "patriotic priests" and "progressive Catholic laymen," to police and administrative harassment of priests and believers, to imprisonment of the Primate himself (in 1953), as well as some of his close associates. On these rough seas, the cardinal always steered his own steady course, constantly strengthening the Church's grip on the souls of this overwhelmingly Catholic and increasingly anti-Communist nation. In fact, the political authorities were obliged to reckon with his power to such an extent that they were forced more than once to "go to Canossa" and ask the Primate for help in calming the rebellious populace.

Throughout the book, one comparison recurs like a refrain—the comparison of Wyszynski and the Hungarian Cardinal Mindszenty. Unlike the latter, "a man of great character and principles, but entirely devoid of flexibility," Wyszynski owed his historical greatness (according to the author) to "steadfastness of principle combined with flexibility of action." Mindszenty, in Micewski's view, lost his battle: "Despite his personal heroism he achieved for the Hungarian Church not even a fraction of what Wyszynski achieved for the Polish Church." Wyszynski, on the other hand, came out on top. Picking his tortuous way between defiance and reconciliation, stepping back whenever necessary and advancing whenever possible, making truces with the Marxist-Leninist devil (such as the 1950 Church-State agreement) but never signing pacts with him, he led his church to its present and unique stature as perhaps the most indestructible of the many institutions that the Communists have tried to destroy. If today's Poland is a one-of-a-kind example of a country ruled by a totalitarian apparatus but inhabited by a people who are virtually immune to totalitarian ideology (and do not attempt to overthrow the system only because of the presence of Soviet tanks), Wyszynski's personal contribution to this state of affairs cannot be overlooked.

There is a question, however, that Micewski never asks: If the long-term victory has been Wyszynski's, was he equally triumphant in every individual action he undertook? What was the price that he (and the entire Catholic Church of Poland under his guidance) had to pay for his victory? What is, from today's perspective, the ratio of losses to gains? And finally, what actually was Wyszynski's legacy, and what has become of it?

The late Primate's idea of the Church's coexistence with a Communist state could be visualized, I think, in terms of an image of a besieged fortress. True, the commanders of the fortress were open to negotiations with the enemy (although they would never have considered the possibility of surrender). Still, life behind fortified walls is sooner or later bound to mold in certain ways the mentality of the besieged—and particularly of those in charge of the defense.

First of all, there emerges a natural need for a strong center of command, for a charismatic and decisive leader who will be responsible for an efficient defense, even at the price of assuming dictatorial power. Wyszynski was such a leader, and the fortress of the Polish Church defended itself splendidly under his command. But the principle of hierarchical subordination (modified to a considerable extent, to be sure, by the element of pluralism secured by the episcopate's role in making decisions) is liable to have certain aftereffects. In every dictatorship, for instance, obedient subordinates have a much greater chance of being promoted than independent spirits. Sometimes a yes-man can become the dictator's handpicked successor and eventually leave behind nothing but a smoking trail of political gaffes and blunders.

Second, successful defense of the fortress requires the unity and the unanimity of the besieged. This can be achieved by creating a common bond of ideas and beliefs, which are made more accessible, in turn, through a set of popular symbols. (Wyszynski, as his biographer points

31

out, assigned such tasks to the Marian cult, which forms the essence of traditional Polish Catholicism.) Again, the Polish Church has been extremely successful in achieving this. But in order to preserve the ranks, it is sometimes necessary to give the cold shoulder to those who discuss too much, think too much, complicate things too much. Thus, the obverse of Wyszynski's striving for unity of the believers was always his mistrust of intellectuals (in 1956 he mentioned explicitly in one of his articles that "intellectuals pose a danger when they want to overintellectualize the Church . . . The Church must minister in a language everyone understands"); of laymen with their own ideas of Christianity (see the history of his reluctant reconciliation with Znak, and important group of lay Catholics); and of possible allies from non-Catholic camps (especially that of the liberal left, with which the cardinal had a long history of mutual misunderstandings, analyzed several years ago in Adam Michnik's excellent book *The Church, the Left, the Dialogue*). In other words, Wyszynski treated dissenters within the fortress and potential helpers who were ready to fight the same enemy outside the fortress with equal suspicion. It is proof of his greatness, however, that in the last decade of his life he did finally acknowledge the role of and offered support to lay organizations of Catholic intellectuals, as well as to non-Catholic human-rights groups.

Third, the most ominous danger that the defenders of the fortress sometimes face is that its defense can ultimately become a self-serving purpose, a goal in itself. In the end, the walls may seem more important than the people they are supposed to protect. It should be said here that the Polish Catholic Church, in my view, has never succumbed to such an illusion. There were many situations, however, in which its position toward issues that concerned Polish society as a whole appeared vague or detached. In 1978, after the election of John Paul II, the philosopher Leszek Kolakowski asked the Polish Church a crucial question: did it oppose the totalitarian system because of its atheism or because of its totalitarianism? The answer is important, since it is quite imaginable that the system could offer considerable concessions, or even grant privileges, to the Church. If programmatic atheism, then, ceased to be a component of the system, would the Church continue to oppose its totalitarian component?

But Kolakowski's question remained unanswered. It was not fully answered, for instance, by Wyszynski's unfortunate and confused sermon of August 1980, which seemed to the striking workers to be more a redundant appeal for rejection of violence (was there any violence?) than an expression of support for their defense of human dignity. It has not been answered by the current situation either, in which the present Primate of Poland far too often assumes the role of mediator between society and its oppressors (admonishing the former too much and the latter too little), rather than that of protector of society against its oppressors.

But the Catholic Church of Poland is not identical to its Primate. As I write, the flowers on the grave of Father Jerzy Popieluszko are still fresh, even though the priest was murdered a few months ago; hundreds of anonymous believers visit the grave every day. What is the true legacy of Cardinal Wyszynski—Archbishop Glemp's "flexibility" or Father Popieluszko's steadfastness? Is it still possible to combine these two qualities? Where is the boundary, under present circumstances, beyond which the Polish Church will have to pronounce another "*non possumus*"? These questions, I'm afraid, will also have to remain unanswered. But not for long.

[1984]

Praying and Playing

Two of the world's most powerful men were once actors. But only one of them was also smart enough to write his own lines. The appearance in English of *The Collected Plays and Writings on Theater*[1] reminds us that before he became John Paul II, Karol Wojtyla's extraecclesiastic pastimes included not only philosophy, poetry, acting, skiing, and hiking but also playwriting. To paraphrase Stalin, how many diversions does the pope have?

Wojtyla stopped writing plays years before he moved to Rome. Between 1940 and 1964 he wrote six plays altogether, of which five have survived. Of these, three were written after he had become a priest. Only one, *The Jeweler's Shop*, was published (under a pseudonym) before his election to the papacy. Naturally all five were eagerly unearthed by the Polish Catholic publishing house Znak in the wake of the rejoicing in 1978, and were included in a volume of Wojtyla's collected poems and plays published in 1980. The poems have been available in English translation for several years; the present edition collects the plays and six brief essays on theater, all translated, annotated, and introduced with extreme care by John Paul's appointed English translator, the London-based poet and critic Boleslaw Taborski.

Though Wojtyla was virtually unknown as a playwright before 1980, the drama was for him an even more essential form of expression than poetry. As an eight-year-old he was involved with an amateur theater in his hometown of Wadowice; as a teenager he acted in some ten plays staged by his high school theater. After moving to Krakow and entering the university in 1938 (he majored in Polish literature), Wojtyla continued to perform with a semiprofessional theater group.

The outbreak of the war did not dissuade him from his literary and theatrical pursuits, even though the Nazi Occupation forced Polish cultural activity underground. Working by day in a quarry and in a chemical factory, by night Wojtyla continued to study at the university, now clandestine, and to write poetry. In December 1939 he wrote his first play (eventually lost), *David;* in 1940 came *Job* and *Jeremiah*. In these first years of the Occupation he was also involved with an underground group of young actors, who staged plays in private apartments. These efforts were institutionalized, though still covert, after August 1941, when Wojtyla and his older friend Mieczyslaw Kotlarczyk founded the Rhapsodic Theater in Krakow.

The Rhapsodic Theater was not just another clandestine means of keeping Polish culture alive. It was an artistic experiment aimed at creating a special "theater of the word," in which scarcity of visual theatrical effect (a natural scarcity, under the circumstances) was part of a deliberate aesthetic. The performances were based on recitation rather than acting, and the repertory consisted of poems rather than plays. As Kotlarczyk put it, it was an attempt "to revolutionize theater through the *word*."

Wojtyla took part in all twenty-two wartime performances of the Rhapsodic Theater. After 1946, when he was ordained a priest, his ties with the Rhapsodic Theater became looser, of course, but they were never completely severed. On the contrary, he supported and defended it throughout its postwar existence, which was particularly difficult during the years of Stalinism, until its final closure by the Gomulka regime in 1967.

The idea of a "rhapsodic theater," or "theater of the word," clearly informs Wojtyla's three later plays, *Our God's Brother* (written in 1945– 1950), *The Jeweler's Shop* (1960), and *Radiation of Fatherhood* (1964). Compared with these works, his beginnings as a dramatist seem decidedly conventional. *Job* and *Jeremiah,* both written when he was twenty, expose the workings of the young author's mind and show his familiarity with the Bible and with the Polish Romantic and Neo-Romantic traditions, but they are not artistic feats in themselves. *Job* reflects on the problems of evil, suffering, and punishment, viewing Job's fate as a prefiguration of Christ's passion, and of mankind's martyrdom during the Second World War. *Jeremiah* fuses biblical allusion with a segment of Poland's turbulent history in the early seventeenth century, thus creating a messianic vision of the nation's downfall and resurrection. *Job* is structured like a Greek tragedy, whereas *Jeremiah* is closer to Symbolist theater.

It is in their style, however, that both these plays are most marked by the future pope's attachment to a particular tradition, the choice of which was not exactly, well, infallible. Both plays, especially in the original, appear heavily influenced by the worst aspect of the work of Stanislaw Wyspianski, the greatest Polish Symbolist playwright, namely his artificially elevated and pseudo-archaic language. These stylistic qualities are greatly toned down in Taborski's sensitive translation, but stiltedness remains. *Job* and *Jeremiah* were written by a twenty-year-old sophomore, and in the Polish edition of Wojtyla's work both plays were listed as juvenilia.

The reader who opens this book in order to see the future pope's mind at work might well begin by reading Wojtyla's next play, *Our God's Brother.* As Taborski notes in his introduction, this play is unique if only because it seldom happens that a playwright has the chance to beatify his play's protagonist. Wojtyla's lifelong fascination with the figure of the legendary Brother Albert (Adam Chmielowski, 1845–1916), a painter and political insurrectionist, protector of the homeless and founder of the order of Albertines, resulted first in his writing a play about him. More than thirty years later, his hero was finally beatified by the Church, and it was John Paul II who announced the event to the one million people who came to hear him in Krakow during his second papal visit to Poland.

Our God's Brother opens the main chapter in Wojtyla's dramaturgy; it breaks with the conventions of Symbolist theater and offers a more innovative approach. The principles of "theater of the word" are already put into effect. The dramatic action and the stage movement are reduced to a minimum; the characters serve mainly as exponents of different ethical attitudes, presented in extensive philosophical exchanges. At the same time it is an example of what Kotlarczyk and Wojtyla called "inner theater." As an attempt to "penetrate the man" rather than simply to illustrate the course of his life, the action takes place in the inner space of the protagonist's mind. The dramatic scenes (if that is what they are) occur as if they belonged to external reality, but in fact they are reminiscences played out on the stage of the hero's thoughts.

Wojtyla took a further step in this direction in his two plays written in the early 1960s, *The Jeweler's Shop* and *Radiation of Fatherhood*. These two plays mark a decisive shift toward the mystery play. Their protagonists are modern Everymen of both sexes, who mediate on the problem of their entanglement in the web of relationships with God and other humans, and ponder the fundamental mysteries of love, marriage, and parenthood. This is indeed a theater of the word or an even more ascetic theater of ideas, one that tries to prove, as Wojtyla put it in one of his essays on theater, that "not only events but also problems are dramatic."

Thus, it is mainly the problem that "acts" here, while the actor serves mainly to "carry the problem." The dramatic action is minimized even more than before; each play is in fact composed of long monologues, which, though interrelated by their content, are monologues nonetheless. Taborski notes properly that these are not monologues of the Harold Pinter variety, where the isolation of utterances serves to stress the characters' inability to communicate. Rather, these are monologues merely because meditation can be done only in solitude. On another plane, though, these separate meditations form a universal dialogue that permeates the human and divine world—"a conversation of prayers," as Dylan Thomas put it.

From a purely literary standpoint, Wojtyla's plays may provoke different reactions. Certainly not everybody needs this much seriousness and solemnity in art. But they should be required reading, along with his poems and philosophical writings, for anyone who wishes to understand the man, certainly for anybody who wishes to pass judgment on him. I don't mean that the plays clarify John Paul's specific ideas. (Although they do that too: *Our God's Brother,* for instance, contains a revealing discussion of the problem of social injustice and revolution, which corresponds intriguingly to the pope's pronouncements in Latin America thirty-odd years later.) I mean that they illuminate the character of this pope—particularly his openmindedness, so seldom comprehended by those who are unwilling to see behind the rigid façade of the institution he represents.

Openminded? The pope? I won't be surprised if I hear a roar of protest. The recent papal visit to the United States, and its largely moronic coverage by the media, left behind two images of John Paul II: a Great Communicator and a great guy, or a reactionary bogeyman who denies the benefits of progress to women and gays. Between a lawn sprinkler in the shape of the pope marketed by some fast-thinking entrepreneur ("Let Us Spray," it was called) and the practice target of the left there is really not much difference: both are made of plastic.

Behind those flat images, an infinitely more complex personality waits to be discovered. What we usually see is John Paul the former actor. We should also see John Paul the former playwright—someone for whom theater means not so much showmanship as dialogue. The mind of a man for whom the theater has been a primary means of expression can hardly be dogmatic. Even when he has shifted from plays to encyclicals, his outlook is still imbued with his recognition of the world's dramatic plurality. The playwright's natural element, after all, is dialogue, the confusion and conversation of our prayers.

[1987]

Walesa: The Uncommon Common Man

It was only seven years ago last August that an obscure unemployed electrician climbed the wall surrounding the Lenin Shipyard in Gdansk, Poland. In jumping down from that wall, he jumped into the limelight of History. Seldom does the course of human events depend so much on an individual's decision as it did that August morning in 1980. Had Lech Walesa not joined the shipyard strike to lead it to its triumphant conclusion two weeks later, and had he not served as his nation's unofficial leader throughout its subsequent seven-year ordeal, our world would look different today.

To be sure, Solidarity would not have emerged, either, had it not been for the long-suppressed aspirations and needs of millions of Poles. Walesa himself is the first to admit that his chief talent is to "know instinctively what most people want." He has always been a man-in-the-street, maybe a little cheekier and more outspoken than the average. He is not a political theorist who concocts an ideology and then tries to gather an army of followers. Rather, he is one of those people who, in the midst of an angry yet uncertain crowd, step up on a soapbox and yell something that suddenly gives the crowd a focus and determination. In this, Walesa, the greatest common man in modern history, is unmatched.

Still, if someone needs just a couple of weeks to institute a ten-million-strong independent union in a totalitarian country; if he wins sixteen months of liberty for his nation and changes its collective mentality forever; if he remains a major actor on the political stage even after a crushing defeat, we cannot help asking: Who is this man, anyway? What makes him tick? *A Way of Hope,* Walesa's autobiography published this year, first in French and now in English,[1] offers the most complete, if not fully satisfying, set of answers to these questions. Walesa's "secret project," on which he worked (no doubt helped by numerous collaborators) over the last three years, the book became the object of an international controversy over the right to publish it first, made headlines throughout the world, and has already sold hundreds of thousands of copies in Europe. The publishers' hype is at least partly justifiable. Even though the book reveals few political secrets, it offers an invaluable look from both inside and atop Solidarity's structure. And even though Walesa has given thousands of interviews, this is by far the most comprehensible self-portrayal of the man to date.

It is the personal side of Walesa's incredible-yet-typical story that appears most revealing and, at the same time, touching. His beginnings were anything but exceptional. Born in a rural province of Nazi-occupied Poland, he was raised in a large peasant family cemented by strong faith and nourished by patriotic reminiscences. As a child, he went through the experiences common to all his generation: the ravages of war (which claimed the life of his father) and the misery of the postwar years. After vocational school and military service, he worked as a run-of-the-mill, though skillful, village mechanic, repairing anything from grandfather clocks to farm equipment.

Walesa's being an expert repairman is probably one key to his personality. A person becomes a mechanic because he is fond of the straightforward logic and functional efficiency of machines. On the other hand, a person like that could only regard People's Poland—where, as an ironic result of central planning and an arbitrary one-party system, nothing has ever seemed to function properly—as an intolerable mess. Such was Walesa's impression when, on the spur of the moment, he left his village in 1967 and went to work as an electrician in the Lenin Shipyard. The pages that depict the horrendous working conditions and exploitation of the workers in this leading enterprise of the "workers' state" at that time are among the most telling in the book. It was no accident that this very shipyard, brimming with bright and skilled yet hopelessly exploited young people such as Walesa, became a hotbed for a violent protest that swept the Baltic Coast in December 1970. Walesa, then twenty-seven, was one of the protest's leaders.

Since that time, through the founding of the first independent trade unions in the late 1970s, the creation and flourishing of Solidarity in 1980–1981, and its underground existence after the 1981 military coup, he has been dealing with a material that is far more delicate than nuts and bolts or electrical cables: the fabric of society and the stuff of human hopes. Walesa has made many mistakes in the process. Some of them he admits (like the errors of inexperience he committed in 1970); some of them are charges he vehemently rejects or decisions he eloquently defends (such as the accusation of his growingly dictatorial role in Solidarity throughout 1981 or his killing of the idea of a general strike in late March 1981, which, in the opinion of many, was the last opportunity for Solidarity to prevent its subsequent defeat). There are also some controversial problems in recent Polish history—for instance, Solidarity's relationships with the Catholic hierarchy and its attitude toward earlier human-rights groups such as KOR—which the book diplomatically smoothes over. Anyone seriously interested in these issues would be better advised to read, in addition to Walesa's, other recent books on Poland, such as Timothy Garton Ash's excellent *The Polish Revolution: Solidarity,* Jan Jozef Lipski's *KOR,* or Adam Michnik's *Letters from Prison.*

Walesa, to reiterate, could be accused of various mistakes before and during his involvement with Solidarity, but those were the years of his maturation as political leader. During the disastrous days of martial law he appeared calm, collected, and cunning. While held incommunicado by Polish security forces, he again "knew instinctively what most people wanted" from him and did the only right thing: he refused to appear in the regime-owned media. Walesa's silence then, as well as his words and actions after his release, made a profound impact on the minds of his fellow countrymen. More than perhaps anyone else but the pope, he helped them continue to resist political oppression without ever resorting to violent means. From this point of view, the 1983 Nobel Peace Prize could not have been awarded to a better man. It could not have been handed to a better woman, either: Walesa's wife, Danuta, who received the prize in Oslo for him, is Poland's veritable First Lady and the force behind Lech's strength and endurance. The book is, among other things, a moving tribute to her and to millions of other Polish women whose courage and determination she epitomizes.

Today, the Polish regime's spokesmen find a perverse satisfaction in

41

referring to Walesa as just an electrician working again in the Lenin Ship-yard—"an ordinary citizen." They do not realize that Walesa's appeal lies precisely in this. Yes, he is an ordinary citizen—one who has thirty million ordinary citizens behind him. He is like most people—and that's exactly why he understands so well, much better than any politician or ideologue, what most people want. What they want is a normal life, a life free from fear and deceit, a life that won't trample on their human dignity, a life worth living. Walesa's example teaches them how to demand this kind of life—and, more important, how to live it.

[1987]

On Adam Michnik

The face on the TV screen hasn't changed at all since I last saw it, in person, the night before my departure from Poland eight and a half years ago. There is some sublime oddity in my sitting in an American living room and catching a glimpse of my coeval and friend setting among other representatives in the Polish parliament while applauding the nomination of People's Poland's first non-Communist prime minister. During those years, I was somehow always convinced that all this would come to pass sooner or later; yet now that it has, I'm still unable to believe it. Adam, are you really a Sejm deputy? Come on. Such animals don't exist in nature (as someone once said looking at a giraffe). No kidding, you really are? So why are you still wearing that old jacket of yours?

It's hard to believe how many things he managed to pack into a mere forty-three years of his life. A total of six years spent in Polish prisons between 1965 and 1986. Countless arrests, detentions, interrogations, searches, and beatings. An inspiring role in virtually all the major acts of antitotalitarian protest in Poland since 1968. Occupations ranging from student to factory worker to editor of underground periodicals and lecturer at an underground university to one of the top advisers to Solidarity and now the editor-in-chief of its *Gazeta Wyborcza* (The Election News). Seven books, most of them written in prison cells (he claims this is the only place he can concentrate). Legendary acts of personal courage, such as the one in 1981 when he faced an angry mob to save the lives of two policemen who were on the verge of being lynched. Millions of pages of everything from Abelard to Zhdanov stored in his photographic memory, thousands of nights spent in clouds of stale tobacco smoke quarreling with friends on everything from avant-garde art to Zionism, hundreds of witticisms he coined and anecdotes about him that have been making the rounds in Poland for the past twenty years. And, maybe the most characteristic thing, thousands of friends all over the world. I am only one of them.

We first met in 1972 in the city of Poznan. I was teaching at a university there, and Adam, who had just spent eighteen months in prison and almost two years working in a lightbulb factory, was commuting from Warsaw as a special student to complete his M.A. in history. (As a leader of the March 1968 student rebellion, he was still considered dangerous enough to be barred from studying at the University of Warsaw.) His studies consisted mostly of passing one exam after another with the greatest of ease and dazzling professors with his irreverent yet exceptionally solid performances. If he happened not to know the answer to a question during an oral exam, he usually responded with such a well-aimed question of his own that the puzzled professor had no choice but to give him an A+ just to get rid of him. It was thanks to our encounters then that I can claim today that I and my wife are probably the only people on this planet who saw Adam Michnik wearing a necktie on at least a dozen occasions. His friends know that his usual appearance is marked by a certain disarray, but before each of his Poznan exams he always went to enormous lengths to look decent, even to the point of borrowing a necktie from me.

I, like so many of Adam's friends, can say that my life took a different turn after I met him. There is probably no other man living to whom I owe so much. Adam's personal influence has always been contagious and irresistible. It was not only that, like many others, I was under the spell of his personality, of his intellectual brilliance combined with his straightforward manner and great sense of humor. And it was not only the fact that Adam introduced me—again, like so many others—to the world of forbidden books and prohibited ideas. What was even more unique and admirable about him was his unwritten résumé, which young Poles like myself knew by heart: founder, at the ripe age of fifteen, of the Club of the Seekers of Contradictions, a discussion group of high school students, subsequently condemned by Wladyslaw Gomulka himself; expelled from two high schools in a row; accepted by Warsaw University; arrested along with Jacek Kuron and Karol Modzelewski in connection with their "Open Letter to the Party"; suspended at the university, reinstated, suspended again; expelled from the Union of Socialist Youth; reinstated as student again; expelled from the university and arrested again in 1968, to be finally sentenced to three years in prison as a punishment for his refusal to cooperate with the investigation . . . We knew all this, and more: we knew that throughout these events, his actions were always the direct consequences of his thoughts.

In that respect, there was at the time no one like him in the entire country. In the early seventies the intellectual community in Poland was, in many ways, completely paralyzed. As a result of the crushed protest of intellectuals in March 1968 and the bloodily suppressed workers' rebellion in December 1970, a discrepancy arose between thought and action. On the one hand, every thinking person had become convinced that the system was based on exploitation, brute force, and lies; on the other hand, the fear of persecution was so widespread that no one dared raise any objection.

Everybody realized this discrepancy, and many people were quite ashamed of themselves—a state of mind that by itself would not have spurred them to any action, had it not been for an obnoxious young man by the name of Adam Michnik. In the atmosphere of general apathy that prevailed in the mid-seventies, he alone had the nerve to pester the venerated luminaries of Polish culture and ask them for their signatures on this or that letter of protest. He also had the nerve to ask them simple yet very disquieting questions: Why are you complaining of censorship when you could easily create an uncensored publishing network of your own simply by using your wits and your typewriters? Why are you lamenting the sad state of official education when you could simply start offering unofficial courses in your own apartments? Why are you shedding tears over the growing split between intellectuals and workers when you are doing nothing to reach those workers?

He was rewarded for his efforts by getting beaten up by "unknown perpetrators" and arrested dozens of times, but that was the price he was prepared to pay. And he was lucky enough to see his labors bear fruit very soon. Had it not been for his individual initiative and persistence, the famous "Letter of the 59" that started it all in December 1975 would never have seen the light of day. The same is true of many other collective actions in the late seventies, such as the creation of independent publishing or the Flying University. They were collective all right, but I'm quite sure none of them would have been undertaken (at least not at that point in time) had it not been for Adam's unshaken belief that the impossible could be achieved if one really wants to, and his conviction that living in truth is actually simpler for a human being than wriggling among lies.

I remember one scene with particular vividness. It was July 1976. We stood—Adam and a group of friends—in a corridor of a Warsaw court where the participants of the June strikes in the city of Ursus were being tried. No one was admitted into the courtroom except close relatives of defendants, mostly the workers' wives. We did not know what was going on inside the courtroom, but after an hour or so we heard a sudden outburst of women's crying pierce the walls. And a while later those weeping, wailing, cursing women left the courtroom and made their way through the crowd—each of them stupefied by the fact that as a result of this sham of a trial she wouldn't see her husband for the next two, three, five years and that nothing, nothing could be done about it. I stood next to Adam at that moment. His eyes were dry but I knew him well enough to see that he had just hit upon one of those ideas of his— ideas that at first seemed foolish even to his friends and then somehow always turned out to be right. The same afternoon he started collecting signatures for another letter of protest. KOR, the Workers' Defense Committee, was formally founded a few months later, but for me that July afternoon will always remain the actual beginning of KOR and everything that happened in Poland afterward. It began not with any-one's political program or ideological statement. It began with a simple impulse of compassion.

And this is how Adam has always been. Today's Poland has no short-age of extraordinary people, but what makes Adam Michnik someone special is, I think, that amid all the politics he is involved in he has never lost sight of what human rights are about: the individual human being. It is individual people and their freedom that he cares about, not ideol-ogies or political agendas. In more peaceful times he would probably be not an activist-cum-writer but just a writer, and a darn good one, too. He just happens to have spent the forty-three years of his life in an epoch and a country in which the most basic acts of human compassion were considered a political offense. That's why he took to politics: he was too intelligent to overlook this idiocy. He was also conscientious enough to stick to his kind of politics even when it seemed hopeless. And he has enough of a sense of humor not to take himself too seriously, now that it has turned out that he was right and the whole situation was not hopeless after all.

As I write on this twenty-first of August 1989, I don't know yet what role, if any, Adam is going to play in the Solidarity-led government that is about to be formed. It's quite possible that they'll make him a minister of culture or something. In such a case, he will be another historic first in the Eastern bloc: the first minister who doesn't wear a necktie. Still, Adam: the jacket must go.

[1989]

The Absolute Horizon

Centuries from now, some historian of the ancient culture of the twentieth century will probably say that among the literary genres cultivated in our epoch the most accomplished was the prison letter. Happily disengaged from the bloody mess from which our culture arose, and able to look at its products from a safe distance, this scholar of the future will view them as nothing more than applications of the theoretical principles of aesthetics. And indeed, if aesthetic accomplishment is to be measured by the degree of the author's dexterity in playing with restrictive rules, then a letter penned by a twentieth-century prisoner of conscience rotting in some Czechoslovakian, Argentinian, Chinese, Cuban, or South African jail surely beats the most finely wrought Provençal *cansos,* Japanese haiku, or classical tragedies. Even more than these genres, the prison letter in countries ruled by oppressive regimes is governed by a detailed set of strict prohibitions and injunctions regulating its size, structure, style, tone, and content. The author's mastery lies precisely in how he handles these rules, complying with them yet managing to slip his message through, remaining within the limits of a standardized model of utterance yet imbuing it with the urgency of his individual voice.

The only difference is perhaps that your average Provençal troubadour operated within restrictions produced, as it were, by the medium of the *canso* itself, and resulting from the genre's own intrinsic refinement. Compared to that, the present-day prisoner is bound by rules drawn up by rather extraliterary and not too refined types such as the chief of secret police, the warden, or that one-of-a-kind contribution of modern penitentiary systems to civilization's progress, the so-called education officer (whose task, as the appellation itself makes clear, is to censor correspondence). Well, to be exact, there is one more difference. If the troubadour had failed to observe specific rhyming rules or a prescribed stanzaic pattern, he risked nothing more than finding himself outside this or that genre; if the prisoner fails to abide by the rules imposed on his letter writing, he risks finding himself definitely on the inside rather than outside, namely in solitary confinement with his visiting privileges rescinded. Not to mention the fact that his letter will never be sent out.

Naturally enough, like every literary genre, the prison letter has its specific generic subdivisions. There are basically three of these. The first category represents pure potentiality—that is, it comprises letters that do not exist at all. Their would-be authors happened to live under systems that were too busy building their respective versions of the radiant future to fritter away their energies on censoring prisoners' correspondence; as a consequence, these systems chose an economical alternative, namely they prohibited correspondence altogether. The nonexistent letters of inmates of the Nazi death camps or certain Siberian labor camps belong in this category, as do the nonexistent letters of selected individuals held incommunicado by other regimes. The second category includes letters that, although theoretically prohibited, have nonetheless been written (if not on paper, then on other available material such as cigarette tissue or bedsheet shreds) and smuggled out. The third and most common category consists of prison letters officially allowed by more lenient regimes—which, all their leniency notwithstanding, are as a rule also prudent enough to officially censor them.

Contrary to what one might surmise, the art of writing these "open" (in a double sense) letters of the third type is by no means less complicated and demanding than the art of writing secret ones. If anything, the smuggled letters form a relatively simpler subgenre of prison correspondence: their generic restrictions have to do mainly with their physical size. Compare that with the intricate regulations the Czech playwright Václav Havel had to comply with while writing officially allowed letters from his consecutive prison cells in 1979–1982. In his case, rules and restrictions governed virtually every aspect of the letters' poetics. There were, first, restrictions of frequency: he was allowed to write only one letter a week. Second, restrictions of space: the letter was not to exceed four pages. Third, restrictions of the addressee: the letter could be addressed and sent only to the writer's immediate family. Fourth, restrictions of subject matter: only "family matters," not a word about prison conditions, much less about politics and other subversive stuff. Fifth, restrictions of tone: humor was strictly banned, since it would have undermined the gravity of the punishment. Sixth, restrictions of vocabulary: no foreign words or expressions were tolerated. Seventh, restrictions concerning handwriting: letters were to be legible, with nothing crossed out or corrected. Eighth, pedantic as they might seem, restrictions concerning punctuation and graphic design: margins of such and such a size, no quotation marks, no underlined words. This list is far from complete, and one must also take into account the separate list of unwritten self-restrictions that the writer, aware of the watchful presence of the censor's eye, had to observe for pragmatic or emotional reasons. He could not, for instance, refer to his fellow dissidents' activities lest they be implicated in his case or otherwise persecuted; he could not open up too much, for instance by allowing himself too much intimacy in writing to his wife; he could not afford, in short, to make others and himself more vulnerable than they already were.

Given all these restrictions and self-restrictions—indeed, infinitely more demanding, and entailing an incomparably greater risk, than the troubadour's juggling of quintuple rhymes and fanciful stanzas—it might seem a miracle that a prison letter gets written, sent, and delivered at all. It might seem a miracle of the second degree that the letter's message makes any sense. But then, as we know, the chief wonder of art is that it thrives on overcoming difficulties. Being bound by countless rules immobilizes the author and sterilizes his expression only if he does not have much to say in the first place. If he does have something important to say, it may happen that coping with rules and restrictions leads him— no, not necessarily to create another symbolic, circumlocutory language, but rather to invent ways of compressing more meanings into his words and sentences than is possible in normal speech, making his message more relevant and semantically charged than the usual communication. This is, in fact, the essence of all poetry, but it is also why some of the prison letters written in the twentieth century are, in addition to being sources of direct human testimony, literary monuments as well. The art of writing a prison letter is founded on the same principle as, on the one hand, the earthy art of preparing a parcel for a prisoner or, on the other, the sublime art of composing a sonnet. If you have a bare minimum of space at your disposal, you have to fill it with what really matters. If you are allowed to write just four pages a week and prohibited even to underline words, you have to pack these four pages with meaning and make a word's importance so self-evident that there will be no need to underline it. Prison may not be the most comfortable place to write, but it certainly is a good school in which to learn the value of the written word.

It may serve as the ultimate symbol for the futility of any oppression of human thought and speech that it was precisely the Czechoslovakian authorities' malicious regulations concerning prison correspondence that pushed Václav Havel into enriching his 144 letters with so much eloquence and profundity. Had he been given free rein in writing, he would most probably have produced another informative account of prison life or another moving document of a prisoner's love for the woman who waited for him outside the walls. In an oblique way, *Letters to Olga*[1] is all this, but also something more. The restrictions made Havel focus on the most essential part of his experience, its irreducible metaphysical core. What seemingly remained a sequence of letters, addressed to his wife Olga and dealing with "family matters" (including very down-to-earth reports about his health or instructions specifying what to put in her next parcel to him), also managed to be a philosophical treatise in weekly installments, addressed to the world at large and dealing with universal questions of human identity and responsibility. Ironically, restraints put on Havel's personal freedom helped him create one of the most powerful arguments for the defense of human freedom in modern literature. This paradox, needless to say, should not be misconstrued as a general cause-and-effect law. Persecution does not necessarily breed art and thought (in fact, it is usually more successful in killing it). Rather, art and thought are sometimes able miraculously to survive and thus render persecution's efforts null and void.

Something like that has certainly happened to Havel's letters. To be sure, party secretaries, policemen, and wardens bent on suppressing him and silencing his writing (goals that in Gustav Husák's efficient police state had been, in many other cases, achieved with no special difficulty) found him more than their match. When he was arrested in June 1979, charged (along with five other signers of Charter 77) with the crime of subversion of the republic by means of distributing illegal written material (mostly announcements of the charter's outgrowth, the Committee to Defend the Unjustly Prosecuted), and several months later, after a travesty of a trial, sentenced to four and a half years in prison, he was already a seasoned practitioner of both the art of writing and the art of doing time for political offenses.

His involvement dates back to 1956, when, as a twenty-year-old poet, he made his first important public appearance defending unorthodox older writers who had been "forgotten" by official publishers and critics. Since 1960 he has tied his career to the theater, working in Prague first as a stagehand and then as a playwright and consultant at the innovative Theater on the Balustrade; in 1963 and 1965 his first plays, *The Garden Party* and *The Memorandum,* initiated a long string of successes as playwright on the stages of both Czechoslovakia and the West. At the same time, beginning in the mid-sixties, he was becoming increasingly active in the radically democratic circles of young Czech intellectuals, serving as editor of the literary magazine *Tvár* and later, during the Prague Spring, founding the so-called Circle of Independent Writers within the official Writers' Union. Having been much less gullible and much more far-reaching in his political criticisms than most of his moderately "revisionist" fellow writers, he soon became a target for attacks and the object of harassment. A year after the Soviet invasion of Czechoslovakia, he was for the first time charged with "subversion" for his protest against Husák's policies, though the trial was adjourned indefinitely.

This was, however, only the beginning. In the seventies, during which Havel wrote what have thus far proved to be his best plays and political essays, the forms of harassment aimed at him started multiplying rapidly. His famous open "Letter to Dr. Gustav Husák" in 1975 did not immediately bring direct punishment, but not much later, particularly after the emergence of Charter 77, Havel became one of the most endangered Czech intellectuals. Endangered not merely in the sense of being frequently detained, interrogated, followed, bugged, and harassed in a variety of other ways, but also in that he was apparently singled out for special treatment: his unquestioned moral integrity needed to be defiled as soon as possible in order to compromise the entire movement he represented. In early 1977 Havel was arrested, and several months later, still lacking the necessary experience of a political prisoner, he committed a rather foolish mistake by sending the authorities what seemed to be a routine and insignificant request to be released. Fragments of this request, taken out of context and maliciously misconstrued, were immediately made public, and Havel's subsequent release was officially interpreted as a reward for his giving in. (Several years later, in *Letters to Olga*, Havel was to reflect upon this affair as a traumatic experience that had caused him a lot of pain and humiliation but also helped him define his moral stance more clearly. Since that time, his "intractable politeness" in dealings with the regime and its agents has always consisted in his courteous yet steadfast refusal to meet them halfway in any sense of the word. After his arrest in 1979, for instance, the authorities suggested that he would be immediately released if only he agreed to accept an invitation to the United States; he categorically rejected this barely masked offer of emigration.)

The 1977 attempt to discredit Havel fell flat, however, and after his release he was active in dissident circles to an even greater extent than before. Arrests and trials followed: in October 1977 he received a fourteen-month suspended sentence for "subversion"; in January 1978 he was arrested, and released a couple of months later. Another incredibly pertinacious and petty-minded campaign of personal harassment ensued, which included round-the-clock police observation, damage to his car by "unknown perpetrators," and other such forms of gentle persuasion. The 1979 arrest and trial may be viewed, in fact, as results of the regime's sheer desperation: Havel simply could not be broken or compromised, and the only option left to his persecutors was to place him behind prison walls. The four and a half years he was supposed to spend there, particularly in the hard-labor camp in Ostrava, seemed a fail-safe way to soften up the recalcitrant dissident. Yet the whole plan misfired again. Havel and his codefendants somehow withstood the harsh conditions, and even their cellmates, most of whom were hardened criminals, treated them with respect. The only thing that finally yielded in Havel was his physical resistance: after a long series of health problems he fell seriously ill in January 1983, and thanks to a wide campaign of support in the West he was finally released after three years and eight months spent behind bars.

The fact that, during these three years and eight months of coping with debilitating illnesses and exhaustion from hard labor, Havel was also able to think and write is by itself an everlasting testimony to the endurance of the human spirit. He wrote his letters mostly on weekends, in extremely cramped and distracting conditions, interrupted by the guards' searches as well as the inmates' banter, usually trying to write down, at one sitting and without corrections, everything that he had thought over during the week. He could not keep copies of the letters, so he had to commit their contents and their logical sequence to memory. And, of course, he did not have much reference help from the prison libraries, in which non-Marxist philosophers were, understandably, poorly represented. In spite of all this, his entire system of thought, as presented in these letters, is a striking example of consistency and lucidity and a scrupulously detailed exploration of all the vistas that his mind discovered on its way to understanding.

This orderliness of Havel's mind is an intriguing counterpart and complement to his courage. I have no firsthand knowledge of his reception in Czechoslovakia in those years, but I remember vividly the broad-based popularity and unanimous respect he enjoyed in the late 1970s among the dissidents in neighboring Poland. This is particularly true of the period following the underground Polish publication of his 1978 essay "The Power of the Powerless," arguably the best work ever written on the intricacies of consent and dissent in Eastern European societies.[2] Still, what struck us about Havel then was primarily the courage of his political convictions. *Letters to Olga* proves that these convictions—and this courage, too—are a direct outgrowth of a consistent philosophical system.

To be sure, Havel does not consider himself an original philosopher. His thought is founded squarely on the basic categories of phenomenology and existentialism, particularly those of Heidegger ("Being," "existence-in-the-world," "thrownness," and so on), which were rooted in his mind thanks to both his earlier readings and the personal influence of the legendary Czech phenomenologist Jan Patocka. On the other hand, a systematic approach to the matters of Being and existence seems to suit his natural inclinations. Characteristically, he approaches the raw material of his experience, including his situation as a prisoner, the way a creative artist does—or, to be more exact, a playwright. He treats it first and foremost as a chaotic substance of events that needs to be put in some kind of meaningful order, and his theatrical imagination seems to serve this goal particularly well. On several occasions, Havel reflects upon the reasons he became a playwright. Besides his aversion to "disrobing in public"—that is, emotional subjectivism, to which theater's way of objective presentation is an antidote—the chief reason is theater's idea of order: "As one who always feels a little outside the given order, or on its margins, I have, understandably, a heightened sense of order (wasn't that, too, characteristic of Kafka?). The importance of structure, organization, composition that is proper to theater—I simply mean the importance of its order—cannot fail to attract me. (Who should be more interested in order than one who is constantly disputing it?)"

Just as a playwright does, then, Havel tends to interpret his existential situation, his being "thrown" into the world, in terms of dramatic structure, with its fundamental categories of time and space. The crucial ones among these are his concepts of "memory of Being" and concentric "horizons" surrounding the individual. Contrary to many thinkers, obsessed with the issue of the origins of evil, Havel begins with the opposite question: How is human good possible at all? What makes us sometimes behave decently when there is no reward in sight? A characteristically concrete image serves him as an illustration of this problem: someone boards an empty, conductorless streetcar for a one-stop ride and, even though nobody sees him, puts his fare in the box. What makes him do it? The pressure of inherited norms of social behavior? The "inner voice" of his conscience? Yes, but what created these norms and what is it that the voice of his conscience speaks for?

The only possible answer, according to Havel, is that man is never completely on his own. He may be alone in the physical sense, but even then he feels the presence of an "observer," an "investigating eye" that evaluates and gives meaning to every action of his. What makes us human beings is precisely the fact that, alienated from Being as we are, we nonetheless look up to the order of Being as a "system of coordinates" to which we can relate our individual beings, a system infinitely more stable and universal than the norms of our environment or the dictates of our conscience. Even when stripped of the closer and more tangible "horizons" of what he considers his physical or spiritual "home," man still orients his existence with regard to the "absolute horizon," which is the "memory of Being."

This particular term encapsulates the essence of Havel's outlook. His basic assumption is that "nothing that has happened can ever unhappen," every human act remains in the "memory of Being" that both records it and serves as an immutable point of reference, "the final court of appeal." The experience of "being in touch with the absolute horizon of Being," Havel writes in one of the letters, "is the 'suboceanic mountain range' that gives coherence and integrity to all those isolated 'islands of meaning' adrift on the ocean of Nothingness, the only effective defense against that Nothingness."

At this point, the question naturally arises whether the "memory of Being" should not be simply called God. In fact, faith is exactly what Havel has in mind while talking about relating to the "absolute horizon" as a defense against what we perceive as the absurdity of existence. The only reason he does not speak overtly about God lies in his striving for honesty and precision. "I have not had the mystical experience of a genuine, personal revelation, that supremely important 'last drop.' No doubt I could simply substitute the word 'God' for my 'something' or my 'absolute horizon' but that would hardly be responsible. I am trying to describe the matter as precisely as I can, as it appears to me and as I feel it; in other words, I don't wish to feign certainty where none exists."

Characteristically again, even in matters of metaphysics Havel prefers to stand with both feet on the ground. As a person, he makes no secret of his enjoyment of the pleasures of life (even the meager pleasures of prison life, such as making himself a cup of strong tea); his politics result not from any fanaticism or pursuit of martyrdom but from his need to restore normalcy to an abnormal world. Similarly, his faith is not that of a mystic. It has to do with the tangible realm of human affairs on this earth rather than with the thin air of heavenly spheres. Havel realizes full well "the profoundly paradoxical nature of human existence: the 'I' can only approach the kind of Being it longs for (i.e., the fullness of Being) through its own existence-in-the-world, and the manner of that existence." Consequently, he views our awareness of the "memory of Being" as the source of our most concrete sense of responsibility. Since "nothing that has happened can ever un-happen," the "Last Judgment is taking place now, continuously, always," with each and every human deed. And responsibility, in turn, "establishes identity": "Indeed: if I know what I have done and why, and what I do and why, if I can really stand behind this and (in private, perhaps) own up to it, I am thereby constantly relating to something stable, something I 'win' from my 'unstable' surroundings, and thus I myself ultimately become 'relatively stable'—

something graspable, something that possesses continuity and integrity. In short, I am 'someone,' i.e., identical with himself."

In that sense, the very identity established through the sense of responsibility, through relating to the "absolute horizon," puts man on the side of the "order of Being" and against the "order of death" or Nothingness. One must take full notice of this argument if one wishes to see what mechanism drives the seemingly inconsiderate behavior of lonely heroes such as Havel in their apparently hopeless fight against crushing odds. For the disillusioned observer who thinks he knows the ways of this world, their quixotic struggle seems nothing short of suicidal. Yet in fact people like Havel—in the beginning indeed lonely, inasmuch as they believe that "responsibility cannot be preached, but only borne, and that the only possible place to begin is with oneself"—are by no means lonely in the long run:

> It is I who must begin. One thing about it, however, is interesting: once I begin—that is, once I try—here and now, right where I am, not excusing myself by saying that things would be easier elsewhere, without grand speeches and ostentatious gestures, but all the more persistently—to live in harmony with the "voice of Being," as I understand it within myself—as soon as I begin that, I suddenly discover, to my surprise, that I am neither the only one, nor the first, nor the most important one to have set out upon that road . . . Whether all is really lost or not depends entirely on whether or not I am lost.

The idea of "the power of the powerless," which Havel has so memorably put into words and whose validity he has so convincingly proven by his own example, only seems to be a paradox. As an extension of his metaphysics, this kind of politics makes perfect sense. For its point is not the pragmatic, shortsighted vision of success or victory. Or perhaps we might say that its vision of victory is of a much longer-range sort and lies on a plane that is completely different from the one politicians are ever likely to imagine. In fact, "the power of the powerless" is just a human manifestation of something ultimately irrepressible and indestructible: the power of the "order of Being," confirmed and fortified by every individual act of human responsibility.

[1989]

Censors and Sense

Big Brother's Red Pencil

The affair began like a Le Carré novel, but its outcome makes one think more along the lines of Kafka and Orwell. In February 1977, an inconspicuous Polish citizen arrived in Sweden by ferry for a two-week vacation. The only peculiar thing about him was his luggage; he brought along, in his pockets and in plastic bags hidden under his clothes, some six hundred pages of top-secret documents from the files of the Polish government's censorship office. The tourist's name was Tomasz Strzyzewski, and he was an employee of the Krakow branch of the Main Office for the Control of Press, Publications, and Public Performances. In other words, he was a censor who had had enough—a Polish version of Winston Smith. He had copied the documents during his two years in the censor's office. Once he had arrived safely in Sweden, he got in touch with the Poland-based human-rights group KOR and requested that the documents be made public. KOR mimeographed the whole collection, provided an introduction, and distributed hundreds of copies among Polish bishops, academicians, writers, artists, and journalists. *The Black Book of Polish Censorship* was subsequently published in the West as well by the émigré publishing house Aneks. As a result, an even greater number of copies made their way back into Poland, smuggled in by other tourists.

As I remember it (I was one of the KOR members who wrote the original introduction to *The Black Book*), the reaction of the first readers was horror—horror that was unmixed with disbelief. Everybody who read the documents was genuinely struck by the extent and meticulous elaboration of the censor's guidelines and reports. The documents proved that censorship had literally every kind of publication under its control, from wedding invitations to circus posters to obscure quarterlies dealing with Mediterranean archaeology. At the same time, no one was really surprised. The iron grip of censorship had been tightening in Poland over the previous few years, and even its absurdities were considered an element of everyday life. To draw on one of my own experiences, I was not particularly shocked when a censor confiscated my translations of John Donne and George Herbert, which had been about to appear in a literary weekly. The reason was not the seventeenth-century poets' incompatibility with Communism, but the simple fact that I was the translator. My name had been included on a blacklist of Polish writers, which was, of course, never officially revealed to me, though I was well aware of its existence. When in 1977 I found the original list among the Strzyzewski documents, therefore, I felt a certain degree of pride (I was in a good company) and a certain degree of horror (I realized how many of my famous colleagues were blacklisted), but I felt no surprise.

Thanks to Random House, *The Black Book of Polish Censorship* is finally available in English[1]—a belated but highly welcome event. Even though the Strzyzewski documents cover the years 1974–1977 (that is, they derive from the middle phase of the so-called Edward Gierek decade, an almost immemorial past by the standards of the recent Polish *accéleration d'histoire*), the book may still be a revelation for the Western reader. It is invaluable as an inside view of the workings of Communist censorship. Moreover, in its English version *The Black Book* is not merely a collection of documents; it is actually Jane Curry's analytic study of censorship in modern Poland, sprinkled with extensive quotations from the Strzyzewski file in her translation.

In speaking of this, I cannot help mentioning that Curry's commentary is not free from minor, though irritating, inaccuracies. She obfuscates, for instance, the circumstances of *The Black Book*'s first Polish appearance by failing to note KOR's role in it (KOR, by the way, was never an "underground organization," and it could never have "forced the regime to retreat from its plans to increase food prices" in June 1976, because it was formed only in September of that year). The complex story of censorship in Independent Poland (1918–1939) is compressed into one paragraph and greatly oversimplified. It is not true that in Stalinist Poland "there were no purge trials where the defendants were put to death"; what Curry wanted to say was probably that in Poland, as opposed to other Eastern European countries, such trials had not affected the highest echelons of the party. Her remark that Julian Kornhauser and Adam Zagajewski's *Unknown World* (its title would be more accurately translated as *The World Not Represented*) "was never actually made available for sale in Poland" is also inaccurate; the book was published and made available in Polish bookstores in 1974. Vladimir Bukovsky is hardly "a Soviet *artist* who *emigrated*." The weekly *WTK* was an organ not of the independent Catholic group Znak but, on the contrary, of the pro-regime organization Pax. Curry's sample of "intellectual weeklies, dealing critically with cultural, political and economic issues" in the 1970s is rather dubious, since it includes *Prawo i Zycie* (Law and Life), a decidedly hard-line Communist weekly whose only distinguishing feature was rabid anti-Semitism; its editor-in-chief, Kazimierz Kakol, could hardly be counted among "Poland's most respected . . . journalists and intellectuals."

On the whole, the journalistic world of the seventies was much shadier than Curry imagines; although *The Black Book* offers many examples of censorship in numerous articles critical of the regime, we must realize that in a typical Communist country every honest journalist has at least a dozen colleagues whose sycophantic articles need no censoring whatsoever. But even this equation oversimplifies reality. In fact, there are no black-and-white moral divisions among those who work for the censored media; there are, rather, varying degrees of compromise. This was finally understood, incidentally, by a large number of pro-Solidarity journalists after the 1981 crackdown: to remain morally untainted, they had to quit their jobs.

Apart from such errors of fact and judgment, however, Jane Curry's commentary and thematic organization of the documents does indeed help the reader grasp the mind-boggling nature of totalitarian censorship. For even though Poland in the seventies was more than once defined as "totalitarianism that, thank God, messed up," its censorship without doubt epitomized the essence of pure totalitarianism. Strzyzewski's escape has often been compared to another famous defection— that of Jozef Swiatlo, a colonel in the Polish secret police during the Stalinist period. But Swiatlo's confessions had revealed only simple, though horrifying, facts of lawlessness and torture. Strzyzewski's documents, more than two decades later, dealt with the infinitely more intricate matters of the concealment and distortion of truth. What is purely totalitarian about Communist censorship is, first of all, the very extent of that distortion and concealment. Not only all means of publication but also every possible kind of publishable information, from world news to the metaphors of a surrealist poet, from economic statistics to satirical cartoons, appears to be under the supervision of an army of censors.

The following is a sample of guidelines that every Polish censor between 1974 and 1977 kept on his desk and knew by heart:

> Until the results of the elections are announced, no figures on the number of persons entitled to vote should be published.

> In mentioning the capital of the GDR, the term "Berlin" should be used, to differentiate it from "West Berlin."

> Information concerning ceremonials and performances and other forms of commemoration of the Bicentennial being observed in the United States, foreign countries, or our country may be reported only through the intermediary of PAP (Polish Press Agency). Information on this subject from other sources should be eliminated.

> All information concerning the participation of representatives of Israel in congresses, international conferences, or performances organized by Poland should be cleared with the GUKPPiW (Main Office for the Control of Press, Publications, and Public Performances) leadership.

> No material concerning the Hippie movement in Poland may be permitted for publication if it expresses approval or tolerance, does not take the question seriously, and so on. Only unequivocally critical material may be published.

> Information on direct threats to life or health caused by industry or chemical agents used in agriculture, or threats to the natural environment in Poland, should be eliminated from works on environmental protection.

> Numerical data on the nationwide increase in alcoholism should not be permitted for publication. Such data may be permitted to appear only in serious specialized publications.

> It was discovered that harmful substances were being emitted from material used to seal the windows in School No. 80 in Gdansk. Classes have been suspended in that school.

Absolutely no information on this subject should be permitted.

No information concerning Poland's export of meat to the USSR should be permitted. This prohibition is intended solely for the benefit of the censorship teams.

All criticism of Marxism should be eliminated from religious publications . . . All material critical of the religious situation in countries of the socialist community should be eliminated.

Another purely totalitarian feature of Communist censorship is its self-contained nature, which is combined with a highly complex internal structure. It is a state within a state, with its own secret rules, hierarchies, codes, and systems of controlling the controllers of the controllers. The Main Office for the Control of Press is not only Orwell's Ministry of Truth but also Kafka's Castle, self-contained and impenetrable from the outside. The above-quoted instruction "This prohibition is intended solely . . ." means that in practice the author or publisher has no right even to know the regulation on the basis of which the work has been censored; besides, this knowledge would not help him, because he does not have the right to appeal. The Strzyzewski documents include guidelines as to what precisely "should not be permitted for publication," as well as periodic "Reports on Materials Censored" (reprints of eliminated texts, neatly grouped by theme and supplied with commentaries for the sake of party authorities and the censors themselves) and special analyses—to be studied by censors—of individual decisions, right or wrong, compiled by the Bureau of Second-Level Control, that is, the censors of the censors. All of this serves to create a hermetically closed circuit of information; the only people in the know are censors and their party superiors.

Under these schizophrenic circumstances, the oddest ideas seem logical. One of the most untamed of Polish writers, Stefan Kisielewski, made a habit in the seventies of writing his most important statements in a deliberately outrageous way, so that they would undoubtedly be censored and thus would make their way into the classified bulletins. This seemed to be the only way to tell at least the leaders of the country—assuming that they read those bulletins at all—that Poland was heading toward disaster.

As we know today, even these desperate measures did not help much.

The popular explanation—that the Communist leaders are ruining their countries simply because "they don't know," "they are misinformed," "they are cut off from the real world"—is only half true. In fact, they schizophrenically *both* "know" and "don't know." The real information is at least partly available to them, if only in the bulletin of "materials censored" which they find every second week on their desks. At the same time, their access to this information has no impact whatsoever on their policies. In totalitarian thinking, there is no objective truth and no objective reality; only those facts and objects exist which are allowed to exist by the ruling power. As Jan Kott recently observed, "It's as if censorship as a system brings to its logical conclusion the poststructuralist principle that reality is only a message, which can be transformed at will according to definite rules." Information about, say, an epidemic is crossed out by the censor's red pencil not because the regime fears mass panic; it is deleted because the epidemic *was not supposed to happen*. The totalitarian rulers resemble some poets in this unconditional faith in the creative/destructive power of the word. Any phenomenon, be it the deterioration of the economy, the publication of a dissident author's book, industrial pollution, or an airplane crash, can be magically made nonexistent if no public mention of it is allowed (even though real people stand in lines, read underground books, suffer from pollution, and die in airplane crashes.) Inversely, the wishful thinking of the leaders can magically become reality if the mass media, statistics, posters, and pop songs all project the image of a flourishing, dissent-free, clean, and fail-safe country (even though, again, real people stand in lines, read underground books . . .).

This is, at least, the totalitarian rulers' dream. Censorship is necessary simply in order to let them keep dreaming. And the most frightening think is that here, in the less schizophrenic part of the world, we most often discuss the "views," "personalities," and "policies" of these dreamers as if they were wide awake, as if they really knew and wanted to know what is going on in their countries. In fact, their Castles are as impenetrable from outside as ever before. There could be no better way to commemorate both Kafka and Orwell in 1984 than to publish the *The Black Book of Polish Censorship*.

[1984]

Renouncing the Contract

On one of the first days after martial law was declared in Poland in late 1981, Polish television broadcast a supposedly "live" news report of a police search of the evacuated Solidarity headquarters in Warsaw. The stage had been elaborately set and all the props were in place: the eye of the camera swept over a neatly arranged assortment of half-emptied vodka bottles, stacks of foreign currency, and, horror of horrors, underground publications. Needless to say, only the latter had indeed been found by the police in the abandoned office; in fact, as close-ups of the covers demonstrated, the publications were quite genuine products of the Independent Publishing House (NOWa) that had just come out and that were awaiting distribution.

But according to eyewitness reports, the TV program resulted in something completely contrary to its original objective. Its aim had been twofold: intimidation and vilification. The average TV viewer was supposed to realize simultaneously how easy it was for the police to confiscate "illegal" publications and how outrageous the conduct of the Solidarity people was—why, they not only drank gallons of vodka bought with U.S. dollars generously supplied by the CIA, but they were also brazen enough to print books without asking for the censors' permission! Yet totalitarian propagandists seldom keep pace with society's evolving attitudes. When there are rapid changes in the collective mentality, they are usually a step behind. The hopelessness and terror that prevailed in December 1981 could still intimidate a great many people, but it was simply too late for vilification; during the sixteen months of Solidarity's existence, the notion of "illegal" publishing had already lost all its negative connotations. This particular segment of TV news did indeed become the talk of the town, but in a peculiar sense: it was received as an unintentional advertisement for the latest uncensored publications. "Have you heard that NOWa finally managed to publish that history book by Barbara Torunczyk? Yes, I saw it on TV the other day! Any idea where one can get a copy?" These were, I'm told, the most common reactions of Warsaw folk.

If we consider that all this happened in the first days of martial law, at the lowest point of society's hopes, in an atmosphere of authentic fear and despair, the significance of this anecdote will become even clearer. It shows that something truly incredible has emerged in today's Poland as an ironic result of decades of constant indoctrination, persecution of free speech, and official backing of obedient quasi-writers and quasi-artists. Despite all this, or perhaps because of it, the phenomenon of independent culture (rather, I should say "culture" without any qualifications, since culture that is not independent becomes a pale imitation of itself) has been able not only to survive and develop but also to secure its position successfully. The image of people making their way through the snowy streets of Warsaw past tanks and police patrols, talking animatedly about a recent history book published underground, is one of those tangible symbols which remind us that even in Communist-ruled countries History occasionally starts up again. And some of its steps forward are irreversible.

I have just used the phrase "to survive," but the notion of culture's survival needs some elucidation. To use this expression implies that the very existence of culture as such would be mortally endangered were it not for its own will and struggle to survive. This sounds true, but it is true only insofar as authentic, independent culture is concerned. What complicates the picture is the fact that even the most ruthless totalitarian regimes are interested in maintaining the semblance of a vivid cultural life, in preserving and supporting some degree of creativity—provided that it is kept under control.

The reasons for this are practical rather than moral or aesthetic. Sometimes this kind of substitute culture is viewed as a potentially useful vehicle for propaganda; sometimes the international image of the system is at stake; sometimes what matters is culture's entertainment value, which can divert the people's attention from more serious issues ("If there's not enough bread, let them at least have some circus"). The relation between suppression and control on the one hand and tolerance or even support on the other may also vary historically—that is to say, there is likely to be change over the course of time, sometimes quite rapid, in accordance with variations in the political climate.

Whatever the particular reasons for this and whatever its individual manifestations, the relationship between a Communist regime and its nation's culture can be seen as a dynamic model based on certain predictable elements. The most important of these is the fact that the regime is constantly suspended between two extreme policies: between the total silencing of culture and a total lack of control over it. Although the former option may well be one of the sweetest of the dreams that totalitarian rulers privately cherish, in fact neither of these two extremes can realistically be implemented. The optimal situation for a Communist regime is one in which some kind of culture and some degree of cultural life do exist but remain under strict and efficient control. From the perspective of the sender of an artistic message, it is a situation in which artists are deprived of creative freedom but not altogether silenced. From the point of view of the receiver, consumers of culture are barred from its authentic spiritual value but are still exposed to its potential for indoctrination and entertainment. Finally, from the point of view of the message itself, this is a situation in which cultural products are largely meaningless but in which their circulation continues; they are not even completely devoid of a superficial attractiveness. We may be reminded of a well-known fictional example: that of George Orwell's *1984*, with its vision of a special ersatz culture for the proletarian masses. But we may also cite actual, real-life examples of officially sponsored cultural (or quasi-cultural) productivity in countries such as Poland in the 1960s or 1970s. I have in mind, for instance, the genres of the popular song or the detective novel, which are the epitome of what a totalitarian regime expects from culture. They are devoid of artistic value yet superficially attractive; they don't force the consumer to think, yet they imperceptibly indoctrinate him; their authors enjoy the opportunity to create (and to make a decent living), yet they remain under state control.

The eminent Czech author Antonin Liehm once suggested that the relative stability of Communist rule in Eastern Europe was the result of what he called "a New Social Contract." On the strength of an unsigned agreement, the regimes guarantee their citizens some basic degree of well-being and safety, while the citizens, in exchange, do not rebel against the system's injustice. This concept can be applied to the narrower field of cultural life. The unwritten Social Contract also provides that artists get published and paid, and that consumers are supplied with cultural products—all on one condition: that they will not rebel and start demanding fancy goods like creative freedom and genuine artistic value, goods the system cannot afford to permit.

What has developed in Poland over the past decade is an initially timid and sporadic but gradually more stubborn and widespread renunciation of the New Social Contract by one of its parties—by society. After all, the other party, namely the regime, proved to be unable to fulfill even the basic provisions of the contract, that is, to assure a minimum of well-being and safety. Exactly the same thing has happened in culture. As it stands now, Polish culture is characterized by a growing number of both producers and consumers of cultural goods who have, at one point or another, decisively renounced the unwritten contract. At the cost of giving up protection, they freed themselves from control.

The watershed date was, to all intents and purposes, 1976, the year in which independent culture went public. It is often overlooked, however, that even prior to 1976 there had been many cases in which individuals took up a more or less independent cultural stance. In fact, there has been no single period in the cultural history of People's Poland in which culture has been totally subordinated to and in conformance with the regime's official policy. Even during the darkest years of Stalinism, the remembrance of which makes many Polish writers, artists, and scholars blush with shame, there still existed some indestructible enclaves of creative independence. Whoever imagines the years 1949–1955 as the triumphant period of Socialist Realism should also remember that those were years during which certain writers, like Czeslaw Milosz, chose exile rather than conformity; others, like Zbigniew Herbert, chose "internal emigration," retiring from public life to write "for their desk drawers"; still others, such as certain Catholic novelists, confined themselves to the theme of the past, since it was impossible to publish any truthful work on contemporary subjects. These were also the years when jazz musicians were giving clandestine concerts, when the poet Miron Bialoszewski began to stage performances of his avant-garde Separate Theater in his

70

private apartment, and nonconformist painters kept on with their work even though they could not exhibit it.

Even during the worst periods, then, totalitarianism was never able to completely suppress the residues of independent culture—that is, of the only culture deserving the name. And these barely visible residues eventually turned into a specific stock of tradition—seldom spoken of by the official histories of postwar culture, but nevertheless highly important as a kind of moral yardstick for the decades that followed. I personally know quite a few writers whose resistance to censorship was aided by the fact that they could measure their efforts against this yardstick. When, say, a censor threatened to withhold a book's publication unless certain "necessary corrections" were made, one could always say to oneself, "Well, if Zbigniew Herbert could do without publishing during the Stalinist years, I can do without it in the seventies." Czeslaw Milosz once mentioned that it would be perfectly possible for someone to write a companion volume to his *The Captive Mind;* this would be a book about the intellectuals' striving for creative freedom in postwar Poland and might be entitled *The Mind Set Free.* (In fact, such a book has recently been published in Paris: I have in mind Adam Michnik's collection of essays *From the History of Honor in Poland,* written, appropriately enough, in a prison cell.) The attitude of comfortable submission, however prevalent, has always been defied by individuals who refused to conform, even at the cost of years of oblivion, isolation, or harassment.

It is a commonplace of Polish cultural history to view October 1956 as the symbolic date for the great "thaw." True, since that date the methods of centralized management of culture have never been the same as they were in the Stalinist period. Especially just after 1956, censorship did indeed loosen its grip, and Poland—like the Soviet Union but to a much greater extent—experienced a genuine explosion of new artistic trends, combined with a revival of certain previously suppressed elements of the cultural past and a renewal of contacts with the West. The brilliant debuts of young and not-so-young poets, the so-called Polish School in cinema, the theatrical triumphs of old masters of the avantgarde like Stanislaw Ignacy Witkiewicz (Witkacy) and new playwrights like Slawomir Mrozek, the emergence of a strong group of modern composers and the overwhelming success of jazz, new tendencies in the visual arts—all this has always been associated in the collective memory with that legendary October. However, from today's perspective it is obvious that, for all its victories, the "thaw" was short-lived and illusory. By the early 1960s censorship restrictions were becoming so annoying once again that they gave rise to the first collective protests by intellectuals (beginning with the 1964 document known as "Letter of the 34"). By March 1968—the date of the brutal suppression of the student demonstrations and writers' protests prompted by the censorship ban on the Warsaw performances of Adam Mickiewicz's *Forefathers' Eve*—no one could have any doubts that the "thaw" was over.

What was new in this situation was the phenomenon I would call "selective silencing." After 1956 the increasing suppression of culture's independence affected mostly its political, ideological, and moral messages, while various avant-garde trends (provided they were ideologically neutral) were given relatively free reign. No one has described this better than one of those poets whose very names had been symbols of the "thaw": Zbigniew Herbert. In one of his prose poems he speaks of "the lowest circle of hell," which "contrary to prevailing opinion . . . is the refuge of artists": "Throughout the year competitions, festivals and concerts are held here . . . Every few months new trends come into being and nothing, it appears, is capable of stopping the triumphant march of the avant-garde . . . Beelzebub supports the arts. He provides his artists with calm, good board, and absolute isolation from hellish life."[1]

In the fall of 1976, exactly twenty years after the 1956 "thaw," came an unprecedented series of events that gave the notion of cultural independence a whole new meaning. Prior to 1976, freedom of expression could only be *given;* now for the first time people simply *took* it, without waiting for it to be given. Prior to 1976, Polish culture, for all its liveliness, had been generally passive in its dealings with the regime and with cultural policies. It had confined itself to taking advantage of the occasional loosening of the proverbial screws and to protesting helplessly when the screws were tightened again. In other words, during all those years culture had been the object of, rather than a partner in, the state's cultural policy. And no wonder, since the state had had a total monopoly over the publication and distribution of cultural products (the limited circulation of émigré publications and hesitant attempts at *samizdat* did not really contradict this rule). As a result, it could always blackmail the

72

writer, artist, or scholar into submission by simply denying his or her work the right to public existence.

The revolutionary change in this state of affairs which occurred in the fall of 1976 consisted of the equally simple act of drawing practical conclusions from thirty years of experience. Since the source of the regime's success in subjugating culture had been its monopoly on publication and circulation, it was necessary to break this monopoly. It was necessary to go from weak and futile protests against abuses of censorship to creating a network of publishing and circulation which would remain outside the regime's control. In other words, previous attempts to broaden the sphere of creative freedom had confined themselves, as a rule, to the first link in the author-publication-distribution-readership chain; now for the first time such attempts embraced the whole process of artistic communication.

All this was possible thanks to the clearsightedness, personal courage, and energy of certain intellectuals, but was also due, to a large extent, to a fortunate convergence of favorable circumstances. The creation of independent publishing would not have taken place had it not been for the increased *need* for such an undertaking, a need that in the mid-1970s was felt by both authors and readers. The abuses of censorship had become so blatant by then that the public—and not only the censored authors—became aware of the dangers inherent in the regime's uncontrolled rule over culture. Moreover, by 1976 the gradual changes in the political mentality of the younger generation had already produced a sufficient number of people who were willing to take the risk of serving as underground printers, editors, distributors, and so on. For the first time in postwar history, all the links of the chain of communication fell into place: there was someone to write for the independent circuit, someone to manage the process of independent publishing, and someone to read independent publications (and thus to form an independent market for them).

The brief but colorful history of independent publishing in Poland is already well-known in the West, so I need not dwell on details. Let me merely point out that what had started in the field of literature and journalism soon spread to other fields of culture. Naturally enough, in arts like the cinema or theater there are, from the purely technical point of view, far fewer opportunities to communicate directly with the public.

No wonder that in the first years after 1976, attempts to liberate culture were more or less restricted to the channels of the printed and spoken word (by the latter I mean, for example, public lectures in private apartments, organized by scholars associated with what was popularly called the Flying University). They were also limited socially and geographically, as their influence was restricted mostly to intellectual circles and to cultural centers such as Warsaw or Krakow. But the state's cultural monopoly had been broken, and whatever happened afterward merely broadened, however dramatically, the sphere of freedom that had already been won.

Here I refer, first of all, to the events of August 1980, which brought about the most impressive gains thus far. The emergence of Solidarity resulted in, among other things, a radical shift in the accessibility of independent culture. From being restricted, it became virtually unlimited. The circulation of uncensored publications spread rapidly to all social milieus and even to the remotest corners of the country. Uncensored public lectures on history, political science, economy, and literature became the most popular public events. Finally, arts other than literature also found their own specific channels of independent communication (such as uncensored theatrical and musical performances and art exhibits). The new spirit affected even those professional artists such as painters and actors who in the past had been most dependent on the state's monopoly on employment and commissions, and who therefore had been most often accused of servility.

The best proof that the self-liberation of Polish intellectuals is an irreversible process lies in the fact that, contrary to what we might expect, even the imposition of martial law has not fundamentally changed the cultural situation. In saying this, I am perfectly aware that the Jaruzelski regime does its best to get away with murdering not only "dissident" priests and schoolboys but also cultural freedom. We all know that hundreds of leading writers, artists, and intellectuals were interned in camps or forced to emigrate; that all the important creative organizations have been disbanded; that people have been given three-year sentences just for possessing an "illegal" leaflet; that there has been a barely masked regression in the regime's policies to the methods of personal blacklisting, campaigns of slander, and even arresting authors for what they have written (as the case of Marek Nowakowski, who was only recently released from prison, demonstrates). But at the same time we all should remember that, although there is no substantial difference between the Stalinist period and the present so far as official cultural policy is concerned, there is an enormous difference in the attitude of both the makers and consumers of culture. Culture as such now refuses to be owned by the regime. Both the artists and their audience have decisively and unequivocally renounced the New Social Contract. Gestures of defiance like the famous actors' boycott of television, or the boycott of the officially sponsored substitute for the disbanded Polish Writers' Union by the overwhelming majority of important authors, are truly unique in the Eastern bloc in that they are not isolated and individual but interconnected, well-organized, and supported by the public.

Granted, the regime still has some powerful means of exerting pressure at its disposal. It can not only directly threaten and punish the individual artist, but also attack the material and organizational roots of the resistance by, for instance, refusing to publish or employ selected groups of intellectuals and banning all forms of organized assistance for them. In fact, many writers and artists in Poland would be reduced quite literally to destitution were it not for occasional support from the Church, from émigré communities, and from Western sympathizers.

Even these difficulties, however, can be overcome at least in part through the continuance of the chain of unrestricted communication between the makers and consumers of culture. The demand for independent culture still exists—and this demand, in turn, constitutes a cultural "market" in the full sense of the word. The reader is willing to pay for a book published underground, and the underground publisher is able both to support himself and to pay an honorarium to the author. As a result, despite all the risk of persecution, the existence of an independent market of cultural goods offers authors and readers a basic alternative. The awareness of this alternative can even affect the way in which official culture is controlled. In fact, what sometimes seems to be unexpected leniency or a mistake on the part of the censors—for example, the publication of a previously prohibited book—is more often than not a decision forced upon the censors and their superiors by the realization that prohibiting a book under the present circumstances will only spur the growth of underground publishing: the book will be published "illegally" anyway.

All this does not mean that my views on the chances of independent culture's survival are simplistically optimistic. As a matter of fact, I am often disturbed by the signs of certain inherent dangers characteristic of a culture that must develop under abnormal conditions. Continual confrontation with a powerful, relentless, and cunning enemy produces a specific "fortress mentality," which can be particularly damaging in the realm of culture. Spontaneous creativity thus often yields to collectivist restrictions; the obligation to defend a certain set of values (which the enemy indeed intends to destroy) makes one forget that, as Joseph Brodsky once said, the poet's only obligation to society is to write well.

These dangers can sometimes be seen in Polish independent culture, and their presence is understandable in the circumstances. One could say that although culture tries to return to normalcy in the very way it functions, it is still far from normal, well-balanced, or well-proportioned so far as its content is concerned. But it might be argued that culture itself produces antidotes to any poison; and there is reason to hope that in this particular case, health is only one step away from sheer survival.[2]

[1985]

The Godfather, Part III, Polish Subtitles

Here's a little exercise in imagination-stretching. While sipping his breakfast coffee one bright morning at the end of his second term, President Reagan reads in his favorite astrologer's column: "A good day for settling old accounts and restoring order in the universe." The next thing we know, he puts a finishing touch on his hairdo, calls his advisers to the Oval Office, and begins with all the force at his disposal to crack down on the National Actors' Guild. As it happens, this very morning the guild's representatives are supposed to reconvene for the third day of a national conference on "How to Save American Culture and Not Lose Money at the Same Time." When they arrive at the convention site in downtown Manhattan, they find a crudely scribbled note taped to the door: "CONFERENCE CANCELED DUE TO REASONS OF NATIONAL SECURITY. GUILD SUSPENDED. GET LOST. MAYOR KOCH." They don't know yet (but they'll soon find out) that even as they rage and fume, the FBI is engaged in a nationwide hunt, arresting scores of leading actors from Gregory Peck to Eddie Murphy and putting them in special internment camps in North Dakota. Ed Asner does his best to protest and, at the risk of his own freedom, personally brings a petition to Ed Meese's office, but he is helpless. The only thing he manages to obtain is the release of Arnold Schwarzenegger, because of his frail health, and Spuds MacKenzie, whose sway over the minds of Americans makes Meese think twice. As the months go by, Reagan's apparatus of terror repeatedly ignores the actors' feeble protests and feeds the media and the public with the same old line time and again: the latest election for members of the guild's executive board was illegal because the wrong people got elected. Eventually the interned actors are released, and some of them are even allowed to appear in local used-car commercials in Cincinnati. But then comes the cruelest blow. An official announcement dissolves the guild "for its lack of cooperation," even though it wasn't allowed to operate in the first place. As a substitute, a new guild is soon formed, consisting of carefully screened actors from B-movies, none of whom have any more acting talent than Pia Zadora. It's called S.N.A.G., which stands for Superior National Actors' Guild. It comes as no surprise that Joan Collins gets elected—or, to be exact, appointed—as S.N.A.G.'s president. In her acceptance speech she states that membership in the new guild and permission to return to the screen may be granted by the federal administration to all actors, even Paul Newman, but first they must mend their ways.

Sounds farfetched? But this, give or take a few details, is roughly what did happen in reality several years ago—only the crackdown's mastermind was dressed in a general's uniform, the suppressed organization was a writers' union, and the place was not present-day America, of course, but Poland under martial law. Granted, my fleshing out the structure of this story with American substance might be judged a poor joke: the sheer impossibility of such a turn of events in a democracy is as obvious as its occurrence in an Eastern bloc country appears trivial. This is, however, exactly the point I wanted to make. Ironically, the more the Western observer knows about the abuses of power in the Communist world, the more apt he is to accept subconsciously even the most flagrant of them as an intrinsic—therefore natural, therefore in turn unavoidable—part of the system. More ironically, this silent acceptance ("That's the East— what else would you expect?") extends to facts that even the absurdity-inured inhabitants of Eastern bloc countries themselves deem shockingly unacceptable. As the death tolls of totalitarianism go, the 1983 destruction of the Polish Writers' Union is, needless to say, infinitely less momentous than the famine in Ethiopia or the Cambodian killing fields, but it is grave enough to deserve a moment of reflection. Lost in the glare of Soviet *glasnost* with all its miraculous resurrections of murdered writers and shredded books is, after all, the fact that in one of the Soviet Union's satellite countries a perfectly legal and highly respected professional organization of intellectuals with its democratically elected board was forcibly put to death five years ago and has been denied its right to resurrection ever since.

What makes the matter more notable is that this particular organization has always been much more than just a union of writers. In fact, while trying to patch together my fictitious story of Reagan's revenge, I searched in vain for a name of an American institution whose significance in this country would be remotely comparable to that of the Writers' Union in Poland before 1983. Surely no writers' organization in the United States has a commensurate grip on public consciousness, and even American actors, as a professional group, are in no way equal in status to Eastern writers in their own countries (though admittedly Jack Nicholson beats any Polish writer in terms of individual recognition among his compatriots). Established as a strictly syndical association in 1920, ZLP (the union's Polish acronym) soon grew into a peculiar institution combining down-to-earth professional concerns with a self-imposed obligation to stand up and be counted whenever freedom of speech or other human rights were at stake. This obligation was clearly an extension of the nineteenth-century concept of the writer's public role, which had emerged as a result of the fact that literature had become a substitute for partitioned Poland's nonexistent political life.

Inevitably, such a tradition of taking an independent stand made ZLP a major thorn in the side of postwar Communist leaders. Throughout the first forty years they tried more than once, with a varying degree of success, to pacify, infiltrate, bribe, divide, manipulate, or intimidate it, and at times even to get rid of some of its members. But until 1983, they never tried to shut it down and replace it with a new union of literary toadies. Something like that had happened in Czechoslovakia fifteen years earlier. In Poland the "Czechoslovakian solution," often hinted at by way of a threat, was nonetheless never taken seriously. The union, all its weaknesses and internal divisions notwithstanding, still was too strong to be crushed and still seemed too much of a cherished national tradition to be quietly disposed of.

No wonder that the 1981–1983 crackdown continues to stir up emotions among today's Polish readers. Witness the vivid reactions to the latest of the three books—all of them, significantly, nonfiction—that were the greatest sensations of Poland's literary life in the past couple of years. The earlier two of these, made available almost simultaneously by both underground and émigré publishing houses, are collections of interviews: Teresa Toranska's *Oni* (published eventually by Harper and Row as *They*) is a chilling record of her frank conversations with former Communist dignitaries; Jacek Trznadel's *Hanba domowa* (Domestic disgrace) contains a series of controversial confessions of prominent writers on the subject of their involvement in or resistance to Stalinism (the book remains untranslated, but its most fiercely debated interview, that with the poet Zbigniew Herbert, appeared recently in *Partisan Review*). The popularity of these two collections in Poland doubtless reflects the sudden growth of interest, particularly among the young generation, in the history of the early 1950s—the only period, fortunately a very brief one, when Poland seemed, at least on the surface, resigned to its fate as a Soviet vassal, and many Polish intellectuals succumbed to the totalitarian temptation. The third book, Jan Jozef Szczepanski's documentary memoir, published underground and titled rather colorlessly *Kadencja* (Term of office),[1] deals with the more recent political and cultural history of Poland, but, in a more profound sense, it seems to share its subject with the other two. It, too, penetrates the dark vaults of the Communist bureaucracy's greed for absolute domination, even though the author's own personality has always been sharply divorced from such appetites and his book appears at first glance to be nothing more than a matter-of-fact account of his "term of office" as the last president of the Polish Writers' Union before its demise.

It's a shame, by the way, that Szczepanski's more typical books—his novels, short stories, and essays—have, quite inexplicably, not yet found their way to the American reader. One would probably have to point to the daunting spelling of this author's last name as the only reason in sight, since both the perspicacity of his vision and the lucidity of his prose make him not only one of Poland's best contemporary fiction writers but also one who might be expected to turn out extremely well in translation. Born in 1919, he experienced, as a young man, the Second World War (he fought against the Nazis first in the regular army and then in a Home Army guerilla unit) and postwar Stalinism (to which he was ideologically immune thanks to the strength of his liberal upbringing). As a writer, he emerged belatedly in the mid-fifties with several excellent novels and collections of short stories, thematically revolving for the most part around the ethical and psychological issues raised by wartime savagery. His favorite theme—individual human fate confronted with dilemmas brought about by History—remained Szczepanski's trademark in his later works, some of which delved into the nineteenth-century past whereas others reflected more modern concerns. Throughout the sixties and seventies his renown grew steadily, boosted especially by the 1975 publication of *Przed nieznanym trybunalem* (Before an unknown tribunal), his widely discussed collection of essays on such disparate figures as Joseph Conrad, Father Maksymilian Kolbe, and Charles Manson. Even though all his books before *Term of Office* had come out in official circulation, his closeness to the circles of liberal Catholics and dissidents, his completely non-Marxist and non-Communist past, and, above all, his well-known personal integrity and intellectual honesty always made the authorities look upon him with suspicion. It goes without saying that exactly these qualities made him, on the other hand, more and more of a moral authority in the eyes of his readers and fellow writers. In spite of this kind of reputation, Szczepanski, a reticent and peace-loving loner, managed for quite a long time to stay away from exposed public roles and instead concentrate on writing.

It's necessary to keep this background in mind while reading *Term of Office.* Apart from its value as a historical record, this account may also be viewed, from another angle, as a psychological self-analysis, a penetrating study of the feeling of inadequacy. Being president of the Polish Writers' Union was the last thing he would have wished for himself, Szczepanski tells us, and whoever knows the tiniest bit about him has no reason to doubt the truth of his words. A series of unexpected coincidences led, however, to a situation in which his colleagues made him an offer he could not refuse. In March 1980 Jaroslaw Iwaszkiewicz, the longtime president of the union, died, having left no designated heir capable of continuing his morally equivocal yet admittedly skillful policy of finding compromises between the State's demands and the writers' interests. Meanwhile, the political situation itself changed dramatically. In August 1980, Solidarity triumphantly emerged, and the majority of Polish writers were drawn, even more irresistibly than the rest of the nation, into the vortex of rapidly developing events. Their community, which since the late sixties had already been increasingly vocal in its protests against censorship and human rights abuses, needed another leader now—someone different from the compliant Iwaszkiewicz, someone

81

prudent enough not to be rejected out of hand as a negotiating partner by the regime, yet fit to serve as an unquestioned moral authority and staunch champion of literature's interests. The next election of the union's president and governing board was to take place at a congress of delegates scheduled for the end of 1980. Unbelievable as it sounds, among the union's more than 1,300 members Szczepanski was the only viable candidate for president. He was the only one who stood a chance of being accepted both by the majority of his fellow writers and, more grudgingly, by the regime, who—so the reasoning went—could consider him a lesser evil compared to some of his radical colleagues.

I happened to serve as one of the delegates to the December 1980 congress (those were my last months in Poland) and I remember vividly how much Szczepanski hated the very idea of his candidacy. It looked as if his logic had persuaded him that there really was no other choice, but his imagination kept feeding him with grim images of troubles that lay ahead. Yet even he could not foresee the truly unimaginable course of events. In its passionless, documentary manner, *Term of Office* unfolds a chronicle of the regime's ensuing moves which reads like a Polish version of *The Godfather*, with party hacks cast in the roles of pocket-sized Corleones. Even during the year of relative freedom, between the December 1980 congress and the December 1981 coup, the union's governing bodies were constantly vilified and their demands largely ignored. The outcome of the congress—the emergence of the union's legally and democratically elected governing board, with Szczepanski as president and mostly non-Communist writers as members—was met with a frenzied smear campaign in the official media. Szczepanski' efforts to establish close cooperation between ZLP and workers' unions were viciously portrayed as attempts to throw Polish literature at the feet of Solidarity radicals (in fact, he had impartially extended an offer of cooperation to all the existing unions, including the regime-sponsored ones, but only Solidarity accepted). Those writers who were party members were summoned to special conferences, where they were given instructions on how to resist the new Board's initiatives.

On December 13, 1981, writers, artists, and intellectuals who came to attend the third day of the Congress of Polish Culture in Warsaw found the door to the conference room locked. Martial law had just been imposed and all the associations suspended; the congress itself had been canceled by the mayor of Warsaw. As riot police busied themselves smashing printing presses with sledgehammers and countering street demonstrations with tear gas and nightsticks, writers tried feverishly to locate their missing colleagues, many of whom were in the process of being transported to internment camps. Over the next few months, the activities of the union officially came to a halt—under martial law, even its most innocent operations such as running a writers' cafeteria were made illegal—while Szczepanski and other members of ZLP's presidium spent virtually all their time trying to intervene on behalf of their interned colleagues. Food parcels were sent to the camps, and the general in charge of the Ministry of Internal Affairs was pestered by Szczepanski's petitions and visits, but that was about all that could be done.

By the end of 1982 the military regime, now more assured of success, switched to cruise control; all the interned writers were released. Even before that, however, the authorities started another campaign aimed at discrediting the board, and Szczepanski in particular, and forcing them to resign. The means of persuasion included such subtle methods as slander in the media, personal intimidation, stonewalling all negotiations on the reactivation of the suspended union, and spreading false rumors. The list of incredible instances of this sort of behavior would be too long to present here, but one such fact, told by Szczepanski in meticulous detail, definitely takes the cake: in February 1983 a letter, complete with his signature and typed on the union's stationery, was forged (certain unmistakable signs pointed to the secret police as the forger) and sent to the chairman of the Council of State. The letter, immediately made public, contained a skillfully stylized pack of threats and abuse; it was an all-too-obvious attempt to portray Szczepanski as a radical lunatic and thus alienate his undecided and pro-regime fellow writers. Szczepanski wrote a statement to the press, but it was confiscated by the censor; it finally did appear, but only after a week and only in two periodicals.

Several months later the Polish Writers' Union, which had so often made history, was itself history. After sixty-three years of existence, it was dissolved by a decree of the authorities, just as other associations of artists and intellectuals had likewise been eliminated earlier, in analogous campaigns. A new union under the old name hastily came into being, taking over, as a matter of course, all the financial and structural assets of its predecessor. A writer who remained outside the new union had no access to its system of grants, pensions, medical care, vacation houses, foreign travel opportunities, and even facilities such as a library or an inexpensive cafeteria—modest privileges which nonetheless had been of vital importance to many. In fact, they were even more essential now that numerous dissident writers, fired from their jobs or facing difficulties in publishing their work, were deprived of means of support.

In spite of this financial blackmail, the new union turned out to be a spectacular flop as far as its membership drive was concerned. Virtually no first-rate writer has joined it so far; the names of its consecutive presidents and board members add up to a pitiful list of literary failures, party activists turned literati, authors of military songs or Socialist thrillers, other figures unknown even to the best literature experts, and a few dozen writers old enough to fear a pensionless retirement. Boycotting the new union continues to be a basic mark of decency and a sort of recognition badge for those who stick to the simple point: no one may disband a union or recall its elected governing body except the union's members themselves. It is a point of order but also a point of honor. Just as by publishing their works underground or abroad Polish writers demonstrate their unwillingness to accept the absurdity of censorship, they refuse to join the new union in order to expose and reject another absurdity: that of a regime trying to make literature a state-owned industry with appointed executives at the helm and writers as obedient employees.

Jan Jozef Szczepanski's dry yet fascinating account of the Polish Writers' Union's struggle, defeat, and moral victory would make, if translated, much-needed reading in the West. Apart from the weight of its factual material and the wealth of its insight, this portrayal of a clash between freedom-obsessed literature and power-obsessed bureaucracy underscores one truth, perhaps not so obvious to someone who envies the intellectuals under Socialism the material advantages of their position: as a state employee, an intellectual may well be better off than he would be otherwise—provided that he thinks only the way the State wants him to think.[2]

[1988]

The State Artist

Several months after my graduation from a Polish university in 1969, I happened to meet on the street a former fellow student, not a particularly close friend, but a guy whom I like for his literary interests, his ability to play ragtime on piano, and his good sense of humor. He, too, had majored in Polish literature and, like myself, had already made his debut as a critic in the press. As was natural for recent graduates, we talked about the job market. The general prospects for humanists were grim, and I considered myself lucky to have been offered a position as a teaching assistant at my alma mater. "How about you?" I asked. "Have you landed any decent job?" "Naah," he groaned. "There was this position as junior editor in some publishing house, but someone snatched it before I had a chance. I heard something encouraging yesterday, though. They say there's an opening in the Office for the Control of the Press. I guess I'll give it a shot." "You mean you want to work as a censor?" I asked tactlessly. He winced at the sound of it but nodded. "Yeah, why not?" "So there's a chance you'll censor my article one day, right?" I persisted. His sense of humor did not fail him. He guffawed heartily and said once again, "Why not?"

Why not, indeed? Had our conversation continued, my fellow humanist would probably have uttered the Polish equivalent of the famous phrase "It's a dirty job but someone's got to do it." Another familiar plea would have followed suit: "It's better for this job to be done by people like me than by some stupid apparatchiks." And if we had quarreled, he might have pinned me down with a clinching argument: "If I were an editor instead of a censor, I'd have to screen your articles anyway, wouldn't I? And what about you writers? Don't you censor your works yourselves?"

He would have had a point. Even as we talked on that autumn day in 1969, hundreds of identical conversations were, in all probability, taking place in the streets and cafés of Warsaw, Prague, Budapest, and East Berlin. And in each of those exchanges the would-be censor and the would-be author could easily have switched roles: there was no distinct moral difference between them, not to mention the fact that who was to become the censor and who the censored was largely a matter of blind chance. True, things were to change soon, at least in Poland. But eighteen years ago we had no inkling of that.

While thinking of the workings of censorship in Eastern Europe, the Westerner is, as a rule, prone to commit a fundamental mistake at the very outset. He begins by imagining a system in which the censor and the author are not only two different characters but natural opponents: the censor's job is to suppress; the author's job is to rebel against suppression. The typical truth is more complex and, at the same time, more ominous. In fact, censorship and culture—to repeat, in usual and typical situations—are not two opposed and separated extremes but rather two cooperating parts of the same mechanism of Socialist cultural life. The controllers of culture are by no means interested in eliminating expression altogether; on the contrary, they sponsor and promote it, provided that it serves their goals. The producers of culture are by no means making their right to free expression an absolute priority; on the contrary, most of them deliberately cede a large part of that right in exchange for some other privileges. Instead of hostility, one should rather speak of a "mutual embrace" of censors and artists.

Miklós Haraszti's *The Velvet Prison*,[1] from which this expression is quoted, is one of the most frightening books on Eastern Europe recently made available to the Western reader. This is so even though—or perhaps because—the book speaks of an apparently flourishing culture rather than artists' arrests and torture; of the "mutual embrace" of the oppressed and the oppressor rather than bloody persecution of the former by the latter. Haraszti can by no means be suspected of beautifying the system's image or sugarcoating its inhumane nature in order to deceive the Western audience. His name, along with Václav Havel's in Czechoslovakia or Adam Michnik's in Poland, has long been a symbol of utmost defiance and moral courage; it stands for what is most independent in Hungarian dissident thought. Born into a Communist family in 1945, he has lived all his life in Hungary, and a better part of this life has been stigmatized by his continuous conflict with authority. "A born dissident," as his friend George Konrád calls him, he was expelled from the university and (another close similarity with Adam Michnik's life) went to work for a year in a factory; the result of this experience was his famous book *A Worker in a Worker's State*. Its underground publication in 1973 earned him a trial and the status of a nonperson in Hungary's official public life. Nonetheless, he has become a leading figure in dissident circles, spreading his ideas mostly through *Beszelo*, a samizdat periodical of which he is an editor and contributor.

Haraszti, however, is not only the dissidents' dissident but also a dissident among the dissidents. He is able to look from a critical distance and without self-delusion at the dissident movement itself; he never falls prey to a typical Eastern European dissident's simplified vision, according to which the entire world is divided into "them" (the ruthless totalitarian persecutors) and "us" (the innocent victims and their chivalrous defenders). His mind is perspicacious and honest enough to fully realize the unpleasant truth: "they" would not stay in power for a single day if not for a measure of acquiescence from "us." The perfidy of modern totalitarianism lies precisely in the fact that it imperceptibly blurs the difference between the oppressors and the oppressed, by involving the victim in the process of victimization.

In order to convey that message, *The Velvet Prison*, though a political essay, employs a narrative device that reminds one of characteristic techniques of Eastern European poetry: a sort of dramatic monologue in which a protagonist presents his arguments only to unwittingly debunk himself. Like a ventriloquist, Haraszti filters his own voice through the lips of a puppet. This puppet, however, is his antagonist rather than his alter ego: it represents a typical intellectual who is clear-sighted enough to be cynical about Socialism but cynical enough to build himself a cozy nest in the Socialist state.

The basic assumption of Haraszti's narrator is this: no one can deny that a system such as Hungary's in the 1970s is something qualitatively different from that of the Soviet Union in the 1930s or even that of Hungary in the early 1950s. In other words, the days of Stalinist terror are long gone. The present-day state Socialism, although formally still based on the same ideological foundations, offers a completely new set of sociotechnical tools for ruling society. One of the most handy tools of this sort is what the book calls "a new aesthetic culture," in which the old method of commanding culture from above (and executing those fools who dare disobey or are not eager enough) is replaced by a "symbiotic" relationship between artists and the modern Socialist state. In cultural as in political life, the old principle of "he who is not with us is against us" has been modified into "he who is not against us is with us." If previously cultural life was characterized by a stark opposition between censorship and artists, the present situation can only be described as a steady disappearance of censorship aimed at its total elimination. More precisely, censorship will soon be superfluous as an institution, since the artists are already censoring themselves. "Censorship professes itself to be freedom because it acts, like morality, as the common spirit of both the rulers and the ruled."

This leads Haraszti's narrator to musings on the relationship between art and freedom. He challenges the sanctified opinion according to which freedom is an essential precondition of art. First of all, it has not always been so: Egyptian and medieval European art did pretty well without freedom. So perhaps our present subservience is just a return to art's natural condition? Second of all, in the modern Socialist state the very need for artistic autonomy has been all but eliminated. Independent art is now virtually impossible since there is no independent audience. In present-day society, any manifestation of truly independent art would be automatically rejected as anti-art. As a consequence, for artists themselves the very notion of independence is "simply a recipe for social irrelevance." Hence what the narrator calls the true "liberation of art" (meaning, of course, liberation in the sense of Engels' definition: "Freedom is a realized necessity"). Culture in today's Socialist state has reached a sort of menopause: the excitement of irresponsibility has been replaced by the pathos of responsibility.

How could this come to pass? Haraszti's narrator takes pains to elucidate the historical reasons. The present culture of a Socialist state draws from the tradition of radical commitment of nineteenth-century art. But the pleasant difference is that whereas in the capitalist era the artist's commitment equaled his alienation, Socialism offered him a vision of a state that needed the artist and rewarded him for his commitment. In reality, after the establishment of state Socialism in Eastern Europe, all this turned out to be even more enjoyable than in the initial promises. As the narrator admits, some sticks had to be used in order to persuade the few reluctant artists, but most of them enthusiastically gobbled the carrot. And the carrot was big and tasty: the state demanded a specific kind of art, an art that would indoctrinate, educate, or at least reinforce social cohesion, but whoever provided such art was nicely rewarded for his efforts. More important, art now had the best of both worlds: it could enjoy "both the privileges of power and the legitimizing conceit of serving the people."

As a result, artists' interests gradually converged with the interests of the State. After the Stalinist "errors and deviations" were done away with, artists could be given a relatively free rein. Within certain limits, though: freedom, after all, is a realized necessity. In arts, such realized necessities take on the shape of certain taboos of which every artist is aware. The most important of these taboos is that art must only affirm reality; consequently, not merely dissenting or politically wrong but also "solipsistic" art is excluded from the state's tolerance, not to mention support. But is any formal censorship really necessary to enforce these taboos? Not at all: the artist in a Socialist state—Haraszti's narrator argues—is something of a company employee, very much in the spirit of corporate capitalism. He realizes that what is good for his company is good for him. What deserves to be called "progressive censorship" is actually a form of the company artist's self-restraint. His "creative compromise" and "self-correction" renders the State's open interference needless.

The artist in a modern Socialist state, then, has come to terms with the State's demands: indeed, he internalized them. Moreover, he balks at the very prospect of severing his ties with the State. One of the most revealing chapters in Haraszti's book, "Art and the Economy," tells the unbelievable story of a debate that took place in the Hungarian media in the 1970s. At a certain point, the regime—tired of the unprofitability of lavishly supported arts—had the quasi-capitalist idea of making a part of cultural enterprises pay for themselves, mostly by way of allowing them to rely more on the Western (thus genuinely attractive) model of mass culture. The idea immediately backfired: it provoked a bizarre neo-

Stalinist protest by the artistic community, who quite rightly feared that any introduction of a market economy into culture would endanger the artist's economic security. In a way, the dog bit the hand that was about to loosen his collar. The artists themselves proved that they prefer protection to freedom.

Haraszti's cynical narrator knows his subject thoroughly and has a lot of supportive evidence up his sleeve. He is detailed and precise in describing the aesthetics of "progressive censorship," its specific taboos and principles, as well as in dissecting the infrastructure of state-supported cultural life (for instance, the unified and carefully planned system of art education, or the so-called amateur artistic movement in which, needless to say, "only those with an amateur's license can be amateurs"). He is also confident about the future of the system he analyzes. He points out that while the phenomenon of circumlocutory language and "writing between the lines" is usually viewed as proof of Socialist culture's decay, we should keep in mind that the same phenomenon was characteristic of ancient civilizations that turned out quite durable. Another illusion he ridicules is the belief that dissidents in Socialist countries can play any significant and genuine cultural role; on the contrary, even their presence may be "part of a well-designed strategy." After all, their usual fate serves as an excellent cautionary tale for the more reasonable "state artists": it reminds them of what they have to lose.

It is at this point that we finally realize the enormity of the actual distance between the voice of Haraszti's puppet—who is a consummate "state artist"—and the voice of Haraszti himself. The facts described are facts nonetheless; but the narrator's cynical confidence is the author's pessimism and despair. He is one of those Maverick Artists his narrator ridicules in the final chapter: one of those who believe, against all odds and against a mass of evidence to the contrary, that their stubborn defense of artistic freedom (meant as freedom pure and simple, not as Engelsian "realized necessity") can make a difference.

The funny thing is that this belief sometimes becomes reality. Haraszti wrote his book before the emergence of Solidarity in Poland and before the rapid spread of similar dissident tendencies in his own country: he is the first to admit (in his afterword, added in 1987) that history made at least partial corrections in his pessimistic outlook. I would even say that the creation of a totally independent publishing network in Poland and the refusal of the majority of first-rate writers to join the state-controlled Polish Writers' Union have convincingly proved the uselessness of any once-and-for-all theory of culture under state Socialism.

I do not mean to say that Haraszti's brilliant and biting work is useless. On the contrary, his book will long remain a classic analysis of the "velvet prison" of posttotalitarian culture in Eastern Europe; my prediction is that its categories and distinctions will prove especially applicable to the Soviet Union's cultural life under Gorbachev in the immediate future. I am only saying that words such as "always" and "never" can, of course, be used in a social analysis of Eastern Europe (especially if its purpose is satirical exaggeration) but they should not be taken at their face value. Ultimately, everything comes down to the question of whether we are to agree that Eastern European totalitarianism has indeed produced a new "breed of men who do not wish for liberty," as George Orwell once feared and as some of the later thinkers, such as Alexander Zinoviev, apparently believe. Let us say that this type of man does exist. But will it "always" exist? Will it "never" change? Haraszti's narrator seems to believe so. But Haraszti's own example proves otherwise. So does the most recent history of Eastern Europe.

[1987]

Despair and Order

Gombrowicz: Culture and Chaos

A few days before the fateful date of September 1, 1939, the thirty-five-year-old Polish writer Witold Gombrowicz disembarked from a transatlantic liner that had just brought him to Buenos Aires on its maiden voyage across the ocean. Little did he know that those few steps down the ship's ladder would lead him into an abyss of obscurity. Instead of several weeks, he was to stay in Argentina for the next twenty-four years—a largely ignored writer from the margins of a marginal literature, as exotic and odd to his émigré compatriots as he was to the Argentinian literary salons.

But in some strange way, obscurity and loneliness also acted on Gombrowicz's behalf during that time. Their depths offered him, as it were, enough room to work his way up to prominence. Forgotten by some, made light of by others, and unknown to most, he had no other choice but to fight for recognition, to try to impose his uniqueness upon the world. His post-1939 novels and plays, which began to come out in the early 1950s, and above all his three-volume *Diary*, today considered by many to be one of the most important books in twentieth-century European literature, put into effect his brazen maxim "Writing is nothing more than a battle that the artist wages with others for his own prominence."

Against all odds, he won that battle. Even before his death in 1969 he managed to become a celebrity in Europe (he was widely translated in France and Germany, and, as legend has it, lost the 1968 Nobel Prize by one vote) and an object of a veritable cult among young intellectuals in his native Poland. One of the things about American culture I fail to understand is why he still has to conquer these shores. The fact that his major novels have not been translated into English from the original but, ludicrously enough, have been retranslated from French translations (and lost much of their stylistic vigor in the process) does not fully explain Gombrowicz's so far rather limited impact in the United States. True, an unprepared reader who opens any of his books may have the disquieting impression of encountering a total oddball, but has there ever been a shortage of oddballs in American literature? Can't it assimilate another one, especially since on closer reading he turns out to make quite a lot of sense? One can only hope that the long-awaited publication in English of the first volume of Gombrowicz's *Diary*[1]—which, among other merits, is also the most incisive commentary on Gombrowicz himself—has at last provided the reader with the set of keys necessary to enter this writer's System.

I'm capitalizing this word because, if we are to make anything of Gombrowicz, we need to see not only the apparently grotesque and bizarre side of his mind but its obverse as well: its philosophical toughness, consistency, and precision. This is most evident in his *Diary*, which, contrary to its title, adheres only to a slight extent to the genre's traditional form: a record of everyday events that may or may not resonate with some more profound reflection in the diarist's mind. At one point Gombrowicz even deliberately pokes fun at such a model of the diary by jotting down, tongue in cheek:

> I got up, as usual, around ten o'clock and ate breakfast: tea with ladyfingers, then Quaker Oats. Letters: one from Litka in New York, the other from Jeleński in Paris . . .
>
> At three, coffee and ham sandwich . . .
>
> I make known the above so that you will see what I am like in my daily routine.

But on the whole, *Diary: Volume One,* even though sprinkled with personal anecdotes and reminiscences, is hardly a detailed chronicle of Gombrowicz's "daily routine" in Argentina between 1953 and 1956. What he wrote under the guise of a diary is, rather, a series of neatly interconnected essays, elaborating on various components of his ever-present System. One more manifest difference is that this particular diary was not supposed to wait in the writer's drawer for discovery by posterity; on the contrary, it was addressed to a specific contemporary audience, most of all to the Polish émigré intelligentsia that in the early 1950s formed the readership of the Paris-based monthly *Kultura,* where the *Diary* was initially published in installments.

In this historical and social context, the *Diary* was bound to be received as a no-holds-barred piece of impudence. Consider its immortal beginning:

Monday
  Me.
Tuesday
  Me.
Wednesday
  Me.
Thursday
  Me.

To the Polish exiled reader in 1953, one thirsting in those troubled times for spiritual support and advice from the moral authority that the Polish writer traditionally had been, this monosyllabic confession of egotism sounded like the utmost effrontery. In spite of the outrage of conservative critics and readers, however, Gombrowicz continued unswervingly in the same vein, making himself consistently the center of his diaristic universe. "Do not allow yourselves to be intimidated," he says to other artists:

> The word "I" is so basic and inborn, so full of the most palpable and thereby the most honest reality, as infallible as a guide and severe as a touchstone, that instead of sneering at it, it would be better to fall to your knees before it. I think rather that I am not yet fanatical enough in my concern with myself and that I did not know how, out of fear of other people, to surrender myself to this vocation with enough of a categorical ruthlessness to push the matter far enough. I am the most important and probably the only problem I have: the only one of all my protagonists to whom I attach real importance.

This provocative bill of an egotist's rights forms, at the same time, a constitution for culture at large. At another point, Gombrowicz says: "To be an individual . . . I do not want to say that collective and abstract thought, that Humanity as such, are not important. Yet a certain balance must be restored. The most modern direction of thought is one that will rediscover the individual man."

Today, twenty years after Gombrowicz's death, when numerous biographical books have already appeared dealing in detail with various phases of his life, it seems clear that this individualistic basis for his System had developed as a result of his early obsession with the rigid, schematic, and oppressive Form that emerges in any interpersonal contact. From his early childhood on, he seemed to be destined to clash with and rebel against the various rituals of what he later called "the inter-human Church." He was born in 1904 on his father's country estate in central Poland; even though Gombrowicz Senior soon switched from landowning to industry management and the family moved to Warsaw in 1911, Gombrowicz grew up in an environment that cultivated traditional ways of life, respected social hierarchies, and was full of aristocratic pretenses. The only rebellious and whimsical child in his family, Gombrowicz graduated with some difficulty from high school (which was to be portrayed as an oppressive realm of empty stereotypes in his first novel, *Ferdydurke*) and, acceding to his father's wishes, studied law unenthusiastically at Warsaw University and in Paris. After graduating he returned to Warsaw, where his unorthodox views were already so well known that he was unable to find a job as a lawyer—a situation that he accepted gratefully as a chance to devote himself entirely to writing. In 1933 his first literary effort, a collection of short stories provocatively titled *A Memoir Written in Puberty*, came out to skeptical reviews; almost all of the critics dismissed the book as "immature," even though precisely the exploration and defense of "immaturity" was the author's chief objective. Nevertheless, Gombrowicz won recognition among the more avant-garde authors. By the mid-1930s he already was viewed as a sort of guru by a circle of not much younger fellow writers, who gathered regularly at "his" table in the famous Ziemianska café in Warsaw. It was *Ferdydurke* that finally made a genuinely big splash; published in 1937, this novel was savagely attacked by critics from both the extreme left and extreme right, but it was also acclaimed by some others as one of the most spectacular manifestations of the avant-garde spirit in Polish fiction. *Ferdydurke* was the last book Gombrowicz published while residing in Poland; prior to the war, only a play, three more short stories, and an unfinished novel of his managed to appear, in periodicals; the novel was a hilarious

Gothic parody serialized pseudonymously in a Warsaw tabloid. At this point, Gombrowicz was enough of a celebrity to be invited aboard a newly built ocean liner—ironically, to take part in its trip as a represent-ative of Reborn Poland's young literature, expected to strengthen cul-tural contacts with the Polish émigré community in Argentina.

While in Buenos Aires, he learned of the outbreak of the war and decided not to return. There was more to it than his self-admitted inca-pacity to serve as a military hero. In a sense, it was one of Gombrowicz's many escapes from this or another Form that stifled and immobilized him—this time, from the Form that his entire life up to that point had taken on. The first Argentinian years, however, while indeed offering him inner freedom by cutting off all of his previous ties and obligations and by transplanting him onto the soil of a "young" country with no historical Form of its own, were also extremely difficult due to his isola-tion and financial hardship. To make ends meet, he finally took a poorly paid job as a clerk in a Polish bank in Buenos Aires. In whatever spare time he had, he worked on his new novels and plays, largely unknown as a writer among his Polish fellow exiles but, ironically, finding more and more admirers among young Argentinian literati. A sort of cult fol-lowing that developed in the narrow circle of his Argentinian friends resulted in a collective Spanish translation of *Ferdydurke*. Meanwhile, Gombrowicz returned to the Polish émigré literary scene in 1953 with his new novel *Trans-Atlantyk,* issued jointly with his play *The Marriage* in Paris. This particular novel, arguably Gombrowicz's best and certainly his funniest (it's a shame that it remains untranslated into English), was met with vitriolic attacks from the conservative trenches of the émigré community for its satirical demolition of the most sacred patriotic clichés and general "lack of seriousness." On the other hand, after 1957–1958, when four of Gombrowicz's books had been published in Poland during the brief period of political relaxation, he became an idol for many young writers and critics there.

Between 1957 and 1966, Gombrowicz published, through the same publishing house in Paris, the rest of his most important books written in exile: two novels, *Pornografia* and *Cosmos,* and the *Diary* in three vol-umes, the last of which also included his third and final play, *Operetta.* The sixties finally brought him recognition in Western Europe, where no less than Camus and Sartre had been involved in persuading publishers and theaters to take on his work. In 1963 he received a grant from the Rockefeller Foundation and left for Europe. After some time spent in West Berlin, he moved to Paris and finally settled with his young French-Canadian wife Rita in the small town of Vence in southern France. Translations, premieres, literary prizes, and a growing European reputation came to him, however, even as his health was rapidly deteriorating. After a long struggle with respiratory disease, he died in Vence in 1969.

Gombrowicz's cult in Poland is a special matter. It has been spreading and intensifying ever since the appearance of his books in 1957–1958, but not without some profoundly bizarre twists, affecting particularly the *Diary*. The chief of these is that soon after 1958, and especially after the political attacks on Gombrowicz in the official media in the mid-1960s, his books were to all practical purposes banned in Poland. After the writer's death, the ban was partly lifted, but at the same time Gombrowicz's last will went into effect, a provision of which specified that his work not be published in Poland unless reprinted in its entirety. Since the authorities had objections to a couple of passages in the *Diary* dealing with the Soviet Union and Communism, and Rita Gombrowicz was steadfast in abiding by her husband's will, an insane situation resulted and lasted for seventeen years: Gombrowicz's work was widely read in its smuggled-in Paris editions or underground reprints, critical books on him were published, and his plays were even staged in Polish theaters, but none of his books could be officially reprinted or bought in a bookstore. In 1986 the regime finally yielded and a state-owned publishing house reprinted Gombrowicz's works, but, as a breach of the agreement reached earlier with the writer's widow, the *Diary* appeared in expurgated form.

The lunacy of Poland's censors aside, this was, in fact, a fitting development in the posthumous career of the work that no orthodox and rigid mind could have ever accepted in toto. Not that the *Diary* is an anti-Communist manifesto: Gombrowicz's thought was too all-encompassing to be preoccupied solely with politics, and his critique of Marxism on the pages of *Volume One*, though devastating, is just one particular application of his more general method. Regardless of the domain of existence he is dealing with, the same System with the same fundamental notions and antinomies underlies his vision of the human world.[2]

The basic premise of Gombrowicz's thought is his obsessive awareness of man's solitude and helplessness in confronting the powerful pressure of culture—if we are to understand "culture" in a Freudian sense, as a collective superego that stifles the authentic impulses of the human self. Accordingly, the chief antinomy that underpins Gombrowicz's philosophical and literary System is the ineffaceable, ubiquitous conflict between the solitary individual and the others, the rest of the human world, in particular—all of society's petrified rituals, customs, stereotypes, and institutionalized relationships. The individual's natural need is to remain free, independent, spontaneous, unique, whereas the very presence of others crams him into the schematic framework of whatever is socially and culturally acceptable.

If Gombrowicz had stopped at this point, he would appear to be merely—and not terribly creatively—continuing the arguments of Freud, if not of Jean-Jacques Rousseau and the whole Romantic tradition. But he is much more original than that. His innately dialectic mind immediately counterbalances the argument with its exact opposite. He is equally aware that, contrary to his need to remain free and unique, the individual also fears isolation and desires to affirm himself through contacts with other people, through his reflection in the eyes of others. This contradiction is particularly dramatic in the case of an artist: he wishes to reveal his individual uniqueness to the audience, but in order to be understood, he must resort to a comprehensible language of approved convention, which, in turn, destroys his uniqueness. In other words, each public manifestation of the artists's freedom-seeking self is tantamount to his self-imprisonment in a rigid scheme of finished shapes— and thus, it means his death as an artist.

Yet the situation of the artist, however dramatic, is for Gombrowicz just one version of a more universal paradox of human existence as such. In his view, every individual lives his life in constant suspension between two ideals: "Maturity" and "Immaturity." These two may be variously called Fulfillment and Unfulfillment, Completeness and Freedom, Perfection and Spontaneity, Typicality and Uniqueness, or, perhaps most generally, Form and Chaos. Just like the protagonist of *Ferdydurke,* who sincerely desires to be mature, responsible, and respected but at the same time is secretly attracted to anything that is immature, chaotic, and inferior, virtually all the characters in Gombrowicz's fiction (more often than not, deliberate impersonations of himself and his own neurotic ob-

101

sessions) are torn between their striving for Form on the one hand and for Chaos on the other. As Gombrowicz puts it succinctly in *Diary: Volume One:* "The most important, most extreme, and most incurable dispute is that waged in us by two of our most basic strivings: the one that desires form, shape, definition and the other, which protests against shape, and does not want form."

In both his literary works and the *Diary,* this basic antinomy takes on the flesh of various specific inter-human relations, from politics to religion to sex. The struggle between Form and Chaos may reveal itself, for example, in its sociological version, in which Aristocracy represents perfect (but also petrified) Maturity or Form, while Peasantry stands for spontaneous (but also inarticulate) Immaturity and Chaos. It may also be illustrated by the inequality of civilizations; Western civilization is, in this respect, an embodiment of Maturity, while the "second-rate" civilizations of countries such as Poland, "the poor relations of the [Western] world," represent Immaturity. Or the tension between the extremes of Form and Chaos makes itself felt within the confines of the individual ego, as a self-contradictory, simultaneous yearning for the "perfection" embodied in the complete personality of an adult on the one hand and the "beauty" of a child's or adolescent's spontaneity on the other.

In fact, all these versions of the basic opposition between Form and Chaos have a common denominator in the concept of inequality; each opposing pair can be interpreted as a case of Superiority confronted with Inferiority. According to Gombrowicz, the very essence of human existence lies in the fact that the individual strives all his life for Superiority and Form but in reality is by no means unequivocally attracted by these values, since their ultimate attainment equals spiritual petrification and death. Therefore, the individual secretly desires Inferiority, Immaturity, and Chaos, because only these extremes offer a chance of freedom. Yet on the other hand, the ultimate attainment of this other goal would mean isolation, the impossibility of any communication and self-affirmation. In the final analysis, the conflict is insoluble. It can be only partly overcome and contained, if not fully resolved, by artistic creativity. Even though the artist can neither escape from nor achieve perfect Form, he can at least feel free to *play* with it. He can make both the Maturity of artistic convention and his own Immaturity "visible" instead of concealing them, and thus, by gaining a salutary distance from both, he can liberate himself to a certain extent from their oppression.

Gombrowicz's way of relating everything to human Superiority and Inferiority means, in turn, that the focal point of his outlook is neither the individual per se nor society in general but, rather, what emerges at the point of their mutual clash: the "inter-human Church." His philosophy, as he puts it in *Diary: Volume One,* subscribes neither to individualist nor to collectivist philosophies but to "the third vision" built on the corpses of both: it is a vision of "man in relation to another man, a concrete man, I in relation to you and him . . . Man through man. Man in relation to man. Man created by man."

At this central juncture, however, the consistency of his own argument forces Gombrowicz in his *Diary* to make a number of necessary qualifications and reservations. In order to prove that his philosophy of the individual is itself individual, he has to distinguish his views from those popular philosophies of his time which for various reasons might be suspected of having influenced him. For such a programmatic artist, Gombrowicz was amazingly well-versed in philosophy—in Argentina, he even supplemented his income for a while by giving occasional philosophy lessons—and the philosophical pages of *Diary: Volume One* testify to his impressive intellectual precision. He is perfectly aware that certain elements of his vision put him close to several existing doctrines, but he identifies with none of them—not only for the simple reason that he had developed his own ideas before the emergence of some of these doctrines (such as existentialism), but because neither of them fits completely into his System. On the one hand, for instance, he clearly realizes his proximity to modern Catholicism:

> I am joined to it by its acute sense of hell contained in our nature and by its fear of man's excessive dynamics . . . The Church has become close to me in its distrust of man, and my distrust of form, my urgent desire to withdraw from it, to claim "that that is not yet I," which accompanies my every thought and feeling, coincides with the intentions of its doctrine. The Church is afraid of man and I am afraid of man. The Church does not trust man and I do not trust man. The Church, in opposing temporality to eternity, heaven to earth, tries to provide man with the distance to his own nature that I find indispensable . . . The important thing for me is that it

103

and I both insist on the division of man: the Church into the divine and human components, I into life and consciousness. After the period in which art, philosophy, and politics looked for the integral, uniform, concrete, and literal man, the need for an elusive man who is a play of contradictions, a fountain of gushing antinomies and a system of infinite compensation, is growing.

Yet Gombrowicz, a declared atheist and rationalist, realizes with equal clarity that no authentic communication between him and a Catholic is possible: in the latter, "everything is already resolved . . . , because [he] already knows the ultimate truth about the universe . . . [and] is not allowed to entertain doubt."

On the other side of the ideological spectrum, Gombrowicz is aware that, at first glance, his vision might reveal considerable affinities with two other popular philosophies: existentialism and Marxism. His System indeed seems to have something in common with each of these two—in particular, with the claim of both that their ultimate goal is the demystification of human consciousness. More specifically, Gombrowicz seemingly finds a common ground with existentialism in regard to the important notion of freedom of the individual, whereas his concept of "man created by man" might be suspected of echoing the Marxist idea of man as a product of social conditions. Gombrowicz himself points to these analogies only to deflect the potential accusation of borrowing from the two doctrines by laying bare the inconsistencies or falsehoods inherent in both. He admits that his early work did bear, *avant la lettre,* some superficial similarity to existentialism, but he also points out that there is no room in his System for the notion of authenticity that the existentialists hold so dear:

> I . . . tried this authentic life, full of loyalty to existence in myself. But what do you want? It can't be done. It can't be done because that authenticity turned out to be falser than all my previous deceptions, games, and leaps taken together . . . It seems impossible to meet the demands of *Dasein* and simultaneously have coffee and croissants for an evening snack. To fear nothingness, but to fear the dentist more. To be consciousness, which walks around in pants and talks on the telephone . . . Strange. Philosophy, exhorting to authenticity, leads us into gigantic falsehoods.

Existentialist "authenticity" is an empty concept for Gombrowicz because in his "inter-human Church" nothing is free from the determining pressure of the presence of others. There is no authenticity as such—there are only the masks of authenticity we put on; man has to be artificial so long as he wishes to remain part of the human community. For the same reason, while writing on Camus's *L'Homme révolté,* Gombrowicz assaults the basic tenet of existentialism, its idea of the absolute moral freedom of the individual as reflected in the notion of conscience:

> For me, conscience, the individual conscience, does not have the power that it has for him as far as saving the world. Don't we see again and again that the conscience has almost no voice in the matter? Does man kill or torture because he has come to the conclusion that he has the right to do so? He kills because others kill. He tortures because others torture. The most abhorrent deed becomes easy if the road to it has been paved, and, for example, in concentration camps the road to death was so well trodden that the bourgeois incapable of killing a fly at home exterminated people with ease.

This, in turn, sounds disturbingly close to the premises of the Marxist philosophy of man, and Gombrowicz takes pains to define the differences between himself and the Marxists as clearly and unequivocally as possible. Even though he is instinctively repelled by the horrifying cruelty that results from any application of Marxist principles to a society's life, he dismisses this emotional response as philosophically irrelevant. Equally irrelevant in this sense are all the other traditional reasons—conservative, religious, libertarian—for condemning Marxism. What matters for Gombrowicz is the question of intellectual honesty, of which Marxism is totally devoid. As a philosophy which claims to relentlessly unmask and demystify everything, its ultimate proof of honesty would be an attempt to unmask itself as well. This is, however, exactly what Marxism slyly avoids by refusing to apply its formidable dialectical apparatus of demystification to its own dialectic:

> Let us catch them red-handed. Let us check the cards, how they are being dealt here, and reveal the trick with which this entire dialectics becomes a trap. This dialectic and liberating thinking stops exactly at the gates of Communism: I am allowed to cast aspersion on my own truths as long as I am on the side of capitalism, but this same self-checking is supposed to cease the minute I join the ranks of the revolution. Here dialectics suddenly gives way to dogma as a result of some astounding about-face.

As we read these words, it may be useful to remember that they were written in the mid-1950s. Who else in world literature except this unknown Polish writer stranded in Argentina was then able to achieve, solely on the strength of his own inexorable honesty in approaching the reality of ideas and facts, such independence of judgment, such clarity of perception? Gombrowicz's intellectual boldness, so striking in his *Diary* and still unmatched after more than three decades, is the boldness of someone who has fought and won a relentless battle. He himself preferred to define it as a battle for literary "prominence." But in his case, prominence was merely an outward sign for something more essential: the writer's ultimate right to speak and be heard. The right that is due the writer only when his mind stops at nothing in questioning its own and the world's self-delusions.

[1988]

The Face of Bruno Schulz

Letters and Drawings of Bruno Schulz is a scrapbook rather than a book,[1] a fascicle with photographs and drawings inset on its pages among letters and press clippings. Its design seems consciously to imitate the randomness of an old album, a book of personal memorabilia that swells with cuttings pasted in over the years, a disparate collection of material traces left behind by a long since extinguished existence.

But the randomness, in this case, is owed to the arbitrariness of death, not to the haphazard hustle of life. There is an aura of incompleteness about this book. It is not even an entire scrapbook—just a handful of torn-out and rumpled pages snatched miraculously from the grasp of doom. The fact that we can read *Letters and Drawings of Bruno Schulz* today is a miracle. The spirit of nothingness that, for lack of a better term, we call History wanted these scraps of paper to perish, together with the human hand that covered them with letters and lines. Unlike Franz Kafka, to whom he is often compared, Bruno Schulz did not have to ask a friend to burn his manuscripts after his death. In his time, and in his part of Europe, the task of lighting an all-devouring fire belonged to History itself.

By painstakingly assembling the Polish edition of this book from whatever could be found in the postwar ashes, Schulz's own Max Brod, his tireless biographer and editor Jerzy Ficowski, disobeyed not the writer's last will but the will of the Holocaust. It is largely thanks to him that we are left today not only with Schulz's self-portrayal as it is reflected obliquely in the pages of his two wondrous collections of short stories, but also with Schulz's image in a more literal sense: with his unforgettable face staring at us from the pages of this book.

In the perfunctory, iconic, short-attention-span culture of our day, the ultimate measure of success for a writer is not so much being widely read as being widely recognized. Recognized, that is, visually: as a face or a silhouette, etched in our otherwise scatterbrained cultural memory. Kafka's eyes, icy and pained, in his last photograph; Joyce pouring over a manuscript with a magnifying glass in his hand; Beckett's profile, like that of an aloof bird of prey; old Auden's tectonic furrows and wrinkles: these images have a staying power of their own. Heavy with the symbolism we put into it, each portrait in this gallery of famous faces is a popular condensation of the writer's work, a condensation so immediately and deceptively comprehensible that it promises (or threatens) to outlive the work itself.

Something like that is happening to the image of Bruno Schulz. It is not only for the unquestionable brilliance of his meager but captivating oeuvre that he has been increasingly attracting the cultural attention of the West. And it is not only due to the fact that the rich texture of his background—he was a Jew writing in Polish in a small town in Polish Galicia that was once part of the Austrian empire and now belongs to the Soviet Ukraine—epitomizes the cultural complexity associated with the fashionable concept of Central Europe. There seem to be other reasons, more subconscious perhaps, having to do with the image of Schulz fixed in our collective mind's eye. Forty-six years after he was shot by a Gestapo agent in the street of his backwater hometown of Drohobycz, this morbidly shy high school teacher of arts and crafts who happened to be a great writer appears as another haunting face in the row of the most suggestive portraits of twentieth-century authors.

The difference is that Schulz etched his features in our memory quite literally, by leaving behind a number of graphics and drawings (some of them illustrations to his short stories) in which his own face catches the eye time and again. We owe our knowledge of what Schulz looked like more to these illustrations, in fact, than to the few blurred photographs of him. The surviving photos show his face invariably at a peculiar angle, strangely foreshortened, as if he were glancing coyly upward from some humble, kneeling position (strikingly reminiscent of the actual position of his alter ego's body in etchings such as *Dedication* or *A Book of Idolatry*). His sunken eyes hide uneasily under his prominent, almost simian eyebrows. He looks like the facial epitome of an inferiority complex, of introversion. This is also true of the group photos, in each of which he seems to have just suffered an anxiety attack, withdrawing into himself and striving in quiet panic toward the picture's background or corner even when he actually remains in its foreground.

His drawings or *cliché-verre* etchings, while often bordering on fantasy, show him more revealingly. And more shockingly. True, today's observer would hardly feel compelled to share the opinion of a certain eighty-year-old Christian Democrat senator who, while taking the waters in the resort of Truskawiec sixty years ago, made a ruckus over the alleged pornography in Schulz's graphics exhibited at a local banquet hall. This kind of charge sounds ludicrous now that art, let alone pornography, has reached degrees of boldness which doubtless would have killed the apoplectic senator on the spot. Yet we must concede that even by today's standards Schulz's way of portraying himself is sometimes disturbingly "indecent," in the sense of revealing what society expects to be suppressed, or at least symbolically disguised. In his early graphics, in particular, he sheds all inhibitions and descends into the shadowy depths of his life's central obsession.

Consider *Wild Beasts,* one of the etchings included in the portfolio *A Book of Idolatry* that Schulz assembled and let circulate as a limited edition in 1920–1921 (that is, several years before he finally switched from art to literature). A teenage girl, dressed in a skimpy, pulled-up nightshirt or slip, sits in an armchair, with her legs spread and her hands crossed over the darkness of her crotch. Her left hand holds a whip; her right leg has a black stocking and a high-heeled shoe on, while the naked left leg, touching the floor with its toes, appears almost luminescent against the dense darkness that lurks beneath the chair. The left shoe, apparently kicked off, rests on the floor in the picture's foreground. Also on the floor, crawling in from the right side toward, it seems, both the girl's bare foot and the shoe, is the naked figure of a man with Schulz's features. His eyes are half-closed and his mouth is half-open in animal ecstasy—or is it the pain of someone having just been whipped? The relation between light and shadow, as well as the etching's composition (the girl's commanding, dynamic figure towering over and turned slightly away from the crawling male torso) make the picture brim with compressed, implicit violence.

This is, obviously, as masochistic and fetishistic a self-portrait as you

109

can get. Interestingly, in Schulz's prose the motif of a man's humiliation by a woman (usually by a vulgar female servant named Adela) does occur, but generally in a much less obtrusive and sexually explicit form. This kind of relationship recurs with obsessive frequency, however, in most of Schulz's graphic works and drawings: a woman or a girl, naked, half-naked, or at least provocatively dressed, often in black stockings and high-heeled shoes, long-legged and round-breasted to the point of fashion-magazine idealization, hovers luminescently over the dark, crouched, miserable figure of her male worshiper, who crawls toward her, kneels in front of her, kisses her feet, lets himself be kicked or trampled. In many pictures, the male figure multiplies into a whole tribe of idolatrous admirers of varying ages and degrees of ugliness.

The fact that they mostly form a symbolic representation of Schulz himself is beyond doubt. We are encouraged to identify him in these pictures, not merely on the basis of the facial likeness, but also on the strength of what we know about his actual sexual obsessions. The prudish norms of Polish small-town society between the wars, and the public image he had to maintain as an educator of the young, forced Schulz to suppress his deviations almost totally; they were revealed mainly through his art. Yet even in his lifetime there were people to whom he did open up, either deliberately or against his better judgment. Ficowski has managed to reach and interview some of these people in his meticulous investigation of the writer's life. Some of their reminiscences (not included in this collection but published in Poland as a separate booklet in 1984)[2] correspond amazingly to the motifs and scenes in Schulz's drawings. There is a woman, for instance, who recalls a scene in 1921. She was twelve; Schulz, a family friend, was painting her portrait; according to her, he lost control and behaved for a while not unlike the man in *Wild Beasts*.

Meddlesome and indiscreet though they may be, such pieces of literary gossip reaffirm in our minds the image of Schulz the masochist, Schulz the seeker of humiliation. In the eyes of a detective from some literary vice squad, all the evidence would confirm that Schulz was exactly this in his life, at least in his intimate life. His symbolic image, pasted together from document, art, and gossip, stares at us with the moist eyes of a whipped dog. Yet symbolic images have a tendency to acquire a life of their own. Their way of singling out a crucial element of a personality inevitably results in a focusing on this particular element alone. A living face ends up frozen in a grimace.

Under the spell of his self-created image as a masochist, we may miss the fact that Schulz was also something else. We tend to see the entirety of his life, not merely his intimate life, as governed by a single principle: the search for humiliation and suffering as a perverse source of pleasure. In some of Schulz's admirers this tendency has gone to truly bizarre lengths. The Polish critic Artur Sandauer, whose meritorious role in popularizing Schulz's work should not be forgotten, had a theory that the writer's masochism was tantamount to a drive toward self-destruction. He was killed, Sandauer maintained in all seriousness, precisely because he instinctively sought death, procrastinating endlessly after he was offered a chance to escape from Nazi-occupied Drohobycz. This is biographical baloney, a pseudo-psychoanalytic approach that finds the chief symptom of the patient's death in the fact that he is dead. But the standard legend of Schulz encourages such silliness, with its insistence that he was bent on misfortune and humiliation at any cost.

The full truth, as usual, is more complex. In his life, as in his drawings, Schulz was indeed constantly trampled by sadistic reality. (The Polish word for "reality" is feminine in gender, by the way.) His letters, particularly those written to female friends, frequently reveal his acute sense of inadequacy, unfulfillment, and unrealized potential. He writes to Romana Halpern in 1936, "It seems to me I have been swindling the world by some sort of flash or glitter when there is nothing inside me."

His mixed background alone could not but brand him with a stigma of incompleteness. Writing in Polish made him an outcast among the Jews. Being Jewish made him a stranger in Polish culture. As if this suspension between the guilt of betrayal and the humiliation of nonbelonging were not devastating enough, his everyday existence oppressed him, too: particularly onerous were twenty-seven hours of teaching high school every week, which effectively stunted his creative growth. By 1942, the year he turned fifty, he had written only two slender books.

Schulz's brutal death cut short a life that must have seemed to this exacting man an almost total failure—in terms of emotional ties, family life, wealth, and social respect. The flash of fame he briefly enjoyed in the thirties was confined to Polish literary circles, and it was largely due to a happy coincidence. (It's unlikely that Schulz would ever have been published had it not been for the influence of the novelist Zofia Nalkowska, who reluctantly agreed to read his manuscript at the request of a mutual friend.)

Still, concentrating on what Schulz did not achieve, and losing sight of the fact that he did, after all, write the stories collected in *Cinnamon Shops* (in English, *The Street of Crocodiles*) and *Sanatorium under the Sign of the Hourglass,* distorts his true image quite severely. In the final analysis, the popular perception makes him one of those people who in life irritate everybody with the odor of failure they seem to exude, and who after their death evoke nothing but warm feelings. Unable to enter their already closed lives, we extend to them a vicarious, retroactive sort of help by idealizing them, even if this idealization makes them into ideal failures. Instead of appreciating what they accomplished against all odds, we wonder what might have been had their appointment with success been a little earlier, or that with death a little later.

What might have been: there is a disquieting poem on the subject written a couple of years ago by the magnificent Polish poet Wislawa Szymborska. The man portrayed in the poem is an oldish intellectual sitting at a table in a cafeteria, presumably in the rather paltry retreat that the Polish Writers' Union maintains in the mountain resort of Zakopane. We observe all the minute particulars of his worn-out appearance and his trivial behavior, from his warts and bald pate to the way he studies a newspaper while waiting to be served his noodle soup. Just before the end of the poem someone addresses him by his surname, "Mr. Baczynski." The name rings a bell in every Polish ear. Suddenly the reader understands why the whole poem was written in the conditional tense. It is a poem about what might have been if Krzysztof Kamil Baczynski, a handsome twenty-three-year-old poet of genius, had not died a heroic death as a fighter in the Warsaw Uprising in 1944. Had Baczynski lived in postwar Poland, he might have been, he would have been, one of us— an ordinary, tired, cynical survivor.

A similar poem could be written about Bruno Schulz, even if his withdrawn, humiliated face offers much less of a contrast with his hypothetical fate than Baczynski's youthful and heroic features. What would he have become if he had not been shot in the street in Drohobycz in 1942? What would he have written, had he lived, say, twenty more years, in

Warsaw or in Krakow as a citizen of People's Poland, repatriated from the Soviet Union after the postwar shifting of the country's frontiers? Would he have completed *The Messiah,* the mythical novel he was writing before the war? Would he have written in the fifties in the same vein, and with the same brilliance, as he wrote in the thirties?

Of course, there is no way we can know. We can be sure, though, that the years after 1942 offered, in that part of Europe, no propitious ground for Schulz's kind of art. There is something pathetically symbolic in the fact that after the Soviet invasion of Poland's eastern territories in 1939, Schulz was forced to make his living in Drohobycz by painting gigantic portraits of Stalin for official ceremonies. By a similar perverse turn of fate, he survived for a while under the Nazis, thanks to the dreadful taste of a Gestapo man who hired Schulz to decorate his child's bedroom with kitschy murals. (This seems also to have caused Schulz's death: he was shot by another Gestapo agent who held some petty grudge against the artist's Heil-Hitlering patron. Not that the latter cared too much.)

As for writing, the years of occupation only fortified the depression and the writer's block that afflicted Schulz all his life. One day the legendary trove of papers that Schulz deposited, according to his friend Izydor Friedman, with a nameless "Catholic outside the ghetto" may be found. But what has survived from his wartime correspondence (for the most part, letters and postcards to the young painter Anna Plockier, another female friend and victim of the Holocaust) does not suggest that the trove contains any fiction written after 1939. Had Schulz himself survived and lived in Poland during the years of Stalinism, he would have most certainly become one of the writers and artists whose creativity was irreversibly warped, stunted, or quashed altogether by the suffocating hypocrisy and oppression of those times. Had he escaped the Nazi bullet in 1942, he would have soon found himself, with his kind of ethics and aesthetics, on a collision course with the "locomotive of History," whose mechanical charms the Socialist Realist poets were to idolize a few years later.

Let us reach even farther back. What would have happened if Schulz's life up to 1939 had been just a little less difficult? What if he had lived, for example, not in the God-forsaken town of Drohobycz but in some vivacious cultural center? What if he had not been pushed into marginality by his mixed racial, religious, and cultural background? What if he had been financially independent enough to quit his hated "drudgery" at school and devote himself entirely to writing? What if he had been able to shake off his inhibitions, the paralyzing "lack of self-confidence" of which he complains so much in his letters?

Moved by compassion at the sight of Schulz's tormented face as it appears in his more intimate letters (and also in the official documents, such as his elaborately humble applications for grants sent to the Ministry of Education), we would rather have him happier in his life, if only a little bit. But the literary critic should know better. What made Bruno Schulz Bruno Schulz was precisely the life he had to bear. Had he not been burdened with his provinciality, his Jewishness, his poverty, his inferiority complex, his swarms of other miseries, he would have been a happier man, and a more prolific writer. But probably he would not have been a great writer, and certainly not the unique writer we admire.

I do not mean to take Schulz as proof of the widely held opinion that only suffering makes an artist. That, too, would reduce Schulz's face to a masochist's grimace. The writer we know was the result not only of the life he had to bear, but also of the way he challenged and resisted this life—of the way he fought back.

Letters and Drawings of Bruno Schulz is a priceless book exactly because it brings this paradox to the light of day. Contrary to his masochistic self-portrayals in word and picture, most of Schulz's letters also show him determined to force his way out of the vicious circle of humiliation, isolation, and marginality. Epistolary form was for him the most natural way to use the word to reach beyond and communicate with people—a much easier way, for this extremely shy man and extremely scrupulous artist, than oral communication and *stricto sensu* literature. (In fact, he entered the edifice of literature through the vestibule of his correspondence: his first short stories were actually letters, unfortunately not preserved, to the writer Debora Vogel.)

His correspondence was Schulz's basic way of establishing genuine and durable human contact. "I need a friend," he bluntly begins a letter to the young writer Tadeusz Breza in 1934. "I need the closeness of a kindred spirit. I long for some outside affirmation of the inner world whose existence I postulate." His unquenchable thirst for contact with the outside world made him cling for years to correspondents whose obvious intellectual inferiority made the exchange otherwise a waste of his time. Such was the case with his former schoolmate Zenon Wasniewski, to whose numerous letters Schulz dutifully responded, groping for anything to say and finally composing not much more than tortuous apologies for not having written earlier.

Not that letters to kindred spirits were easier for him to write. There is always something strained about his way of addressing correspondents who achieved any sort of literary prominence, genuine celebrities like the poet Julian Tuwim or decidedly minor writers like the psychologist Stefan Szuman, whose weak poems Schulz makes great effort to praise. His only surviving letter to Tuwim, thanking him for the recognition of Schulz's first book, is particularly telling. Originally written in beautiful but slightly stilted and ornately rhetorical Polish, these few sentences must have cost Schulz long hours of labor. Each of them seems to reflect his complicated inhibitions. He never ceases here to be conscious that he is writing to a celebrity, to an acknowledged master of style, to an influential man of letters. He laboriously tries to strike a balance between modesty and dignity, to prevent his homage from slipping into flattery, to express his gratitude yet dispel the suspicion that he might be asking for further favors.

Schulz's numerous letters to his patroness, the famous and influential novelist Nalkowska, have perished. We can only guess how difficult it must have been for him to communicate with this worldly lady friend, who was as extroverted as he was withdrawn. The feelings involved must have been particularly complicated. We may be sure that Schulz was genuinely thankful to Nalkowska for having discovered and appreciated his work, but also that he could not help silently comparing her conventionally "modern" psychological novels with his own more innovative writing.

Schulz sounds much more at ease in correspondence with the few writers who really were his peers in terms of literary innovation, Witkacy (Stanislaw Ignacy Witkiewicz) and Witold Gombrowicz. Each of these giants of literary modernity was, needless to say, different from Schulz (he himself felt obliged to react to a 1938 review, which claimed he influenced Gombrowicz, by publicly declaring their mutual "autonomy and integrity"). Yet they served as Schulz's ideal readers. Witkacy and

115

Gombrowicz were the authors of the two most penetrating commentaries of his work published before the war. Schulz's surviving exchanges with them are confined to a couple of interviews, essays, and literary polemics; but even in these pieces, intended for publication, he is much more open and spontaneous than in his private letters to the celebrities of mainstream literary life.

His lively exchange with Gombrowicz, a half-serious "polemic" provoked by Gombrowicz's "Open Letter to Bruno Schulz" published in the obscure journal *Studio* in 1936, is highly revealing of the differences between these two writers. Many years later, in his postwar *Diary,* Gombrowicz was to define writing as "nothing more than a battle that the artist wages with others for his own prominence"; and this cheeky maxim already lies at the bottom of his early instigation. Its central issue is the innovative artist's relationship with his audience. Quoting teasingly "a certain doctor's wife" who claims that Schulz is a "sick pervert or a poseur," Gombrowicz prods his reticent fellow innovator to greater forcefulness, to imposing his uniqueness upon the reader more directly. Anticipating Schulz's reluctance and attributing it, not too delicately, to his masochism ("perhaps, indulging in your masochistic tendencies, you will humiliate yourself and fall at the dainty toes of the satisfied doctor's wife"), he nonetheless challenges him to respond to the silly accusations: "One must play the game with people on every level and in every possible situation. Our attitude toward matters of stupidity is perhaps even more important than our attitude toward the great, wise, principal problems."

In his retort, Schulz shows a rare glimpse of good-natured humor. He agrees to go along with Gombrowicz's indiscreet joke: "Certainly, I appreciate and admit with all my heart that the doctor's wife has beautiful thighs, but I put this matter in its own place. I can ensure that my worship of the doctor's wife's legs does not filter down into a totally inappropriate area." What he means by "inappropriate area" is the area of art, where he resolutely—and seriously, this time—rejects Gombrowicz's idea of "playing the game with people on every level":

> You say this is the face of life? You say not only that we, the brighter and better, have the right to make fun of the doctor's wife, but also that you acknowledge her equal right to scorn, disdain, and ridicule? In that case you stand on the side of inferiority against superiority. You try to compro-

mise our actions by casting before our eyes the massive torso of the doctor's wife, and you identify with her thick-headed chuckles. You claim that in her person you defend vitality and biology, against abstraction, against our detachment from life. If this is biology, Witold, then you must mean the force of her immobility; if this is vitality, you must mean her heavy passive mass.

But the avant-garde of biology is thought, experiment, creative discovery. We, in fact, are this belligerent biology, this conquering biology; we are the truly vital.

Here, and in other startlingly trenchant theoretical statements on art and literature scattered throughout the pages of this scrapbook, we finally see Schulz from his other, unexpected side. Instead of the passive sufferer whose sunken eyes gaze at us from his photos, graphics, and epistolary complaints, he looms in these pieces (in particular, in his afterword to Kafka's *The Trial,* his review of Gombrowicz's *Ferdydurke,* and his crucial essay "The Mythologizing of Reality") as the mind we know from his short stories: the tough, "belligerent," and "conquering" mind of an uncompromising artist.

He was much closer, in fact, to Gombrowicz than their polemical fervor, cranked up for the sake of argument, would suggest. In speaking of the artist's "belligerent" and "conquering" attitude, both had in mind the conquest of reality rather than the conquest of "the doctor's wife," the audience of their time. Both were loners: two of the greatest loners in twentieth-century literature. They differed only in their methods. Gombrowicz preferred to unmask reality; Schulz, to "mythologize" it, to intensify its "universal masquerade" and thus reconstruct its "universal Sense."

And they differed in one more essential thing. Gombrowicz's "conquering" attitude in matters of literature was entirely consistent with his life, and his unobfuscated pursuit of his own artistic "prominence." In Schulz, there is more dialectic ambivalence. His personality stretches between two extremes—between a masochistic self-humiliation of his private ego in the face of the world, and a demiurgic imposition of his creative self upon the world. That which gives him reasons for passive suffering in his intimate life is, precisely, the source of his firm grip on reality in his artistic life.

With the former, we associate the wounded face we know from his pictures and letters, many of which sound, in spite of all his shyness and restraint, like desperate cries for help, confessions of unbearable pain, laments over his "profound loneliness." The latter is reflected in the closing sentence of an autobiographical essay he wrote in 1935: "Loneliness is the catalyst that makes reality ferment, precipitates its surface layer of figures and colors." And in the latter, too, we find the absolute, unyielding exactitude of the rhythms and the images he used in his prose to make this fermenting reality seethe forever in our ears and eyes. As a man, he was more vulnerable than most. As an artist, he was as tough as anyone.

[1988]

A Masterpiece of Memory

We would know less about Communism, and Polish literature would not be what it is today, had a forgotten Dadaist poet named Aleksander Wat not suffered a stroke one day early in 1953.

It happened in Warsaw at the height of Stalin's power (nobody could have foreseen that the Immortal Light of Mankind himself would die several weeks later), and it was probably a psychosomatic result of Wat's most recent public castigation for his lack of enthusiasm for Socialist Realism. Wat recovered from the stroke. A burst blood vessel in his brain caused a chronic neurological disorder, however, diagnosed as Wallenberg Complex. Its chief symptoms were unpredictable attacks of debilitating pain in the head and body, which lasted for hours and left Wat exhausted and unable to work. There was nothing the doctors could do except prescribe extra-strong painkillers. Asked about a cure, one specialist answered, "Yes, you can leave this disease behind you—by jumping out a window."

The illness was to keep Wat company for the next fourteen years, during which the recurrent pain succeeded in frustrating his major literary projects before it finally pushed him to suicide in 1967. But ironically, his very pain was also chiefly responsible for the emergence of two masterpieces: Wat's late poetry and his prose work *My Century*.[1] In Wat's poems, physical pain becomes a central metaphor that binds together various strains of human existence. *My Century*, his "spoken memoir"— or, rather, his enormous interview/reminiscence/confession/meditation recorded by Czeslaw Milosz in Berkeley and Paris during 1964, is even more literally a product of pain. It was initially undertaken for therapeutic reasons, to take Wat's mind off his suffering.

"The devil behind my illness is the devil of communism," Wat remarks matter-of-factly in the first pages of *My Century*. He proceeds to define Communism as naturally "pathogenic." Taken literally, this might sound paranoid, but Wat's intent becomes clearer later on, as he expands on the essence of Stalinism as "exteriorization . . . the killing of the inner man . . . the poisoning of the inner man so that it becomes shrunken the way headhunters shrink heads—those shriveled little heads—and then disappears entirely. It doesn't even rot away inside, because the communists are afraid of inner rot. No, it should turn to dust."

Yet Wat was a poet as well as a thinker; and in his mind a metaphor could take on the appearance of an objective truth, something to be taken at face value. He was not above regarding his illness as, quite literally, the body's way of rebelling against decades of mental subordination to unacceptable doctrine. Or, in more metaphysical terms, it was the final link in a long series of providential punishments for having once collaborated with the satanic forces of History. Wat was a modern incarnation of Job, not because he suffered more than the millions of other victims of the century's ideological lunacies, but because he tried persistently to find a reason for his suffering. What was unique in Wat's case was not misery itself, but the encounter between a commonly shared misery and the exceptionally receptive and subtle mind of a poet and thinker.

Still, if not for Wat's illness and Milosz's tape recorder, we would have only an inkling of Wat's greatness. Even before the debilitating disease seized him in 1953, his literary productivity had been weirdly stunted by History's vagaries and his own doubts. Wat's career may well be one of the most disjointed in literature. After his first book of Dadaist poetry came out in 1919, he lapsed into nearly total silence as a poet for the next thirty-eight years. He published a single collection of short stories, and otherwise confined himself to translating and editing other authors. His second book of poems appeared in Poland only in 1957, and his third in 1962. These three slim collections comprise Wat's entire poetic oeuvre published in his lifetime. A year after his death, another collection—the Polish title can be translated as *Dark Trinket* or *Obscure Source of Light*—appeared in the West, containing not only the older work but a number of dazzling new poems, too.

The publication of *My Century* took much longer. After plenty of editing and retyping, mostly done by the poet's widow, Paulina (Ola) Wat, the first Polish edition appeared in London in 1977. Over the past decade, aided by young scholars of Wat's work, Paulina Wat has dug through mountains of her husband's scattered publications and almost illegible manuscripts, and has initiated publication of his collected works. Two volumes, containing his essays and notes, are available so far. In English, Wat was represented until now only by a small collection entitled *Mediterranean Poems*, selected and translated by Milosz and published by Ardis Press in 1977.

This is not much by any standard. Those who knew Wat personally were always intrigued by the contrast between his minute output and his enormous intellectual power, which was immediately clear in conversations and in his oral reminiscences. Something of a child prodigy, Wat had begun to develop a highly complex and unorthodox intellect very early in life. Born in 1900 as Aleksander Chwat to a Jewish family, with famous philosophers and rabbis among his ancestors and a home library full of ancient and modern books, he mastered several languages as a matter of course, and read voraciously in each of them throughout his childhood. He became a rising star in philosophy at the University of Warsaw. But by then he had already become known in literary circles for his iconoclastic writings.

As a nineteen-year-old, Wat made his name as a cofounder of Polish Futurism and author of a shockingly bizarre book entitled *Me from One Side and Me from the Other Side of My Pug Iron Stove*. The book is a long poem in prose that faintly recalls Rimbaud or Lautréamont, but mainly it is Dadaist, relying on the technique of *écriture automatique*. (Legend has it that Wat wrote it in a couple of nights while suffering from a high fever, and never bothered to correct numerous printing mistakes that added to the text's puzzling quality.) But it was distinctly different from other Futurists' work: it explored the dark realms of the subconscious rather than exclaiming over civilization's bright prospects. Still, for the next several years, though writing less and less of his own poetry, Wat remained an active participant in the Futurist movement.

At this point, however, Polish Futurism itself was undergoing a highly characteristic turnabout. In the mid–1920s, its anarchic praise of unrestricted freedom was rapidly turning into its exact opposite, namely a strict subservience to Communist ideology and party discipline, thus re-creating in literature the famous path once envisaged by Dostoevsky's hero Shigalev: "Starting from unlimited freedom and arriving at unlimited despotism." Wat was perhaps not as pure an example of this evolution as his fellow poet Bruno Jasienski, who in roughly two decades went all the way from the anarchic dandyism of his "ego-Futurist" beginnings to wholehearted acceptance of Communism; he emigrated to the Soviet Union, where he became a party dignitary, only to perish not long after in one of Stalin's purges.

Yet Wat, too, turned to Communism, that common substitute for faith during those years of crisis, to fill the ideological void that was evident in his second book, the collection of catastrophic short stories *Lucifer Unemployed* that appeared in 1927. Throughout the 1930s, when he stopped writing poetry altogether and made his living as an editor and translator, he became increasingly close to the Communist Party of Poland. Even though he never formally joined it and, with his individualistic doubts of a typical rotten intellectual, remained a "fellow traveler," the party entrusted him in 1929–1931 with the post of editor-in-chief of its most influential organ, the *Literary Monthly*. A good half of *My Century* is devoted to a pricelessly detailed discussion of this period in both Wat's life and in Poland's political and intellectual history; there is simply no other account available that could recreate the atmosphere of the 1930s in Poland and dissect the mentality of the pro-Communist left with such thoroughness and such surgical precision.

Since the Communist Party of Poland had been formally banned, the *Literary Monthly* was closed down, and in 1932 Wat found himself in the first of the fourteen prisons he was to get to know in the later course of his life. This was a Polish prison between the wars, however, and it was, therefore, even in those years of exacerbated political tensions, a relatively tolerable one. Wat spent only a few weeks there, and at one point he and his comrades even enjoyed luxurious food and drinks sent to their cell by a literary friend who happened to be a big gun in ruling circles. More disconcerting was Wat's confrontation with the close-mindedness of his Communist cellmates, with the unmistakably totalitarian bent in their mental and behavioral subordination to party discipline. It was then that Wat had his first foretaste of Communism's evil, its "killing of the inner man." It was then, too, that he began to rethink his Communist leanings.

Still, his Polish experience of this kind of evil was just a watered-down version of what he was to encounter in the Soviet Union in the coming years. All his pro-Communist past did not save him—indeed, it incriminated him even more—when after the outbreak of war he found himself a refugee in Lvov, the capital of the Polish Ukraine soon captured by the advancing Soviet army and made part of the Soviet Union. After all, the Communist Party of Poland had been charged with treason and dissolved by the Comintern a few years earlier. In any case, someone like Wat, by virtue of his very status as a Polish intellectual, was suspect whatever his affiliations.

The first transports to Siberia did not include Wat or his wife and son, but they did not have to wait long. In January 1940, Wat was arrested, along with a group of other Polish writers (the most prominent among them was the famous pro-Communist poet Wladyslaw Broniewski), after a brawl was staged in a Lvov restaurant by Stalin's secret police. Separated from his family and knowing nothing of their whereabouts, Wat spent the next two years in a number of Soviet prisons, accused of a smorgasbord of crimes ranging from Zionism and Trotskyism to spying on behalf of the Vatican. In one prison he underwent a spiritual rebirth and converted to Catholicism (although the eventual transformations of his religious outlook were to leave him with a rather unorthodox mixture of Judaism and Christianity).

After Hitler's breach of the Ribbentrop-Molotov pact, and Stalin's consequent "amnesty" for Poles who survived his mass executions and concentration camps, Wat was released and evacuated to Alma-Ata, where he was reunited with his family. His refusal to join the Soviet-sponsored Union of Polish Patriots, however, resulted in the family's banishment to a remote settlement in the wilds of a Kazakhstan desert. There Wat was arrested and jailed again, this time for his resistance to "passportization"—that is, the forcing of Polish settlers to accept Soviet citizenship (thus depriving them of any chance to be repatriated).

After Wat's release, the family continued to live for a while in Kazakhstan, coping with destitution, illness, and the harsh conditions of everyday life, until they were finally allowed to return to Poland in April 1946. The Soviet period of Wat's life up to the Kazakhstan years is covered by the second half of *My Century,* a book comparable to Nadezhda Mandelstam's *Hope against Hope,* an incomparably profound and precise analysis of everything from the nature of totalitarianism and the specifics of prison life to the intricacies of human character and the essence of religious experience. (A forceful chapter from Paulina Wat's separate memoir, originally published in 1984, describes the passportization affair in vivid detail.)

Wat's reminiscences stop well before the point of his family's repatriation. He wanted to continue the recordings, but Milosz, his ideal listener and interlocutor, was unable to spend more time on them, and cooperation with another interviewer did not work out. What happened next in Wat's life is known from other sources, including his posthumously published *Diary without Vowels*, a loose collection of notes and reminiscences Wat transcribed in a code that omitted vowels.

In Stalinist Poland, Wat's position was precarious: he was tolerated, but prohibited from publishing his work and viewed with suspicion, particularly after his numerous outspoken criticisms of Socialist Realism. The early 1950s were marked by intensified political attacks against him, one of which probably led to his fateful stroke. Wat's illness and his prolonged stays in Polish hospitals, where speakers mounted in every room blared propagandistic radio broadcasts all day long, cast a grim shadow on this phase in his life. The political thaw of 1956 brought a respite, during which Wat returned to literary life, publishing a book of poems in 1957 and earning high praise from younger poets. An official literary prize he received for the book enabled him to travel to the West in 1959, chiefly in search of a cure and a milder climate. He lived initially in southern France and Italy, then in Paris, writing a few poems (collected in his third volume in 1962) and essays; the latter are innovative meditations on the nature of Stalinism, on the poetics of Socialist Realist literature, and on the semantics of totalitarian language.

By the early 1960s the political pendulum in Poland had swung back to intolerance, and attacks on Wat were resumed; some went so far as to accuse him of faking his disease in order to enjoy life in the West. In 1963 he decided not to return to Poland, even though he had no steady means of support in Paris. In an attempt to help him, his admirers in California, particularly Gleb Struve and Milosz, persuaded Berkeley's Center for Slavic and East European Studies to invite Wat for a year's stay. Wat was initially elated and brimming with ideas and plans, but at Berkeley his health deteriorated further. The attacks of pain and the heavy doses of painkillers left him unable to write for most of the time, and this inability, in turn, made him feel guilty and despondent. It was then that the center's director, Gregory Grossman, and Milosz hit upon the idea of recording Wat's oral reminiscences as a substitute for real activity and a sort of psychotherapy. No one could have expected that the final product of the recording sessions would emerge after many years, along with Witold Gombrowicz's *Diary*, as one of the most important books of nonfiction in modern Polish literature.

[1988]

The Ecstatic Pessimist

Since becoming an émigré in 1951, Czeslaw Milosz the essayist has written basically two kinds of books, distinctly different in terms of their implied readers and rhetorical techniques. The first kind of book, represented by *The Captive Mind, Native Realm,* and the recent *Witness of Poetry,* is addressed primarily to a Western audience. The chief intent of such books is to break down certain mental barriers, to open new vistas by revealing the unique perspective of an outsider-participant, someone who bridges East and West with his individual experience. As a consequence, the nature of these books is paradoxical: while they are—like everything Milosz writes—utterly personal, they also have to be more or less didactic. The other kind, exemplified (to draw on only those works in English translation) by *Visions from San Francisco Bay,* seems to be closer to the traditional genre of "a writer's notebook." If Milosz has in mind any specific reader here, it is a reader intimately acquainted with the author's background, a reader who has shared much of the author's experience and therefore needs less explanation and instruction.

The Land of Ulro[1] does its best to belong to this second category. Its American edition, though it is excellently translated and annotated by Louis Iribarne, begins with a straightforward warning: "Dear reader," writes Milosz in a specially added preface, "this book was not intended for you . . . When writing it, I indulged in a personal whim, dismissing in advance the idea of its publication in English . . . I gave free rein to my meditations and didn't try to reach anybody in particular, except perhaps a few fastidious people able to read my Polish and belonging to the same circle of the literati."

In fact, even Polish critics were perplexed when the book first appeared in the original. When I myself read it back in 1978, I felt overwhelmed and dazed not only by its unconstrainedly meandering manner of presentation, which moves in sudden leaps and turns from one name, epoch, or country to another, but also by the completely new set of ideas and problems it opened to me. I can foresee the same kind of feeling in the American reader. Regardless of cultural differences, we all instinctively expect that an essayistic book, original as it may be, will, at least to some degree, fit into one or another ideological pigeonhole. We want to place it somewhere on our pocket map, the four quadrants of which are usually "left" versus "right" and "conservative" versus "progressive." Milosz shakes off all these labels. "I am fighting," he says at one point, "for the right to exercise my mind outside accepted disciplines." "And outside ideological categories," we might add.

This is possible because the point of departure for *The Land of Ulro* is personal and autobiographical, though the book deals with nothing less than problems in the intellectual history of Western civilization. By asking at the very outset "Who was I?" and "Who am I now, years later?" Milosz ostensibly tries to elucidate the reasons for his own evolution. Since it so happens, however, that the questions he constantly asks himself are questions that centuries of our civilization have tried to answer, his treatise on himself soon becomes a treatise on a certain current of thought, a certain neglected philosophical tradition.

This tradition's invisible thread, which in Milosz's book links such seemingly disparate figures as Emmanuel Swedenborg, William Blake, Feodor Dostoevsky, the Polish romantic poet Adam Mickiewicz, and the French symbolist (and Milosz's relative) Oskar W. Milosz, is the perennial question of *unde malum*, of the origins of evil. Even before Milosz began to search for an answer in the works of philosophers, ranging from the Manichaeans and Gnostics to Lev Shestov and Simone Weil, he had become obsessed by the irresolvable problem of how to reconcile the presence of evil with the notion of Providence. This obsession resulted in his lifelong attitude of paradoxical "ecstatic pessimism." But it also made him sensitive to the fact that Western civilization had for at least two centuries been bypassing the human world into what Blake called the land of Ulro.

Ulro is "the land of the disinherited," "a land where man is reduced to a supererogatory number, worse, where he becomes as much for himself, in his own eyes, in his own mind." Following Blake, Milosz sees the beginnings of the process of such disinheritance in the Age of Enlightenment, with its fundamentally wrong decision to put all of mankind's hopes in the triumphs of science and reason. The age of Bacon, Locke, and Newton saw the first signs of a rapidly widening rift between the inner world of the human imagination and the outer world of science's abstract laws. The ensuing Romantic crisis of European culture, which has continued to our time, has been, in Milosz's view, a phenomenon contained within the walls of the land of Ulro. Only a handful of prophetic seers have attempted, in both literature and philosophy, to seek some effective way out, usually at the risk of being perceived as "abnormal," incomprehensible, or excessively mystical.

But how do their efforts relate to the question of *unde malum?* One common denominator Milosz finds between these thinkers and his own intellectual inclinations is the notion of anthropocentrism combined with a "bias against Nature." In other words, those who try to bring down the walls of Ulro must consider man the center of the universe while being perfectly aware that there is no such thing as innate human goodness. Nature is not a harmoniously working mechanism, as the deists of the Age of Enlightenment liked to imagine it, nor is it a refuge from the troubles of civilization, as post-Rousseau Romantics tended to think. On the contrary, Nature, including human nature, is branded by the unavoidable presence of evil. Whoever realizes this must deem it impossible to create any system of ethics free of religious sanctions. The only way to create an intellectual space that a human society could inhabit is to reconcile the presence of evil with the notion of a providential plan by introducing the idea of "Godmanhood." Not deified man, but precisely the opposite: humanized God. This is the concept through which we can "assent to our existence on earth." Within such a vision, Christ, as in Swedenborg, becomes identical with God the Father, and the moment of Creation is simultaneous with that of the Crucifixion. The God who created the world with all its evil and suffering is the God who also agreed to participate in our pain, who "took on a human form and willingly died the death of a tortured prisoner."

Swedenborg, Blake, Mickiewicz, Dostoevsky, and Oskar Milosz were thinkers who, for all their human limitations and errors, had enough visionary power to give the notion of divine humanity or Godmanhood pride of place in their systems of thought—even to the point of, in Dostoevsky's radical phrase, "choosing Christ over truth" (that is, over the abstract truth of science). Our century, on the other hand, is viewed by Milosz as living proof of "the utter failure of secular humanism, a failure sponsored by the very successes of that same humanism." Ours is the world disinherited of values, the world whose inner void can be—and is—too easily filled with worthless and often antihuman ideological substitutes. The road of Dostoevsky's Grand Inquisitor seems to be taken time and again.

Such a diagnosis does not mean, though, that Milosz readily dismisses every form of agnosticism or atheism as simply disguises for ethical relativism. On the contrary, his polemic with Witold Gombrowicz—which makes extremely illuminative reading, and not only for the student of Polish literature—shows that he fully appreciates the kind of atheism that is "bound by the strictest ethical code" precisely because it does not admit the possibility of divine intervention or posthumous reparation. "Morally speaking," says Milosz, "there is nothing, in my view, which argues either for Christians or against atheists . . . I would even say that if someone can be an atheist, he ought to be one." Would that mean, in turn, that religion can be reduced to a means of intellectual self-defense against an ethical void? Such a concept of religion, albeit theologically rather unorthodox, seems indeed to be quite close to Milosz's views. In fact, his book is a treatise on what Blake called "Divine Works of the Imagination": it finds a possible remedy for the modern crisis of Christian civilization not merely in reanimating the religious spirit but, more demandingly, in broadening the sphere of imagination and thus reclaiming the abandoned space of the human world.

It is to be expected that *The Land of Ulro* will stir up a great deal of controversy among its American readers. Some of this book's concepts—such as the theocracy mentioned a few times as a possible model for societies of tomorrow—are indeed highly unpopular in this country's intellectual tradition. I myself am rather unconvinced, to say the least, by Milosz's overly categorical criticism of what he calls "secular humanism." It would be unfortunate, however, if such controversial details veiled in the reader's perception the more essential issues raised by Milosz's brilliant defense of the imagination and its humanizing power. The central problem of this book—the question of how civilization should deal with the individual's sense of insignificance in the universe—is no small matter, after all.

*   *   *

"All right, but doesn't it all boil down to his conviction that literature should be an *uplifting* business?" I was asked this question by an American friend of mine when we exchanged opinions on the first of Czeslaw Milosz's six Norton Lectures at Harvard. His skepticism struck me as being out of accord with the usual appraisal of Milosz's work. After all, Milosz's name has always been associated by Polish critics with the dark mood of the 1930s—with the "catastrophist" school in prewar poetry. And his more recent poetry and prose hardly show him to be an easygoing optimist. Ironically, Milosz's lectures coincided with the imposition of martial law in Poland—in other words, with yet another attempt to bury Polish hopes.

And yet the underlying theme of Milosz's six lectures[2] is nothing less than hope, and poetry as a possible source of hope. Hope against hope, to be sure, since the author himself realizes that almost nothing in either contemporary poetry or the recent history of our civilization seems to justify such expectations. At least in Western societies, readers as well as poets themselves have long been reconciled with a poetry reduced to confessing its own helplessness.

Milosz begins by looking at the problem from a different perspective. His poetic credo has been shaped, after all, by his experience as an Eastern European poet living in exile in the West. Accordingly, his introductory lecture, "Starting from my Europe" (which condenses the broad range of problems treated in his earlier essays), presents the cultural experience of his youth. The remote Polish-Lithuanian corner of Europe where he lived was strangely situated: geographically between East and West, culturally between Rome and Byzantium, historically between past and future. Here, people had developed a keen sense of historical relativity. None of the disasters that swept over these crossroads of civilizations could seem final and irreversible; every vision of the future had to allow for some eschatology. In that country of historical cataclysms, poetry became "a home for incorrigible hope."

For Milosz, "the witness of poetry" means much more than "poetry as a testimony." A testimony can be wrung out of someone; a witness is born voluntarily, by someone who wants to help justice. If poetry is sup-

posed to bear witness, that means it is considered a form of active participation in mankind's affairs. In the poem "Dedication," written just after
World War II, Milosz did not hesitate to speak of poetry as a potential
savior of both individual and collective souls. The very fact of presenting
the problem in such extreme terms was an act of defiance. It defied Auden and so many others, and it stood against Milosz's own doubts. At
least in this poem, Milosz was sure that poetry could "make something
happen." But can it really? If we leave Eastern Europe for a moment and
consider poetry the world over, we will see that, instead of bearing witness, twentieth-century poetry "testifies to serious disturbances in our
perception of the world." The second, third, and fourth of Milosz's lectures analyze three specific forms of such disturbances.

The first of them is sociological. The birth of artistic bohemias in the
middle of the nineteenth century resulted from the poet's gradual alienation from "the great human family." Since that moment, a schism between the poet and the rest of society has become accepted fact. Culture
has been divided into pure art for the chosen few, and entertainment or
didactic instruction for the despised philistines. The poet has deliberately
chosen to become an outcast, and his work has turned from the pursuit
of reality to various attempts to cultivate art for art's sake. But as Milosz
tries to show, the dichotomy of "reality" and "pure art" is, in fact, false.
It is possible to conceive of a poetry that is at the same time mystical and
yet immersed in history, artistically minded and yet responsive to social
reality, individualist and yet not isolated from "the human family."

Another cause of the twentieth-century crisis of poetry is what Milosz
calls "the lesson of biology." In his view, the progressive application of
Darwinism to the social sciences has thoroughly refashioned our imagination: it has made us more and more disposed to interpret the human
world in the categories of biological determinism. Moreover, the historical upheavals of our times have persuaded us that not only human beings
but also human civilizations are mortal. All of this is totally at odds with
the poet's natural tendency to look at the world, as it were, with the eyes
of a child—a child who still believes in the criteria of good and evil. If
the poet in our century retains such blessed naïveté, he is nevertheless
constantly pressured by cynical "adults" to respect so-called naked facts.
Even though he may instinctively try to resist this pressure, he can no
longer rely on old categories and ideals. As a result, the poet of today is

"ashamed of the child in himself": the "lesson of biology" teaches him more often than not to give up his childlike rectitude.

Finally, the third reason for poetry's vitiated role is described by Milosz as a classicist temptation. The poet can trade in his social bonds for an attitude of haughty self-isolation; he can trade in his moral steadfastness for biological determinism; he can trade in his fidelity to the real world for compliance with ready-made conventions. Common to all three is the choosing of an easy, simple, undemanding solution. Such a charge against classicism may puzzle Milosz's readers for a while. Isn't he himself usually labeled a classicist? In fact, even though he may occasionally have been attracted by classicism, he views it as a temptation that should be resisted. Poetry in our epoch is a battle between realism and classicism, faithfulness to the external world and adherence to the internal rules of art. The use of poetic convention makes contact with the reader possible, but at the same time it builds a glass wall separating the poet from reality. Thus, the division between the word and human experience grows continuously, splitting mankind into "those who know but do not speak" and "those who speak but do not know."

After this general analysis of dangers hovering over contemporary poetry, Milosz turns again to the poetry of a specific place and time. His fifth lecture, entitled "Ruins and Poetry," tells the story of the experiences of Polish poetry during the Second World War. Faced with the threat of physical extermination and the annihilation of culture, Polish authors were compelled to rethink the most essential questions concerning the tasks of poetry and its functions within a community. The apocalypse of the war simplified everything in a positive and creative sense: it created a need to give the new reality a name, to comprehend what seemed to be incomprehensible, to find hope in what was apparently hopeless. Paradoxically, the catastrophe of war restored some hierarchy of moral values and revived realism. It also proved to be a cure for poetry's isolation, since poets were facing the same dangers as other people. One of the unexpected results of the war and the disintegration of the European cultural tradition has been—at least for Polish poets and writers—the renewed belief that "the great schism in poetry is curable."

Milosz's last lecture, "On Hope," opens with a question. "What if the lament so widely spread in poetry today proves to be a prophetic response to the hopeless situation in which mankind has found itself?"

What, in other words, if poetic catastrophism happens to be confirmed by some ultimate catastrophe? As I said before—and as every reader of Milosz knows very well—the author of *The Captive Mind* has never been a thoughtless optimist. In fact, he discerns in contemporary history "a kind of race between the lifegiving and the destructive activity of civilization's bacteria," whose final result is unknown and can be only vaguely apprehended by the prophetic imagination of poets.

In Milosz's view, however, there is reason if not for optimism then for the rejection of hopelessness. He sees humanity as having emerged as "an elemental force," which in our time replaces the anachronistic structures based on class distinctions and social hierarchies. Culturally, this means that "man is opening up to science and art on an unprecedented scale": there is a growing demand for culture as a source of knowledge about mankind's own past. This enormous demand is still not fully realized and satisfied by culture itself. Nevertheless, it offers new opportunities—especially to poetry, which in its function as "the witness" proves to be a particularly ample means of making the past an element of our present and relating universal problems of the human condition to a given place and time.

It would be hard to overestimate the weight and significance of Milosz's six lectures. By the strength of its condensed and lucid exposition, *The Witness of Poetry* provides us with a key to Milosz's poetic philosophy, aesthetics, and vision of history. And Milosz's entire work offers one of the most profound responses to the dilemmas of our century. His opposition to commonplace beliefs, according to which our civilization has no perspectives and the alienation of culture is an irreversible fact, seems perhaps more natural to his Polish reader. After all, in countries such as Poland contemporary poetry more than once proved indispensable to society's existence; its role as a witness to reality, as a defense against oppression, and as a source of hope is not an abstract axiom but the concrete and personal experience of many people. To quote once again Milosz's poem, it is indeed no exaggeration to say that poetry can sometimes "save nations or people." While reading the words about "humanity as an elemental force" one cannot help recalling the sixteen months of Solidarity when poems by Milosz (among others) were printed in workers' newsletters along with unionist appeals and political analyses. Still, the reaction of my American friend seems to me significant, too.

Milosz's defense of hope will most probably provoke even more caustic reactions from those Western intellectuals whose monotonous laments over the helplessness of contemporary culture are their main contributions to it. Let them at least remember that while their despair is one of the easiest solutions, Milosz's hope is hard-earned.

[1983–1985]

Fiction and Action

A Russian Roulette

"I'd like a few books that would give me some idea of contemporary Soviet fiction." Anyone who would approach an American bookseller with a demand like this is bound to leave the store with a bag of books more or less as heterogeneous and mutually incomparable as the six that lie in front of me right now. These are books published almost simultaneously in English and over a span of not more than twenty-odd years in the original Russian, but to read them one after another is an experience that makes one question the very semantic validity of each of the three words contained in the label "contemporary Soviet fiction." If by "contemporary" we are to understand the literature of the last thirty years, it is impossible to overlook the startling cognitive and aesthetic differences between works representative of the post-Stalinist "thaw" or the beginnings of *samizdat* and the major novels of the late seventies to early eighties. The term "Soviet" is a particularly confusing misnomer: each of these six novels deals with Soviet reality, but out of the six writers only one both published his work and lived all his life in the Soviet Union. Another lived there but wrote his novel with no hope of having it officially published; yet another's work was officially circulated, but afterward he fled to the West; and the other three authors wrote their books, completely or in part, while living in the Soviet Union but published them only abroad and are now themselves living in exile. Finally, even the broad term "fiction" seems hardly applicable to each of these six books in the same manner: ironically, the one among them that is formally the closest to the nonfictional "literature of facts" reads like a utopian fairy-tale, whereas the one that apparently reaches the farthest extremes of grotesquely absurd distortion offers, in fact, the most compelling reflection of Soviet reality. The paradoxes of chronology, cultural geography, and literary genre all conspire to overwhelm the American reader of what is sold as "contemporary Soviet fiction" with an impression of a puzzlingly wide range of approaches and styles, covering the vast space between the panoramic epic and the self-centered lyric, between the moralists' sacred truths and the mockers' topsy-turvy blasphemies, between the likes of Alexander Solzhenitsyn or Vasily Grossman on the one hand and Venedikt Erofeyev or Sasha Sokolov on the other.

In my six-book sampler of recently translated "contemporary Soviet fiction," Anatolii Kuznetsov's *The Journey*[1] is a specimen of both the least contemporary and the most Soviet. Its original Russian publication actually marked the debut of the writer (1929–1979), who was to make himself better known later on, first by the appearance of his best-selling war novel *Babi Yar* in 1966, and then by his much-publicized act of defection to England in 1969 (after which he changed his name, revised *Babi Yar,* and condemned his early writing).

First published in the liberal journal *Youth* in 1957, *The Journey* was considered in its time one of the signs of the cultural "thaw." From today's perspective, however, it looms rather as a symbol of how strictly limited the official "thaw" was and how little food for thought was enough in 1957 to make the starved Soviet reader happy. Suffice it to say that *The Journey* is a book on Siberia in which not a single word about Siberian labor camps is uttered. Instead, we have a book based on false pretenses: outwardly, it appears to be a work of nonfiction exploiting the quasi-documentary formula of a writer's travel notebook; inherently, it is a belated example of that most fairy-tale-like genre of Socialist Realism, "the production novel." The first-person narrator, a graduate of a Moscow high school and member of the Union of Communist Youth, rejects the alluring prospects of higher education and a city-based career and sets off by train to Siberia. He ends up in Irkutsk as a worker in concrete at a dam construction site on the Angara. Unaccustomed to tough work conditions and unfit for physical labor, he falls seriously ill and even experiences a moment of doubt, but he is rescued by the tirade of his friend, an idealistic Komsomol member, and promptly reaches the conclusion that "real happiness—is happiness in work." Other workers at the site undergo a similar transformation: in the beginning the brigade still has its share of sluggards, drunkards, and swindlers, but in the end each of them has matured so much that he is ready to throw himself with his cement truck into the waters of the Angara to precipitate the dam's completion. At the same time, the heroic ordeal of the protagonist is didactically contrasted with the portrayal of his former schoolmate Viktor, who has chosen the easy path of a careerist and cynic: he stays in Moscow, studies at the university, wears trendy clothes, and listens to rock and roll.

Its doctrinaire schematism aside, Kuznetsov's tale cannot help offering, be it deliberately or inadvertently, some hints at the existence of Soviet reality's dark side. Behind the marble façade of the "great building site of Socialism" there lurk undeniable facts which the reader is compelled to realize in the course of the narrative: exploitation of the worker, chronic mismanagement and corruption, contempt of the individual, brutality in human relations, the depressing dullness of everyday life. Of course, even if Kuznetsov's narrator realizes these facts along with the reader, he hastens to emphasize that these are remnants of the prerevolutionary past or individual faults of people who do not yet measure up to the demands of the ideology. To blame the system would certainly be too much to expect from a work published in the Soviet press in 1957.

But it is not only a matter of censorship. Kuznetsov's narrator is himself a sincere believer, an example of "the new Soviet man" who is simply unable to think and speak in categories other than those dictated by the official ideology. This is especially noticeable in his language, which reveals him time and again to be a victim of the Stalinist verbal machine: as a matter of course, this young man designates poor women peddling sunflower seeds as "speculators," describes a peasant lad who is furious after being robbed on the train as "avaricious and a *kulak*," and dreams about cleansing the Socialist world of "parasites"; needless to say, he still takes for granted the rather infamous slogan "If you're not with us, you're against us." One could understand why *The Journey* was acclaimed as a literary event in 1957 in the Soviet Union; read in America in 1986, it is nothing more than a piece of bad propagandistic literature, made even worse by the stilted, unnatural language of the translation (which oftentimes, particularly in the dialogues, seems to be a mechanical rendition of Russian colloquialisms and idioms into literal English).

It is almost indecent to speak in one breath of Kuznetsov's debut and Vasily Grossman's famous last novel *Forever Flowing;*[2] the latter is an infinitely more mature, humane, and honest work, by an authentic writer. Even though these two books were produced during virtually the same period of Soviet literary history (Grossman had been working on his novel from 1955 to 1963; he died a year later), they are so different in all their basic aspects, one might think they'd been written on two different planets. Grossman, a man not only a generation older (born in 1905) but also much more harshly tested by history's adversities (he served as a war correspondent and a few years later was viciously slandered in the 1949 anti-Semitic campaign against the "cosmopolites"), was one of the first Soviet writers to recognize the fundamental inhumanity of both the apparatus of power and its ideological basis. This is clearly documented by his war epic *Life and Fate,* but even more so by *Forever Flowing,* which stands out as a shatteringly unequivocal indictment of the more than forty years of Soviet rule. Grossman views it as founded at the very outset—Lenin's period fully included—on a total "absence of freedom" and thus preserving "that link between progress and slavery which has historically been Russia's curse." Chronologically speaking, the development of this kind of unflinching vision parallels the similar evolution of Solzhenitsyn, even though it is only recently that Grossman has been posthumously discovered in the West (*Forever Flowing* was first published in English in 1972, but *Life and Fate* appeared only in 1986).

In its initial scenes, *Forever Flowing* promises to be just a realistic novel about the early years of the post-Stalinist era. Ivan Grigoryevich returns to Moscow after thirty years spent in a labor camp. He returns a forgotten and lonely man; even the woman he loved stopped writing to him long ago. We witness his first encounters with the reality beyond the barbed wire: his uneasy reunion with a relative who in the meantime has made a rather dubious career, his accidental meeting with the man who betrayed him thirty years ago, and so on. The society that is enjoying a long-awaited "thaw" strikes Ivan Grigoryevich as one not very much changed since the years of terror and actually well adjusted to oppression: it has already given up its longing for genuine freedom, and there is no spiritual difference between the worlds inside and outside the camps. The protagonist moves to a small town in southern Russia, where he takes up a worker's job and falls in love with his landlady, a war widow, herself a victim of Stalinism. In the ensuing part of the novel, the

140

details of the plot become more and more sketchy: the book's entire second half is a series of dialogues and meditations by Ivan Grigoryevich and Anna Sergeyevna on the issues of Russian history, the nature of the Soviet system, moral responsibility, and the irrepressiblity of human striving toward freedom.

Grossman's political and ethical outlook, based on the simple but consistent assumption that the need for freedom is something inherent in human nature and that "everything inhuman is senseless and worthless," has lost nothing in value over the years; neither have his images of life under Lenin and Stalin (in particular, his account of the years of "collectivization") lost their staggering power. Considered as a novel, though, *Forever Flowing* seems to be a work as crippled as it is ambitious. The plot, begun in a realistic vein, is apparently unable to contain the scope and carry the burden of the book's problematics, and Grossman, as it were, discards it midway through in favor of a straightforward discourse in which the two protagonists serve merely as mouthpieces for the author's own opinions.

One is tempted to see in this, however, not so much an artistic failure as evidence of Grossman's honesty as a writer: he is indirectly expressing his distrust of the traditional instruments of the realistic novel. Juxtaposed with the bestiality and absurdity of history, the authoritative role of an omniscient narrator—that of a rational explainer, organizer of the plot, supplier of moralistic instruction—could indeed seem impossible to retain in a longer run. Thus, Grossman's narrator is omniscient so long as he confines himself to presenting the novel's setting and initial situations. It is characteristic that he abandons this role for the first time in Chapter 7, which is focused on the issue of the guilt and moral responsibility of people who in the years of Stalinism served as informers. At this point, there is no use for the narrator's authoritative explanation or unequivocal moralistic commentary, precisely because one of the chief evils of totalitarian terror is that under its circumstances the issues of guilt and responsibility become ambiguous and blurred. Henceforth, the figure of an omniscient narrator appears as increasingly inadequate and the only way Grossman can carry the weight of the issues raised in his novel is ultimately through direct and essayistic, rather than novelistic, discourse.

As such, *Forever Flowing* remains not only a profound and honest analysis of the phenomenon of Soviet totalitarianism, but also an important indication of the vicious circle in which the tradition of literary realism has found itself in our age. On the one hand, the enormity of human suffering under totalitarian systems demands realistic description more than any other approach; on the other, the authoritative role of the realistic narrator, which so often accompanies this approach, seems today more inconceivable than ever before.

A writer who seems to have been more acutely aware of this conundrum than most of his contemporaries—and who, while remaining a true-blue realist, found perhaps the most artistically satisfying way out of it—is Yuri Trifonov (1925–1981), whose last novel, *The Old Man*,[3] is a fitting culmination of his unique career. Trifonov was perhaps the only Soviet writer in recent decades who managed to attain the maximum of honesty in his critical depiction of Soviet reality while also managing to stay on the surface of official literary life. All his major novels, including *The Old Man,* have appeared in Soviet periodicals and through Soviet publishing houses, even though in most cases their publication could seem a grave blunder on the part of the censor. Of course, there was a price to pay: especially when compared with works written "for the author's desk drawer" or for uncensored publication, such as Grossman's full-scale investigation of the Soviet system's crimes, Trifonov's books are characterized by a certain deliberate limitation of the field of vision and even by occasional instances of circumlocutory language. It might be argued, however, that what appears to have been self-censorship was in fact Trifonov's individual way of focusing on what he knew and understood best. He didn't have to write openly about Stalinist terror, Siberian camps, or dissidents' trials. His unique role was to specialize in meticulous portrayals of the mentality of an average Soviet citizen; and these portrayals provided the reader with even more horrifying insight into that society's distorted system of moral values than many of the works circulating in the samizdat.

The Old Man is Trifonov's most ambitious and successful attempt of that kind. In this novel, the roots of contemporary evil are discovered—even more unequivocally than in some of his previous works, such as *The House on the Embankment*—in the very beginnings of the Soviet system and in its inherent immorality. It was the Revolution itself, along with its idea of "historical necessity," that first exempted the individual from moral responsibility for his actions. The novel's plot, in its contemporary layer (which takes place near Moscow in the oppressively hot summer of 1973), is the story of the last weeks in the life of Pavel Evgrafovich, a veteran of the Revolution and Civil War, who shares his shabby suburban dacha with the families of his son and daughter. The plot revolves around the complicated maneuvers, legal and semilegal, which several members of the local housing cooperative, including Pavel Evgrafovich's children, initiate in order to obtain another cottage, left after the death of a certain widow (who, incidentally, had herself taken possession of it during the years of Stalin's terror by forcing out a family of an arrested "enemy of the people"). At the same time, a letter received by Pavel Evgrafovich from his old love Anna Konstantinovna provokes a series of flashbacks, in which he recalls the story of Migulin, a Cossack commander of the pro-Bolshevik regiment in the Civil War and Anna's husband. It turns out that Pavel betrayed Migulin by testifying as a witness for the prosecution during his show trial in 1919 and admitting the "possibility" that Migulin had been part of an anti-Communist conspiracy.

These two lines of the plot, the contemporary and retrospective, constitute the novel. But Trifonov's art lies in his subtle way of making them seemingly independent from each other (Pavel is not interested in the intrigues concerning the cottage, just as his neighbors and family are not interested in his Civil War memories) while at the same time suggesting their deeper, ethical affinity. It is significant that even Pavel, who seems to stand morally a little bit above the thoroughly corrupt and materialistic younger generation, never realizes the individual guilt that lay in his act of betrayal. In the final analysis, he too turns out to have been contaminated by the germ of moral nihilism which spawned the bloody immoralism of the Revolution as well as the greedy immoralism of the average Soviet citizen in modern times. Trifonov, with all his dislike for overt moralistic instruction and black-and-white divisions, is a moralist in the sense that, for him, acts of evil are never isolated. On the contrary, they are always rife with consequences—including those that come to the surface of social life generations later. One of the characters in his novel expresses that idea by realizing that "life was a system in which everything, in some mysterious way and according to some higher plan, was interlaced." This concept of the interdependence of various components of reality is reflected in Trifonov's superb narrative technique (well rendered in Jacqueline Edwards and Mitchell Schneider's finely crafted translation). As I have mentioned, he found his own solution to the dilemma of contemporary realism: in his novels, he worked out a highly complex system of shifting viewpoints and the protagonists' indirect self-characterization, thanks to which realistic depiction is preserved without the overbearing presence of an authoritative, omniscient narrator. *The Old Man,* a nearly perfect example of such technique, is a triumph of both the moralist and the artist.

Alas, this cannot possibly be said about another apparently realistic work, which copes with the same dilemma only to fail in both an ethical and aesthetic sense. At the outset, Sergei Dovlatov's *The Zone*[4] seems to offer a unique perspective—it deals with the theme of Soviet prison camps, seen, however, not from the usual viewpoint of an inmate but from that of a camp guard. (The author, born in Russia in 1941 and an American émigré since 1978, was, as a young man, drafted into the army and sent to serve as a guard in a camp for criminal offenders.) This concept is perhaps not so revolutionary as that of the brilliant novella *Faithful Ruslan* by Georgy Vladimov, in which the world of a camp was seen through the eyes of a guard dog. Nevertheless, it does sound promising, and it's a pity that Dovlatov's book does not live up to its promise—in fact, it disappoints in comparison not only with Vladimov but also with more traditional prison camp literature, like that of Solzhenitsyn or Varlam Shalamov.

The Zone is actually a sequence of short stories, interspersed with the author's letters to his Russian émigré publisher. The book is presented as a sort of work in progress, which takes shape as the U.S.-based author receives fragments of his manuscripts left behind in Russia before his emigration and now sent to him clandestinely by his friends. But the function of the letters is not merely to explain the book's genesis or provide a framework that would counterbalance its fragmentary construction. In addition, the letters are used as an opportunity to comment on the stories themselves. And here's the rub: Dovlatov errs in overtly expounding the ideology of his stories instead of incorporating it in their narrative structure. If we read, for example, his explicit statements on the analogies between the inner world of the camp and the outer world of

144

Soviet reality, this observation strikes us as perhaps true but banal. It might not be the case, had we come to the same conclusion themselves, compelled to do so by a convincing plot of a story.

In a sense, then, Dovlatov turns Trifonov's technique inside out: he amplifies the overbearing voice of an authoritative author-narrator instead of letting the reality presented speak for itself. This is an aesthetic as well as ethical error, since the presence of the authoritative outside commentary also muffles the moral impact of the stories. Dovlatov would have shocked the reader more if he had left him face-to-face with the narrator, who is a camp guard and looks at the camp from his own specific perspective. Tadeusz Borowski, author of Polish classics of prison camp literature, did not hesitate to do just that in his Auschwitz stories: his narrator, a camp *Vorarbeiter* bearing Borowski's first name, was able to stir up a moral uneasiness in the reader precisely because he had no qualms about his role as helper to the oppressors. Dovlatov, on the other hand, confronts us with guards who, as conscripts, have been forced to perform their unpleasant duties and are, in fact, no less unhappy than the inmates they guard (and sometimes shoot). This may be, in some cases, psychologically true, but it makes the ethical problematics inherent in such a perspective melt into thin air. In the final analysis, both the guards and the prisoners appear to be victims of the system in almost the same sense and to almost the same extent. The old Socialist Realist formula "It's not the system but the people who are to blame" has thus undergone a complete turnabout: Dovlatov seems to say that it's only the system that is guilty, whereas all the people are its blameless victims.

This six-pack of Soviet fiction makes me think of a literary version of Russian roulette, in which a reader can never be sure whether the next turn of the gun's barrel will deliver an authentic charge or a misfire. The last two novels in this collection, both written in the Soviet Union in the mid-seventies by authors who now live in the United States, are just such genuine explosions of creative talent. They may not be equal in value, but they share a new approach to the dilemma of traditional realism. Both authors, like Trifonov, reject the authoritative voice of an omniscient narrator, but instead of creating a polyphonic mosaic of different points of view, both of them prefer to focus on an individual hero or an individual voice. Trifonov's striving for objectivity thus finds its counterbalance in narrative subjectivity, which is, of course, not without effect for the general vision of reality presented in these novels.

Vassily Aksyonov's *The Burn*[5] is his magnum opus whose publication in the West in 1980 earned him expulsion from the Soviet Union; it appears in English only now, one can guess, because of the immense labor required on the part of the translator due to the novel's length and the stylistic variety of its original Russian. The first pages of this huge work make the reader plunge into what seems to be total disarray: individual characters and plot lines appear only to disappear again, the narration shifts from first person to third person and back, the nature of the motivation for specific scenes (rational or fantastic) is far from certain. Only after some time are we able to grasp the underlying principle of construction: with complete disregard for traditional realistic rules, the novel has five chief protagonists who are five different personages while *also* being the same person. These five are a popular jazz saxophonist, a scientist involved in some mysterious military research, a dissident writer, an unorthodox sculptor, and a doctor who has discovered the so-called "Lymph-D," described as "liquid soul or something like that." All five live in Moscow in the early seventies, and their paths sometimes even cross. In fact, however, each of them is just a different grown-up extension of one single character, Tolya von Steinbock, son of a Russian father and Jewish mother, whose adolescence (shown in a series of half realistic, half nightmarish flashbacks) was spent in Magadan during Stalin's last years, where his mother, released from camp, served her sentence of internal exile. The unity of the five characters (in the novel's last part they again converge into one, called The Victim) is emphasized by the fact that they share the same patronymic, they have the same acquaintances, they belong to the same milieu of Moscow artists and intellectuals and, most important, to the same generation. In both its retrospective and its contemporary layers, *The Burn* is indeed a portrait of a certain generation—of the generation of people, now in their fifties, who lived through a Stalinist childhood, the euphoria of 1956, and the gradually increasing disappointment and cynicism of subsequent years.

Oddly enough, however, the novel's central device, which makes such a collective portrayal of a generation possible, is also the cause of the book's chief shortcomings. The dissociation of Tolya von Steinbock into five different contemporary characters is an innovative device, but it confronts Aksyonov with the need to endow each of these five with individual characteristics and a more or less independent life. This is perhaps too much to sustain for five hundred pages, and the reader suspects on numerous occasions that certain fantastic developments in the plot stem not so much from the author's absurdist vision of contemporary Soviet life as from his pressing need to differentiate the five characters and give them some personal traits. In contrast, it is the relatively most realistic (and, incidentally, most autobiographical) layer of the novel's plot—the story of Tolya's coming of age in Magadan—that engages the reader most. It is so not necessarily because this is the part closest in style to traditional realism; rather, Tolya is the only character in the novel whose inner drama—his being torn apart between longing for freedom and love on the one hand and the desire to be like everybody else on the other—is truly convincing. Compared to him, all his five "extensions," with their more or less imaginative adventures in a world ranging from Moscow's salons to its detoxification stations, seem to be devoid of authentic inner conflicts, and their despair, demonstrated by superhuman indulgence in sex and alcohol, reads almost like something out of the melodramas of Françoise Sagan. Chaotic, overflowing, unbelievably uneven, at turns rambling and farfetched or incisive and compelling, Aksyonov's *The Burn* may well be *the* novel of his generation and is certainly the work of an enormously talented writer. But it never attains the degree of artistic cohesion that would make it something more than a testimony to its times.

In this company of six, it is Yuz Aleshkovsky who, besides Trifonov, turns out to be a decisive winner—even more so as *Kangaroo*[6] is his first novel to appear in English, whereas Trifonov's reputation in the West has been fairly well established for quite a while. This does not mean that these two writers have much in common. Indeed, it would be hard to find two more dissimilar novelists. Whereas Trifonov has often been seen as a modern continuator of Chekhov, Aleshkovsky's work refers back to the neglected tradition of Andrey Platonov: what interests him is not so much psychological or factual realism as the autonomous reality of language, treated as something even more important than the external reality it reflects.

At the same time, Aleshkovsky is a great writer of the absurd; in that

147

sense, his literary pedigree reaches back to the stories of Abram Tertz (Andrey Sinyavsky), and even farther back, to the early novels of Mikhail Bulgakov. What they all share is the method of starting with an apparently absurd situation, but dealing with it and developing it along lines that are completely in accord with the logic of Soviet life. In *Kangaroo*'s case, the logic is that of Stalinism *anno* 1947. The first-person narrator, Fan Fanych, a notorious con artist, in a book-length monologue relates his story to a friend with a similar background. Well-known to the KGB, he nonetheless had never been imprisoned before 1947 because he had been kept in reserve as the ideal defendant in a long-planned great "trial of the future." Finally arrested, he was offered a choice of several different indictments; in order to make the prosecution's task as difficult as possible, he chose the most absurd one, the scenario composed by a malfunctioning KGB computer, according to which he raped and murdered an aged kangaroo in the Moscow Zoo "on a night between July 14, 1789, and January 9, 1905." From that hilarious premise, everything in the plot develops with the infallible consistency of the Stalinist system, in which the prosecution is always right (even if the crime has never been committed) and the case is not closed until the defendant himself confesses his guilt. Fan Fanych is joined in his cell by a tutor, an expert in marsupials; he is drugged so that he can believe *himself* to be a kangaroo; he plays the main role in a film prepared by his prosecutors as an important piece of courtroom evidence; finally he is sentenced (in a huge show trial which is only a slight caricature of the Moscow trials in the 1930s), sent to a special camp for the most distinguished old Bolsheviks, and released only in the years of the "thaw." There is no shortage of fantastic ramifications in the plot (among other things, the hero contributes personally, by stealing Hitler's wallet in 1929, to the birth of Nazism; later, he is able to witness—from a rather strange vantage point—the secret proceedings at the Yalta conference), but, on the whole, one is struck by the paralyzing logic rather than the imaginary nature of the plot's development. Everything that happens here is just an exaggeration of what could have happened in the Stalinist reality; in fact, even the charge of raping a kangaroo is not very far from the preposterous accusations which could be heard in the real-life show trials.

But *Kangaroo* is much more than just a convex mirror which magnifies the absurdities of the Soviet system; in the original, and also to a large extent in Tamara Glenny's excellent translation, it is an orgy of linguistic mockery. The language of the monologue is a hysterically funny result of the clash between official Soviet phraseology and the monologuist's own nonconformist style formed in prisons and interrogation rooms (for instance: "I told him if you subtract the enthusiasm of the twenties from the enthusiasm of the thirties, all that's left is ten years for counterrevolutionary agitation and propaganda"); thus, it provides its own, independent commentary on the nature of Soviet reality. It defines this reality as shaped not only by events and facts but also by ubiquitous *signs*—ranging from propaganda slogans to films or portraits of the leaders—from which there is no escape; the only way for a free mind to cope with this permanent pressure is through parody, through linguistic violence, through an abuse of official language that will overpower it and thus defeat it. Aleshkovsky's narrator may not have raped a kangaroo but he did rape the Soviet language. His creator's offense is as serious as his artistic victory is total.

[1986]

Science Friction

Q: What puts Stanislaw Lem in a category with François Rabelais and Anton Chekhov? A: All three started out in the medical profession. The best-known representative of European science fiction, as well as the most widely translated among Poland's living authors, Lem wandered into literature almost reluctantly. Something of a Polish Isaac Asimov, he can claim an up-to-date familiarity with many fields of science; as the legend goes, he devours professional journals on topics ranging from astrophysics to zoopsychiatry at the rate of a dozen a day. Some of his nonfictional works, such as the wittily yet forbiddingly titled *Summa Technologiae* or the highly technical treatise on literature's cognitive aspects *Philosophy of Chance,* leave the poor literary critic in helpless awe. But Lem's mind works in mysterious ways. Loaded, computerlike, with an intimidating amount of scientific information, it emits a torrent of novels and short stories that betray this computer's unmistakably human qualities, from compassion to an acerbic sense of humor.

For this sort of mind, medicine might have seemed a better outlet than literature. Born in 1921, Lem received as sound a medical education as was possible in the war-ravaged cities of Lvov in the early forties and Krakow between 1946 and 1948. After graduation he tried for a while to pursue all of his incompatible interests at once, by writing everything from poems and short stories to popular essays on science to articles published in professional medical journals. Perhaps the only way to avoid dissociation of personality was for him to make all these fields and genres converge, in science fiction.

In Poland just after the war, that was an adventurous thing to do. For one thing, all eyes were turned toward the immediate past. The memories of wartime inhumanity still smarted. It seemed that for many years to come, literature would be confined to bearing witness to what had happened—to describing, as one contemporary Polish writer put it, "the fate that humans had procured for humans." At the same time, all individual musings on the future (and what else is science fiction if not a private-enterprise vision of the future?) were being more and more strictly weeded out, to be replaced with "scientifically" elaborated prospects, courtesy of Marxism and its aesthetic extension, Socialist Realism. The Polish term for science fiction is, in fact, "scientific fantasy," a *contradictio in adiecto*. In Stalinist Poland, visions of the future were expected to be "scientific" all right, but unhealthy fantasizing was strictly forbidden.

Young Lem was clever enough, however, to outsmart the guardians of Socialist Realism's purity. He created his own version of science fiction and managed to get it past the censors. After the serialized publication of his first, now forgotten, novel *The Man from Mars* in a teen magazine in 1946, the appearance in 1951 of his first published book, *The Astronauts,* brought him huge success. Needless to say, this novel would not have seen the light of day at all had it not been fashioned more or less along the obligatory ideological lines of its time. The global Communist future depicted here is definitely rosy. Space exploration flourishes in the spirit of true internationalism—that is to say, with Russians at the helm. Even in this book, however, Lem's perspicacity somehow has the last word. He manages to pose a number of rather non–Socialist Realist questions concerning the nature of human civilization and the ethical complications involved in the mind's triumphs over matter.

In the post-Stalinist years, naturally, Lem's skill in asking such questions has found incomparably more room to develop. Over the past thirty years he has been developing as a writer with breakneck speed, not only writing profusely but constantly surprising his readers. What strikes Lem's faithful followers most, I think, is his uncanny thematic and generic versatility, combined with a poetic gift for totally unexpected literary approaches. Nobody could have predicted, for instance, that after the success of his first couple of middle-of-the-road science fiction novels, he would switch to pure-nonsensical satires with strong antitotalitarian overtones, as in *The Star Diaries* (1957). Or that alongside his ingenious yet relatively conventional space-exploration novels such as the famous

151

Solaris, he would later publish farcical fables like *The Cyberiad,* Kafka-esque parables like *Memoirs Found in a Bathtub,* or philosophical thrillers like *The Investigation,* not to mention even crazier generic oddities such as *A Perfect Vacuum,* which is a collection of reviews of nonexistent books.

And this is not all. It is merely the Lem available in English. Lem's die-hard Polish fans also know him as more than a science fiction writer. To them he is also a philosopher, a literary theoritician and critic (writing sagaciously on the subject of science fiction itself), a brilliant memoirist, and even a poet (although this early component of his output, unearthed and published in Poland in 1975, was not much more than a surprise gift for Lem's admirers).

Wait a second, there's more. There is also Lem the realist novelist. And quite a traditional realist novelist he is, too. *Hospital of the Trans-figuration*[1] shows us a Lem hardly imaginable to anyone who has read his *Memoirs of a Space Traveler* or *The Futurological Congress.* What we actually see here is the resolute direction of his early writing before it was irreversibly diverted from that straight route by his success with science fiction. *The Astronauts* was Lem's first published book, but *Hospital* was the first mature novel he completed. It had been written long before *The Astronauts,* in 1948–1949, though it was published only in 1955.

The publisher's blurb for the new book never mentions that *Hospital of the Transfiguration* is part of a larger whole. It is the first volume in a trilogy titled in Polish, with an anti-Proustian wink, *The Time Not Lost.* Not that it would have made any sense to have the entire trilogy trans-lated and published here. Its second and particularly third volumes are marred by many flaws; in recent decades Lem himself has condemned these two volumes to oblivion and allowed the Polish publishers to re-edit only the first. Indeed, the closer the reader comes to the final chap-ters of the last volume, the more forgettable this trilogy seems.

The edifying intent is clear in the title. The novel was supposed to be a sort of modern *Bildungsroman,* in which a young man's experiences make him gradually a fuller person, and thus make his "time" of trial worthwhile and "not lost." The trouble, however, was that young Lem had ambitiously decided to set the plot of his trilogy against the back-ground of his own turbulent times. These included not only the war years but the immediate postwar phase of People's Poland as well. In cognitive and aesthetic terms, this was a suicidal decision. Whoever in 1948–1949, or especially in the several years that followed, wished to write a contemporary novel based in Poland faced a brutal alternative: either to write for his desk drawer or to tell lies. Lem attempted to find a middle road by trying to save as much of the picture's complexity as possible, but at the cost of ultimately portraying Socialist Poland as a blessed haven for his troubled hero and his nation.

There were, to be sure, hundreds of far less honest books produced in Poland at the time, and Lem does not really have much reason to blush. Still, it was wise on his part to reduce *The Time Not Lost* to the *Hospital of the Transfiguration*. Read separately, this brief novel, though certainly not flawless, offers Lem's admirers a highly interesting look into his early realistic aspirations and concerns. Rather than emulating H. G. Wells, he is quite visibly inspired here by an entirely different novelistic tradition, one that extends from Dostoevsky to Thomas Mann (the setting and the ideas of *The Magic Mountain* must have been a crucial influence); and if the final results are not quite up to these two names, it is certainly not for Lem's lack of ambition.

Lem's own Hans Castorp is a young doctor fresh out of school, named Stefan Trzyniecki, and his Davos is a hospital for the mentally ill in the Polish provinces during the first months of the Nazi occupation. At the novel's outset, Trzyniecki, having just attended a relative's funeral in the country (his kin are mostly landowning families but he himself is a poor city-dweller), succumbs to a spiritual crisis, caused by many things at once: his realization of the senselessness of suffering and death, his depression after his country's defeat, the instinctive disgust most people evoke in him, and finally the Gombrowiczian sense of his own unbearable incompleteness and indefiniteness. In order to escape from all this he decides, on the spur of the moment, not to return home, and instead to accept his friend's invitation to join the staff of a nearby psychiatric asylum.

Here the book's best part starts. *Hospital of the Transfiguration* proves the old point about realistic literature: whenever the author touches upon the concrete subjects he knows thoroughly, instead of voicing general truths, his writing always gets better, becomes more convincing, not merely in an informative but also in a strictly aesthetic sense. In reading Lem's novel, it is not its philosophical or moralistic import but the raw

153

substance of tangible experience, the fruit of his medical training, that appeals most.

In contrast, the devices Lem employs to drive his *Bildungsroman* points home lend the novel an air of predictability. The book's very title deflates the suspense: we know beforehand that the hospital setting and the symbolic "transfiguration" of the protagonist in it will serve as the novel's pivotal elements. The underlying concept of the isolated microcosm of a hospital as a sort of testing lab where human characters mature or break under pressure, where, despite all isolation, the external world constantly makes its ominous presence felt, where finally the protagonists, all their self-centered escapism notwithstanding, are forced to make a moral choice, quickly becomes too transparent and obvious.

Yet Lem's portrayal of the hospital itself still retains a great deal of literary power, from the stark realism of the ward and the operating room to the hidden mechanisms behind the asylum's functioning—the web of cruelty, intrigue, and indifference that binds the doctors and patients alike, the deranged or unscrupulous behavior of some and the desperate efforts of others to preserve the last vestiges of sanity and humaneness. The pages that depict this world show Lem in his element. The book's final chapter, in which the Nazis take over the hospital and force the doctors to consent to the patients' liquidation, is supposed to provide both the tragic *peripeteia* and moralistic dilemma, but it seems almost conventional by comparison. This novel's plot—which begins with a funeral and ends with an act of physical love—locates the tragic conflict in the human body rather than in the realm of history or ethics; its bitterness is less that of a moralist than that of a physician who knows pain, madness, and death from close personal observation.

This book may provide the answer to the question of why Lem the budding realist switched to science fiction. Was the failure of the subsequent parts of his trilogy an indication to him that under the conditions of censorship the futuristic disguise would help him write more honestly about humanity's contemporary problems? Or did he simply find himself, as an artist and thinker, at realism's dead end? The disparity in weight between the theme of human biology and the theme of human history in *Hospital of the Transfiguration* suggests yet another possible answer. Lem is one of those writers who are interested more in the essential immutability of human existence than in any superficial evolution that history may provide. Paradoxically, he visualizes the future only to find more proof of his suspicion that human fate has remained, will remain, bound by the same laws of pain, love, and death, no matter what space suits we wear or what utopias we build.

[1988]

Wake Up to Unreality

In Polish, the word *rondo* means several different yet similar things: a hat brim, a traffic rotary, cursive writing, a musical form based on a repetitive refrain. Each of these has to do with roundness, circular shape, cyclical movement, spherical self-containment. Kazimierz Brandys' novel *Rondo*[1] is about what happens when someone attempts to create such a self-contained, closed-circuited niche of fictitious reality in real life. Though artificial and therefore seemingly safer than the angular and dangerously open world outside, the fabricated realm that his protagonist creates is marred by one deadly drawback: it can turn with astonishing ease into something terrifyingly real.

Brandys wrote the first draft of his novel in 1974. This was exactly the time when the best of contemporary Polish literature was just beginning to hum under its collective breath the immortal lines of Cole Porter: "Use your mentality / Wake up to reality." Three decades of dealing with thematic restrictions and trying to outsmart censorship had left Polish fiction with a dubious legacy of allusions and disguises. Conceived to get one's message past the censor's eye unharmed, the devices ended up harming the integrity of the message even more than the red pencil would have. There was a powerful need for a more direct presentation of Polish experience. There was a thirst for the real.

At this early stage in literature's return to simple truths and straight-forward realism, to jump one step further, as Brandys did, and discover unreality as the most real presence in Polish life required a paradoxical mind indeed. But then, the complicated course of Brandys' own career had prepared him well to cope with all the paradoxes involved in the clash between fact and fiction. One of the most popular Polish writers in

1974, by that time he had already shed several different novelistic styles, as the political world around him changed, and his views of literature's relation to reality changed along with it.

He launched his career with the novel *A Wooden Horse,* written in Warsaw under the Nazi occupation and published in 1946, a work that owed a great deal to the prewar novelistic avant-garde with its penchant for grotesque irony. Shortly afterward, Brandys' writing turned deadly serious, and anything but equivocal. Switching from his prewar vague leftism to Communism, in the early postwar years he joined the growing ranks of Socialist Realists. A skillful and prolific writer, he began to turn out novels that bore all the required stamps of the official ideology, and then some: his novel *The Citizens,* which appeared in 1954, is still remembered for a rather overzealous episode in which high school students heroically inform the authorities about the reactionary views of their teachers.

Yet the true believer within Brandys turned quite abruptly into the equally true skeptic, an about-face similar to that of many Polish writers at the end of the first postwar decade. The short stories and novels he published during the mid-1950s, some of them even preceding the official "thaw," may strike us today as somewhat naïve in their political diagnoses. Mysterious manipulators of innocent souls are too often blamed for anything found wrong with Stalinism. Some of these works, however, such as the brief political novel known in English translation as *Sons and Comrades,* manage to strip off more than one layer of the system's falsity by the sheer force of their stories and characters. Still in the early phase of his career, Brandys drew on his personal experience with the Stalinist "new faith" to explore the ethical conflicts produced by the pressure of collective beliefs, from totalitarian ideologies to nationalistic dogmas.

It was also at this point that the tension between fact and fiction began to appear in his works. Since the publication in 1958 of his first volume of "Letters to Mrs. Z.," a sequence of half-fictional essays in epistolary form, Brandys has been a certified master at making fiction pretend that it isn't. His numerous books published over the past thirty years may be viewed, in fact, as a series of experiments to that end. Narrative prose is variously disguised in conspicuously nonfictional genres and forms of discourse: a letter sequence, a writer's diary, an interview. We are dealing, to be sure, with a wider novelistic trend of our times, which to the cynical eye may look like novelists' panicky response to losing their readers to memoirs and biographies.

Still, in Brandys' best books the device has an interesting, individual twist, as personal as it is Polish. The novel *Postal Variations* (1972), an untranslatable fireworks-display of stylization, is a highly amusing collection of fictitious letters in which the history of one Polish family over several centuries—and by extension, the history of Poland itself—is offhandedly presented, while the author has a wonderful time imitating the stylistic flavors of the language of consecutive epochs. Unbelievably enough, this flash of literary brilliance provoked an ugly act of political mugging. After the publication of the novel in Poland, the regime's trusted critics staged a campaign of slander, accusing Brandys (not without unmistakable hints about his Jewish descent) of ridiculing Polish history. The pretense of nonfiction was, in a sense, taken at face value and turned against its creator. Brandys' artistic unreality began to function as something unexpectedly real.

Without delving too deeply into psychological motivations, one may safely assume that the idea of *Rondo*—which Brandys started in 1974, then dropped, turning instead to another novel, *Unreality* (published in English in 1980 as *A Question of Reality*), then picked up again and finished—had a good deal to do with the reception of *Postal Variations*. In Brandys' life, the writing of this pair of novels coincided with the beginning of his open participation in the rapidly growing intellectual dissent of the mid-1970s. In 1976 he was one of the founders of *Zapis* (The record), the first uncensored literary journal in Poland. His own books, increasingly free of self-censorship, came out in the late 1970s mostly through the newly founded underground publishing houses or émigré presses in the West.

The device of a nonfictional genre no longer served the purpose of literary experiment; it was simply the most direct and effective way of writing about contemporary events, which in Poland over the past dozen years have certainly been stranger than any fiction. This at least is the case with *The Months,* Brandys' major work in progress, his multivolume writer's diary or personal chronicle of events and reflections. Begun in Warsaw some ten years ago, Brandys continued it in New York, where he was caught by the news of martial law in Poland, and then in Paris, where he moved soon afterward and now lives. (Out of four volumes of *The Months* published in Polish so far, the first has appeared in English as *A Warsaw Diary*, and the third, unfortunately in heavily truncated form, as *Paris, New York: 1982–1984*.)

Both *Rondo* and *Unreality*—they are, in a sense, twin novels—make use of an ostentatiously nonfictional device. *Rondo* is, or at least begins as, a polemical letter written to a historical quarterly to rectify false information in an article; *Unreality* takes the shape of a series of tape-recorded responses by a Polish intellectual to a questionnaire handed to him by a Western sociologist. Overlapping details in the respective plots make the two novels a sort of tandem, linked by the figure of the protagonist: the same man who explains an episode of his wartime past in *Rondo* tries to explain how People's Poland works (or, more accurately, does not work) in *Unreality*.

Two variations on the theme of Polish unreality, *Rondo* is, true to its title, a self-contained whole in a way that its counterpart, in which plot loses out to explanation, is not. More than self-contained: it is based, like a musical rondo, on the compositional principle of close-circuited self-sufficiency. The recurring thematic refrains and the narrative method of circling around key events instead of presenting them in a linear fashion convey a claustrophobic impression of a determined world in which nothing is left open-ended, in which fate cannot be averted. Once events are set in motion, nothing can stop them. Once unreality is created, nothing can undo its very real existence.

This is precisely what *Rondo*'s protagonist tries to explain in his letter to the editor of the historical quarterly. The letter, which soon evolves into a long narrative, has been inspired, we learn, by a pretentiously titled article, "A Chapter in the History of Struggle," by one Professor Janota, which offered a totally falsified account of the wartime activities of an underground fighting unit called Rondo. The protagonist knows all about the strange truth of Rondo for one simple reason: he was its sole creator. He is the only person who can certify that Rondo never existed in reality.

Didn't it? Or perhaps it did exist, but in another kind of reality, one where fictions become hard facts? Brandys' narrator is familiar with this transformation of unreality into reality from his provincial childhood, thanks to persistent gossip that made him a natural son of the national

159

hero, Marshal Pilsudski. The gossip makes even wider rounds when, as a law student in prewar Warsaw, he is accidentally seen by a friend at the entrance to Belweder, Pilsudski's official residence.

The unbidden notoriety turns into unbidden charisma when the war breaks out and many people start viewing the narrator—a man in whom nothing is in fact out of the ordinary save his "insane normality"—as a possibly providential leader. Meanwhile, he develops a powerful attraction to theater, drops out of law school, and makes his living as an extra in one of Warsaw's troupes. This settles his fate: he falls in love with a young actress named Tola, a woman as oversensitive and chaotic as he is calm, collected, and reliable. When they become lovers, it dawns on him that the only way to keep this impossible relationship alive is to make Tola's life a *role,* of which he would be an invisible "director."

After the Nazis come in and theaters are closed down, the narrator's concern is to keep not merely their relationship but Tola herself alive. He is involved in the activities of the underground Home Army, and Tola, always an exalted maximalist, demands to be part of that. Left without any role to play, she is dangerously close to mental disintegration; yet precisely because of her instability she would be too great a risk. While listening to Chopin's Rondo at a clandestine concert, the protagonist hits upon a brilliant idea for saving Tola both from herself and from the Nazis: he will create a nonexistent clandestine organization and make Tola work for it as a secret courier.

Thus Rondo comes into being. Tola is sworn in, given instructions, and periodically sent out with suitcases containing secret messages that are in fact old newspapers and books. She has a role to play, but at the same time she is protected from any real danger. But the danger becomes real very soon. The news of Rondo's supposed existence inevitably begins to spread. Even its accidental name is deciphered as an acronym for a direct military extension of the Polish underground commander-in-chief. The myth of Rondo's exploits, combined with the narrator's unwanted charisma, attracts people who—much like Tola—need a role to play in order to fill their own spiritual void with some semblance of meaning and purpose.

Among the recruits is the protagonist's former schoolmate and the Mephisto of his life, Wladek Sznej. A highly intelligent mind, Sznej nevertheless has no inner resources of his own. He lacks any moral principle; his personality portends the future of Poland, which will soon be ruled by his "tribe of middlemen":

> They served as mediators between truth and falsehood, honesty and fear, conscience and success. Most often perhaps they mediated between themselves and the "objective situation." Almost all these people shared one astonishing feature: flexibility of the line dividing the true from the false. They possessed a highly developed sense of relativity in every judgment (at that time it was called "dialectical thinking"), but in reality they lacked internal foundations. Their consciences were constantly on the lookout for endorsers.

Before the war, Sznej's conscience finds an endorser in the ideology of right-wing nationalism; after the war, in Communism. (This kind of evolution is not a farfetched fantasy. People's Poland has had a share of real-life Sznejs.) In the wartime interim, he grasps at the straw of Rondo's supposed existence with fanatical determination, forcing the protagonist to induct him, too, and immediately pressing him to broaden the base of the organization (which at this point already includes several young people whom, like Tola, the narrator tries to protect from real involvement).

Rondo quickly acquires an increasingly tangible existence. Conceived to save lives, it endangers them more and more. In the end, the roof of the whole structure of unreality falls in for real, burying all of the narrator's hopes. A rival guerilla group bungles the execution of a traitor and instead someone else dies—a famous older actor who happens to have been Tola's idol and one-time lover. Convinced of the protagonist's omnipotence in murky dealings of the underground, Tola cannot be persuaded that he had nothing to do with the victim's death. Her mental illness is just one disastrous consequence of Rondo's nonexistent existence.

There are others. Even after the war ends, Rondo never ceases to cast its long shadow on the lives it once touched. As a bitter irony of fate, the narrator spends several years in a Stalinist jail, accused of, and interrogated about, his wartime membership in an organization that arouses even more suspicion by having been so perfectly undercover that nothing is known about its activity. The all-pervading unreality of Communism absorbs this instance of individual unreality with the greatest of ease.

161

At the time the narrator writes his letter, he has been free for many years; but even though he hopes to reunite with Tola, who is about to return from emigration, evil has already been done and lives have been ruined irrevocably. Professor Janota's article, which ultimately mythicizes Rondo's history and confirms the everlasting power of unreality, is the final insult—especially since, as we learn near the end of the novel, Janota's true name is Wladek Sznej. The role of historian, whose supposed vocation is to dig up the truth, is now played by the man who once said, "Humanity . . . is a chaos we fill with meaning. We create legends and make ourselves believe in illusions. We, the people, use lies to bring some order into reality! There is no such thing as the truth of reality. All the testimonies and accounts are only interpretations."

Thus, *Rondo*'s circular structure comes to its ultimate fulfillment: from the last page we must return to the first. From the first words of his letter, the narrator was aware that Janota was in fact Sznej. While ostensibly trying to defend the truth and to denounce unreality, he knew all along that his explanation would fall on the deaf ears of someone for whom "there is no such thing as the truth of reality." *Rondo* is a novel about what happens when someone or something, an individual or a political system, acts on those chilling words.

[1989]

The Polish Complex

I'm standing in line in front of a state-owned *delikatesy* shop. I'm the one hundred forty-seventh person in line. The huge queue, extending toward Freedom Square, suddenly turns down a side street to avoid the road and crosses Red Army Street in the distance. Rumor has it that a delivery will arrive in a quarter of an hour. Carp or coffee—no one knows for certain. In any case, the lady who is one hundred forty-sixth in line convinces me it's worth joining.

A bleak, rainy day: Christmas Eve, 1977. Half an hour ago I finished my third reading of Tadeusz Konwicki's novel *The Polish Complex*,[1] and went out for a walk to meditate a bit on the book. How did it happen that instead of walking about at random I chose to stand in a line? I'm not sure myself. Maybe simple symmetry: as in the novel, it is Christmas Eve; as in the novel, this is Poland; and therefore, as in the novel, one must stand in line. Whether it's for a hundred grams of sour coffee ("Extra-Select") at sixty zlotys, or for a troublesome fish to store in your bathtub, is the least important issue. A queue is simply ideal for reflecting upon Konwicki's latest novel.

Why does the action of his book—at least the narrative set in the present—mostly take place in a queue? The first answer is embarrassingly simple: because all of Poland today is queuing up. The line, as the central idea of Konwicki's book, is one of those literary strokes of genius which combine everyday ordinariness with symbolic meaning, where a specific situation reflects the general state of society.

But a simple queue—like the one I am standing in—would not suffice as a symbol. The reader has little need for the banal statement that for forty years we Poles have been suffering "temporary difficulties." Konwicki's trick is more treacherous. His line is not a line in front of a food store but a jewelry shop, a *Jubiler*. The heroes await not a shipment of butter or meat but a delivery of gold rings from Russia, investments for their devaluating zlotys. A line for gold—an everyday scene in a Socialist country! Thus, the emphasis shifts from the banality of an economic criticism of the system to a much more interesting insight (artistically speaking) into the system's most significant feature: absurdity, the Great Nonsense that constitutes the main theme of the novel.

I look at the queue in which I am standing, and, as always on such occasions, I feel anxiety mixed with anger. I was one hundred forty-seventh, but what number am I now? The line has swollen; we are no longer standing in single file. The queuers are joined by their friends and the friends of their friends. Always the same. Nothing ever changes in the phenomenology of a line. Take the elderly gentleman less than twenty places in front of me who exclaims with prewar righteousness and post-war helplessness, "But please, ladies and gentlemen, we can't let this get out of hand. We must organize ourselves!" Even he is a constant in a queue. It seems as though I've heard his words many times before. And this old busybody right behind me who says loudly and bitterly, "Yeah, get yourself organized, Grandpa. There won't be enough goods anyway." She, too, never fails to appear on such occasions. And, as always, the line responds in unison with muted laughter—a laughter of people who at once realize the absurdity of their lives. Briefly this sad laughter unites them, hostile and embroiled, in one big brotherhood.

And here we have our second reason. The line in Konwicki's novel is more than a symbol of the Great Nonsense: it is both a model and a cross section of a society approaching the condition of "Madogism" (from "mad dog"), a term coined by Alexander Zinoviev (a Soviet logician who was forced by illogical reality to become a writer of satire). Zinoviev's *The Yawning Heights* contains the ominous sentence, "Queuing is the highest possible form of Madogism." Well, things still aren't that bad in Poland—a typically Polish consolation—but even here, in our country, the line does begin to symbolize our society. It is a society in which everyone is wronged equally but sees no chance of improvement, even through collective action. Hence, the people transform their frustration into aggression or, simply speaking, begin to hate one another.

Konwicki manages to pinpoint the paradox of our society with striking accuracy. A writer, a worker, a plainclothesman, a private entrepreneur, a student, and a professional queuer hired by some pensioner—all enjoy equal rights in the line for Soviet gold. To make the situation all the more funny and real, the author has them joined by a group of Soviet tourists who seem to have come to Poland for the sole purpose of purchasing Soviet goods. Thus, Konwicki gives us a full range of social classes and strata, with a national conflict to top it all off. Yet the animosities that arise between the characters do not come from differences of class or nationality. Each would-be customer, whether he is wealthy or belongs to a privileged group, is victimized equally; there simply are no goods to acquire. Nothing can justify our everyday pains, humiliations, and hustles. Not only are higher goals absent (in fact, they have been long forgotten) but also the simplest, most palpable things desired, the material goods, are gone. What remains is hatred for anyone who, in this senseless queue, has a better place in line, and even more for anyone shrewd enough to bypass the line altogether.

The most delightful, if this word is appropriate, of Konwicki's inventions is his story of Kojran and Duszek. Immediately after the war, the narrator, Konwicki, who has just converted to a new Socialist Realist faith, is tailed by Kojran, who plans to carry out a death sentence passed down by a resistance organization. Meanwhile, Kojran is followed by Duszek, a State Security agent, who finally arrests and tortures him. "You might say we were walking Indian file," states Kojran. When I say this dismal plot is "delightful," I mean it gives the purely aesthetic delight of watching Konwicki develop this motif to the utmost. Nearly four decades later, all three end up standing in line for gold, Konwicki, Kojran, Duszek, in that order, single file. With their places saved, they go to have a drink together. Years of struggle, assassinations, prison sentences, and torture are put behind them and blotted out. Kojran has served his seven years, and Duszek seems to have rejected his past; in any case, he doesn't like to talk about it. Today, they are almost friends. Three sharp human profiles blur, after years, into one nonentity. The values that once motivated them no longer matter. In the past, their "Indian file" relation to one another signified a certain social structure, a paradoxical integrity rooted in political antagonism. By stepping on each other's heels they were connected by an official bond of hostility; their clashes were tangible. Today the "Indian file," treated as a social model, lacks even this kind of integrity. True, agents of power like Grzesio still exist, furnished with blue jeans, but they are not distinguishable by their convictions but rather by their privileged position in line. If they are "nosing" after somebody, it is not ideological fanaticism; it is simply their job. (Stanislaw Jerzy Lec's aphorism is apt here: "He suffered from a persecution mania. He thought someone was following him, and it was only an agent of the State Security.")

A fitting symbol of a conservative hierarchical state would be a human pyramid composed of people standing on one another's shoulders. Similarly, a symbol for an ideal democracy would be a circle of people seated around a table and looking squarely into each other's eyes. The symbol for a state like ours is the queue; each individual can see only the back of the person standing in front of him, and the only movement is an anxious pushing forward.

Here we go! The door to the *delikatesy* has just opened, and a human tide, pushing and trampling, surges over the threshold. The last residual forms of social self-discipline disappear. One might say Konwicki's line was more civilized. Not because it was a line for gold; rather, the difference was in numbers. When attendance reaches a critical point, every queue is transformed into a mob—a desperate mob, since the supplies will certainly fall short of the demand. I am too far back; but how would I act if I were, say, thirtieth in line and saw only ten hams on the counter?

After the first assault on the door, the commotion subsides. Rumors spread down the line that the shipment hasn't arrived, but is expected soon, maybe in a half hour. Most probably carp.

Well, we'll wait and see. Now that we have more time, let's return to Konwicki. To recapitulate: a queue is both a symbol and model of a society that pursues the most mundane values required to justify the pain of daily existence. Since even the simplest of needs cannot be fulfilled— for reasons inherent in the system—the society gradually disintegrates, and the people's frustration is discharged through outbursts of mutual

166

hatred. But not even this hatred is real; the everyday sense of impotence has destroyed all authentic impulses and moral systems. Everything dissolves into the Great Nonsense.

And still, note Konwicki's confession: "I write because in my subconscious there stirs a spark of hope that somewhere there is something, that something endures somewhere, that, in my last instant, Great Meaning will take notice of me and save me from a universe without meaning." It's true, the subject of the novel is not only the Great Nonsense but also human hopes, the struggle to wrestle out of the grasp of the absurd, the anticipation of a miracle, and the efforts to use one's own power to fight the Nonsense.

After all, it is Christmas Eve, the eve of the Miracle. The word "miracle" appears in the novel again and again. "What are you waiting for, a miracle or something?" asks Kojran in the opening scene. To which the narrator answers, "Yes, you're right. I am waiting for a miracle." The colloquial expression suddenly gains here a deeper meaning, and later this phrase becomes a leitmotiv. "I'm quietly waiting for a miracle. I'm constantly waiting for an answer," the narrator explains, but other characters cannot respond with any such certainty. And yet almost all of them are on the eve of something that can, supposedly, change their lives. Each cherishes his or her little hope: Kojran flies to America to start a new life the very next day, and Julia, who claims she's already hit the jackpot, hopes to find a man to share her loneliness.

But let us note that nobody really believes in his own dreams. No character takes his or her hopes seriously, not even the woman whose only consolation is the thought that people elsewhere are just as badly off. The possibilities of a miracle, of escape from everyday existence, are rejected one after another as illusory. Even the narrator's unexpected sexual adventure, which at first seemed to be precisely that miracle—the Assumption, with all its angelic attributes—is diluted into profane banality. Such a disappointment is a constant motif in Konwicki's writing. I would call it the "second-try complex." In the midst of the sexual act, the hero often experiences mystical exaltation, but when he tries to recreate the ecstasy a second time, it's either a complete failure or a disillusionment. The repeated act has only minimal appeal for the hero, and he, "like an old husband," cannot free himself from the ennui. Therefore, there is no real escape to be found in love, or even in death—neither the

167

death that seeks the hero (a coronary), nor the death that the hero pursues at the end of the novel.

Might there be no refuge from the symbolic queue? Is there no escape from the nonsense? There is. Or there might be. But . . .

. . . But in the meantime, news reaches us that the carp has been delivered. As if the pressure weren't already enough, the crowd tries to force its way into the shop. Dantesque scenes take place in the bottleneck of the single half of the door that is opened. (Ilf and Pietrov's law can be applied to all Eastern European countries: when an architect plans a number of entrances, only one, at best, is opened.) Cries and insults are thick in the air. One other aspect of the phenomenology of the line: the participants push forward as though this could hasten their access to the goods. Therefore, I push too. Besides, being pushed from behind, I have little choice.

There is an escape from Konwicki's line. Or rather, there is a way to rise above the level of the line, rise in the most literal sense. The critic Lech Dymarski has written about the "cosmic perspective" adopted in the novel: Konwicki's narrator explains the rules governing our planet and our civilization as though to an audience of intelligent aliens who had strayed into our galaxy. Abandoned after the first pages, this perspective might appear as a rather unmotivated literary device. But in Konwicki's case it is not. The narrator acts as if he were, despite the burden of his fifty years, the only man for whom nothing is obvious: he is a man no longer surprised by anything who suddenly decides to understand and explain everything anew, to get down to bedrock. This perspective appears in Konwicki's earlier books as well. It so happens that it reveals itself most clearly in the two novels that I consider—of course, not only for this reason—to be Konwicki's best achievements prior to *The Polish Complex:* these novels are *The Ascension* and *Anthropos-Specter-Beast.* In both, the narrator appears as a tabula rasa, a person with a limited knowledge of the world's rules. In both, this innocence is provided with a rational explanation: the narrator of *Anthropos-Specter-Beast* is a child; and the story of *The Ascension* is told by a man who wakes in the center of Warsaw with a fractured skull and partial amnesia. These tales are thus similar to the philosophical parables of the eighteenth century, where

168

cultural strangeness (for example, in Montesquieu's *Persian Letters*) or a naïve protagonist/narrator provided such a point of view.

In *The Polish Complex* things are different. The narrator is neither a naïve simpleton nor a visitor from another land. He knows his world like the back of his hand. Nothing can astonish him any more, not even the French anarchist who came to Poland to seek true freedom, or the black man who speaks Warsaw cockney and discusses Lithuanian dishes. And yet he is up against the wall of the Great Nonsense, the only thing he cannot cope with. He can only try to rise spiritually above the wall and regard our moronic planet from the cosmic perspective of an alien. It is only then, perhaps, that he might ascertain the real proportions between the meaningful and the absurd in the life of all earthlings and in his own life.

They've started selling the carp. The line creeps forward, and this limited movement brings consolation. At least something is happening; the line is not so senseless as it was before; we are approaching some goal. But at the same time anxiety grows. The basic feature of attractive merchandise is its scarcity. Since the carp is being sold, sooner or later the supply will run out, and therefore we may not be able to get any. Symptoms of panic appear, the line becomes even more shapeless. Not only do the queuers push forward, but some try to bypass the line, and others lean out so as to have at least a glimpse of the objects they desire. My well-trained eyes register common phenomena: an elderly man, with great dignity and little confidence, produces his handicapped citizen's card. He meets an unyielding wall of arms and elbows and angry comments: "Cripples, stay home!" From the front of the line, where taller heads can already see the counter, furious cries are heard: "One fish per customer! Look at that! She's stuffing her shopping bag!" The lucky ones who've already made their purchases push laboriously toward the exit, fighting the stream of people. They are especially disdainful of the crowd. They complain loudly about the lack of common courtesy and, reaching the street, show each other their torn-off buttons. We regard them with genuine hatred.

Yes, from the viewpoint of an alien, one might comprehend the proportions of human flights and falls. But at this point the deepest, most fundamental dilemma of the book appears. Among the many absurdities of our civilization, the narrator discovers the most astonishing one: instead of uniting rationally, humanity has fragmented into groups called nations, distinguishable only by the language they use. This trifling difference has been the cause of bloody wars, imperial oppression, insurgencies, and uprisings.

And suddenly we must abandon the cosmic perspective: there is no retreat from one's own earthly self. Konwicki's self is molded from Lithuania and Poland, from their common and separate histories, from their suffering and hopes. At this point it becomes obvious that not even the most intelligent alien will understand what our freedom is and how people feel when deprived of it. If freedom did not exist, it would be difficult to understand that the escape from the absurd (which pushes us into the "highest form of Madogism—the queue") should be sought not in naïve expectations of miracles or in philosophical elevations but, ironically, in a domain that has shown so many absurdities, errors, failures, and betrayals. In other words, a Polish writer—if he is not a blind nationalist—can see best that the history of an oppressed nation abounds in irrationality. At the same time, a Polish writer has more occasions to single out those situations in which, against all odds, people have managed to conquer the absurd and to create meaning. They are the unknown people who, in Konwicki's words, "drowned in the sea of anonymity fulfilling their tough human duty, people who, in the darkness of despair, barred the roads against the floodwaters of evil, time, or history with their own bones, who in pain and labor gave birth to me so that I could shout as loud as I could, so that I could howl to the very ends of heaven and earth, so that I could save myself and God."

To show those who fulfilled this "tough human duty," Konwicki calls on history by way of two sudden and seemingly unmotivated subplots set in 1863. One story concerns Zygmunt Mineyko, the leader of a handful of insurgents who disperse after the first shots are fired. Mineyko himself is delivered by his compatriots into the hands of a Russian soldier. The other is about Romuald Traugutt, the dictator of the failed uprising, who knows he has been defeated but nevertheless must fulfill his duties to the end. Both the minor insurgent and the leader have lost, but in a sense they are both winners. When Traugutt explains, "I don't know if there was any sense in it. I do know that it had to be done," he gives, perhaps, the only answer possible to those who question the sense of struggling against the Great Nonsense.

In order to prove, in an ironic reversal, that one must not be "ashamed of a fondness for freedom even though it was . . . the freedom which leads to a ruin," Konwicki inserts two striking episodes. The first is the discovery of a desperate letter from a friend living in a remote country— a country from which freedom has been so completely banished that the question of its meaning and value no longer troubles anyone. The second episode is more restrained and ordinary, though in my opinion more astounding—in fact, it may be the most alarming scene in the whole book. Here the narrator meets his alter ego, a relative from beyond the eastern border, a Socialist Labor hero and the foreman of a pig-farm in Soviet Lithuania. When asked, "Are you satisfied with your life?" he answers, "I never think about it. It could be worse . . . Man is created to work . . . The rest is bunk."

Their destiny will be ours, Konwicki seems to say, if we likewise stop asking ourselves that very question again and again, if we get accustomed to the Great Nonsense, if we sink into silence, which so far is our only right. "Previously a slave was entitled to cry out; today the slave has been assured the right of silence, muteness. Crying out brought relief as it does for a newborn baby. Silence and muteness cause degeneration, they suffocate, kill. Previously when a captive nation regained its freedom, it was not hindered in joining the great family of free nations. Today, if by chance it is set free, it will no longer be fit for life and will perish from the poisons accumulated during the dark night of captivity."

I'm finally inside the state-owned *delikatesy*, and now we learn that the carp is sold out! The news has the speed and impact of an explosion. What follows is a collective moan of disappointment. So we will have no carp on our table this Christmas Eve. Once again we are cheated, fooled, humiliated. No miracle this time.

We leave the shop in silence.[2]

[1978]

171

Rhyme and Time

Searching for the Real

At first sight, Czeslaw Milosz's most recent collection[1] reminds one of the *silva rerum*, or "forest of things," the seventeenth-century term for a fascicle containing loosely arranged notes, occasional poems, copies of letters, and memorable quotations. In the same way, *Unattainable Earth* consists only in part of Milosz's poems. The rest of the volume is filled with his prose notes or aphorisms, letters from his friends, and what he calls "inscripts"—fragments from sources as diverse as the *Corpus Hermeticum*, Casanova's *Memoirs*, Zen philosophers, Lev Shestov, Oskar Milosz, and Simone Weil. There are even several poems by Walt Whitman and D. H. Lawrence, translated by Milosz into Polish in the book's original edition and here restored to their English versions and included as "an homage to tutelary spirits."

A veritable mosaic, then; yet its diversity is carefully arranged. Unlike Milosz's three previous collections in English, each of which offered a mix of his older and more recent poems, *Unattainable Earth* is a faithful replica of his latest Polish book, published in 1984. A few minor omissions and additions are all that distinguish the translation (a splendid job done by Milosz himself with the help of one of his steady collaborators, the poet Robert Hass) from the original. The overall composition of the book, however, remains intact. This fact alone indicates that Milosz's "forest of things" is not as wild as it seems to be; that, as the author says in his preface, "under the surface of somewhat odd multiformity, the reader will recognize a deeper unity."

What provides this unity is, first and foremost, Milosz's basic philosophical dilemma, compressed in the two words that form the book's title. In its Polish version, the meaning of the title is, more precisely, "an earth too huge to be grasped." This notion is, indeed, the key to Milosz's poetic philosophy. On the one hand, his is a poetry obsessed with the very fact of the world's being. "What use are you? In your writings there is nothing except immense amazement," he addresses himself in one of his prose notes. Despite the ironic tone, there is much truth in this self-description. Milosz's constant, perpetually renewed "amazement" with the richness of "the Garden of Earthly Delights" (as he calls the world in a poem that borrows its title from Hieronymus Bosch's triptych) can often reach the heights of an ecstatic hymn of praise and thankfulness: "You watch what is, though it fades away, / And are grateful every moment for your being."

On the other hand, Milosz's certainty that the earth is something real and tangible is coupled with his incessant awareness that the earth is "unattainable," "too huge to be grasped." We humans have our share in it, but we are separated from its essence by the dim screens of our imperfect senses, our fallible memory, our limited language.

Even what is enclosed in our consciousness can be, then, only partly expressed; moreover, our human consciousness is itself "weak" and limited. We are able to perceive only the external surface of things, and we but vaguely sense the existence of its "other side":

Fat and lean, old and young, male and female,
Carrying bags and valises, they defile in the corridors of an airport.
And suddenly I feel it is impossible.
It is the reverse side of a Gobelin
And behind there is the other which explains everything.

Here we encounter Milosz the metaphysical and religious poet, one who is able to note down, apparently with an approving nod, this statement from the philosopher René La Senne: "For me the principal proof of the existence of God is the joy I experience any time I think that God is." But he is also able to record this thought: "A decent man cannot believe that a good God wanted such a world." That is because the world—both the world of nature and the world of human history—is tainted by the constant presence of evil. In other words, the earth is not only "unattainable" to our imperfect senses, intellect, or language; it is also "unattainable" because the coexistence of a good God and unwarranted suffering is something beyond our comprehension.

For Milosz, one answer to the problem of evil is the very act of being aware that "good is an ally of being and the mirror of evil is nothing," and that what we call the devil is actually "the Great Spirit of Nonbeing." As a consequence, "searching for the Real," futile and unsatisfactory as that usually is, is the only defense of the good that is accessible to the poet. He affirms being through naming it, and this affirmation has, by itself, an ethical dimension.

But the poet's search for the Real, if it is to bring any result at all, cannot take place within the narrow limits of one mind, one place, one language, one epoch. It must involve his repeated attempts "to transcend [his] place and time," to "multiply" himself and "inhabit" objects and people, so that finally the voice of the poet speaks on behalf of all the things of this world, all forms of being, past and present, dead and alive. This is why the ultimate aim of Milosz's unique development as a poet has been, paradoxically, to pursue the ideal of dissolving his individual voice in an all-encompassing polyphony—in the immense dialogue of different voices, his own and not his own, that is heard in the pages of *Unattainable Earth*.

* * *

As I write this essay, a minor but highly unusual controversy involving its subject is raging on the pages of *The New York Review of Books*. At first glance, what is happening seems to be pretty common: in a letter to the editor (*NYRB*, July 21, 1988), an author is taking exception to the opinions of a reviewer of his book. Neither this nor the fact that the author is Czeslaw Milosz and the reviewer is the well-known British critic A. Alvarez would by itself raise any eyebrows. What makes the situation exceptional and a little strange is that the author is by no means protesting against any harsh treatment from the reviewer. On the contrary, Alvarez's long and detailed review of Milosz's *The Collected Poems, 1931–1987*[2] (*NYRB*, June 2, 1988) was nothing if not warmly appreciative and even enthusiastic. Milosz does not complain of not having been praised enough; rather—and here's the rub—he complains of having been praised for the wrong reasons. In his opinion, Alvarez's review, entitled "Witness," helps trap his work within the worn-out and outdated concept of Eastern European poetry as primarily a moralistic reaction to the pressures suffered at the hands of History and Society. A longer quote is necessary here: "History. Society. If a literary critic is fascinated with them, that's his choice; if, however, he is insensitive to another dimension, he risks to curtail his right to reflect on literature. Perhaps some Western writers are longing for subjects provided by spasms of historical violent change, but I can assure Mr. Alvarez that we, i.e., natives of hazy Eastern regions, perceive History as a curse and prefer to restore to literature its autonomy, dignity, and independence from social pressures . . . The voice of a poet should be purer and more distinct than the noise (or confused music) of History. You may guess my uneasiness when I saw the long evolution of my poetic craft encapsuled by Mr. Alvarez in the word 'witness,' which for him is perhaps a praise, but for me is not."

Milosz has been known for the contrariness with which he often demolishes critical stereotypes about himself and his work, but the fierceness of his resistance to the "witness" formula may puzzle us a little. Hasn't he himself written a book called *The Witness of Poetry*? And yet, whoever has closely followed the latest, truly breathtaking stages of Milosz's soaring poetic career realizes that he has a point here. The key word in his polemic is "evolution." His poetry has indeed come a long way from the 1930s, wartime, and the years of Stalinism, and today it cannot possibly be defined solely in political or moralistic terms borrowed from his *Native Realm* or *The Captive Mind*. To quote Milosz's letter once more: "Poetry should not freeze, magnetized by the sight of evil perpetrated in our lifetime. My objection to Mr. Alvarez's method of literary criticism is that he seems to be impervious to the dynamics at the very core of any art: after all, a poet repeatedly says farewell to his old selves and makes himself ready for renewals."

At a closer look, Milosz's seemingly curious protest against being praised for the wrong reasons is, then, perfectly understandable as the self-defense of an artist pushed into a compartment which he has already outgrown. It becomes more and more justifiable as we leaf through the book in question. A few years ago, Alvarez or any other Western critic could still claim the validity of the "witness" label by pointing out that this was exactly what Milosz himself propounded in his essayistic books made available in English, from older works such as *Native Realm* up to his Charles Eliot Norton lectures of 1981–1982, and what also transpired in the majority of his translated poems. After the publication of *The Land of Ulro* in 1984 and *Unattainable Earth* in 1986, however, such claims no longer hold water. These two books have finally revealed to the English-speaking audience what the Polish reader had grown accustomed to since at least the mid-1970s: they reveal Milosz's true identity as first and foremost—let us use this imprecise term for the sake of brevity—a metaphysical poet. And a careful reading of the five hundred pages of *The Collected Poems* backs this conclusion with a great deal of supportive evidence.

For *The Collected Poems,* although the fifth book of verse Milosz has published in English, is actually the first book that can finally give the English-speaking reader a fairly accurate idea of what his poetry really is, both in the sense of the breadth of its thematic and stylistic range and the uniqueness of his more than half-century long creative evolution. This has been achieved in three ways at once. First, a significant number of important poems from earlier periods, previously unknown in English, have now been translated (mostly by Milosz himself in collaboration with Robert Hass) specially for the purpose of incorporation in the present edition. This group includes several poems that to the Polish reader seem indispensable for any attempt at grasping the essence of Milosz's work, such as the prewar "The Gates of the Arsenal" and "Dawns," the immediately postwar "Song on Porcelain" and "A Nation," the 1957 "Treatise on Poetry" (here represented, to be sure, only by three brief fragments), the 1962 "I Sleep a Lot," the 1968 "Higher Arguments in Favor of Discipline," and so on.

Second, the very latest, astonishingly profound and brilliant phase of Milosz's career, known to the Polish reader through his recent volume *Kroniki,* has also been well represented here, since the book ends with a number of hitherto untranslated new poems, including such crucially important longer sequences as the cycle "La Belle Epoque" and the "Six Lectures in Verse" (these two, in my opinion, being among the highest achievements of Milosz's art).

Third, odd as it may sound, this is actually the first book of Milosz's poems in English that presents his output in strict chronological order and indicates the original books that the poems came from. With the exception of *Unattainable Earth,* which was a translation of Milosz's single Polish volume published in 1984, his previously published *Selected Poems, Bells in Winter,* and *The Separate Notebooks* made a deliberate point in mixing old and new poems, thus blurring the outlines of the poet's evolution. This has often resulted in confusion among English-speaking critics, as openly admitted by, for example, Donald Davie in his recent book *Czeslaw Milosz and the Insufficiency of Lyric*.

To realize to what extent *The Collected Poems* may be successful in elucidating, complementing, and otherwise straightening out the image of the poet's work, it is enough to look at the numbers. The book contains more than one hundred eighty separate poems ranging from two-liners to extremely large and complex works such as the sixty-page poem "From the Rising of the Sun" (here published for the first time in its entirety). Out of these one hundred eighty, as many as forty-nine appear for the first time in this edition, twenty-nine of them being recently translated older poems (written before *Unattainable Earth*) and twenty of them new poems (written in 1985–1987). Not all of Milosz's previous collections of poems in English have been completely superseded by the present edition: *Unattainable Earth*, for instance, is still worth reading as a separate book, since it includes a number of prose fragments, notes, letters, verses of other poets, and so on which are omitted in *The Collected Poems*. By and large, however, the latter book comes as close as a selective translation possibly could to achieving the ideal goal of making Milosz's poetic oeuvre available to the English-speaking reader in all its variety, inner complexity, and historically evolving shape.

In order to understand why this goal was not achieved earlier, one has to take into account that the Western recognition of Milosz as a poet had been slowed down, ironically, by his early international success as a novelist and essayist. In contrast to the case in his homeland, he was known in the West for many years as the author of *The Captive Mind* rather than of any poem, which was due both to political and technical considerations—that is, to the immediate thematic appeal of his prose and to the relative difficulty in adequately translating his poetry into any foreign language. Moreover, in the first two decades of his émigré phase he was little concerned with translating his own poetry: instead, he spent a great deal of time and energy introducing other Polish poets to the English-speaking audience. (As he himself likes to remember, before being awarded the Nobel Prize he was known in American literary circles as a translator of Zbigniew Herbert rather than as a poet in his own right.) The first American translators with whom he began to work on his poems seriously were his Berkeley students: for some of those, like Richard Lourie, Louis Iribarne, and Lillian Vallee, this was the beginning of their careers as highly successful translators of Polish literature. Lillian Vallee went on to collaborate with Milosz on the translation of his *Bells in Winter* (his previous collection, *Selected Poems*, had been a mixed bag of translations done by various hands).

Since 1980 Milosz's work on translation of his own poetry has greatly intensified, thanks to both the increased demand and the efficiency of his new collaborators. A new translating team which took shape in the 1980s consists of Milosz himself and two first-rate California poets, Robert Hass and Robert Pinsky; at various times Hass and Pinsky, who do not know Polish, also worked in a "trio" with Renata Gorczynski, or Milosz relied on collaboration with another Berkeley poet, Leonard Nathan. The results of this collective work have more often than not been splendid. Hass and Pinsky, in particular, never hesitate to tackle the most demanding exigencies of rhyme and meter (although, interestingly, Milosz thought it better to include in *The Collected Poems* not their rhymed version of the long poem "The World," published earlier in *The Separate Notebooks*, but rather a "less ambitious but literal" version done by himself). The English versions of the "Song on Porcelain" (Milosz-Pinsky), "Treatise on Poetry" (Milosz-Hass), "Lauda" (Milosz-Nathan-Hass), "Rivers" (Gorczynski-Hass), and "Six Lectures in Verse" (Milosz-Nathan), to cite but a few of the most impressive examples, give a whole new meaning to the words "poetic translation," particularly in this country, where translating a poem so often means turning its living flesh into processed meat—bland prose divided into lines.

In addition to the inclusion of numerous previously unknown poems, the generally high level of translation contributes significantly to the fact that *The Collected Poems* finally gives the English-speaking audience the chance to grasp both Milosz's complexity and consistent evolution. To repeat, he emerges from this volume as a primarily metaphysical poet or, to be more exact, a poet whose existential and metaphysical concerns have always been dominant in his work, even when accompanied by moralistic obligations or temporarily overshadowed by a sense of necessity to focus on the ominous course of modern history. From "Dawns," written when he was twenty-one, to the recent "Six Lectures in Verse," his paramount theme is the universal essence of the human condition: its complex entanglement in various unresolvable conflicts at once—in paradoxes of history and society, yes, but also in paradoxes of time and space, nature and divinity, good and evil, experience and communication, existence and cognition.

From the point of view of its evolution, Milosz's poetry certainly seems to have gone through many more or less radical changes. In particular, two segments of his career—the earliest period, represented by his 1933 debut, *A Poem on Frozen Time,* and the years between the end of war and his emigration (the poetic harvest of which was collected in *Daylight* in 1953)—strike the observer as two phases during which his poetry frequently deviated from its central obsessions, steering toward direct social and political concerns and sometimes being overtly didactic. Regardless of these thematic variations, however, the philosophical outlook of his poetry taken as a whole turns out to be a highly consistent system. It is a system based, as it were, on three fundamental premises— a metaphysical, an ethical, and an aesthetic one. The first premise may be construed as follows: In spite of the fallibility of our cognition, external reality does exist objectively, and its very being is a constant reason for our admiration of the world. The second premise: In spite of all relativistic theories and nihilistic ideologies, the borderline between good and evil also does exist objectively, and the existence of evil is a constant reason for our abomination with the world. And the third premise: The task of poetry is precisely to bring into relief this irresolvable paradox and to find the means of expression that would be able to cover the infinite distance between admiration and abomination, between metaphysical rapture and ethical repulsion.

The publication of his *Treatise on Poetry* more than thirty years ago ushered in Milosz's most accomplished phase, which has continued to the present. During this phase, despite all the specific strains of his continuous evolution, his work has been characterized by the ultimate fusion of its metaphysical, ethical, and aesthetic concerns. On the one hand, his poetry continues to be an euphoric hymn to the beauty of objectively existing things, of everything that *is* (see "Esse," "An Hour," and many other poems). Many of these poems can be defined as epiphanies—sudden illuminations that reveal a sacred truth of Being hidden behind the external appearance of an object, landscape, or human face. In poems like these, the ecstatic tone is not merely a matter of the speaker's emotional state of rapture; rather, it is motivated by his actual discovery of the "holiness of being" which makes the poem a confession of religious faith. As an aesthetic consequence, this utter respect for the holiness of being has a tremendous impact on Milosz's concept of poetic language, which strives for extreme concreteness in naming things and reflects, by means of dramatic polyphony, the bewildering richness of the world's various "voices."

On the other hand, this ecstatic admiration of the world comes into conflict with Milosz's sober awareness that reality—not only the reality of History but also the reality of Nature—is tainted by the unalterable presence of evil. The Manichaean roots of such a vision have been pointed out by many critics and by Milosz himself: evil is for him the ineffaceable shadow of all that exists, including, perhaps above all, the poet's own ego (see, among other examples, the poems "Temptation" and "Account"). If the "earth" seems "unattainable" to him, it is not merely in the sense that the essence of its being cannot be grasped by our imperfect senses and intellect or reproduced by our imperfect language. Earth is also unattainable in that the coexistence of a good God and the indelible fact of unwarranted suffering is something beyond our comprehension. Whatever can be said about the human predicament on this earth must end with the conclusion that an individual existence is not rationally justified; rather, it is doomed to senselessness.

Yet Milosz at the same time never loses sight of the fact that, just as God agreed to take on human shape in order to share suffering with the Creation, human beings are able at least to "tame" their "affliction" and thus to imbue their apparently senseless existence with some kind of divine sense. And again, numerous aesthetic consequences spring from his conviction that one means of "taming affliction" is through poetry, through "searching for the Real" and trying to give the Real its true name—which is, in fact, the only means the poet has for defending Being against Nothingness and Good against Evil.

In the final analysis, the appearance of *The Collected Poems* does not, of course, invalidate the popular interpretation of Milosz's poetry as "witness" to his epoch and to the political, social, and moral dilemmas brought by the course of modern history. This function has been performed by his work more than once, and it has been performed magnificently, as many specific examples from "Campo dei Fiori" to "The Titanic" would easily prove. Yet it is essential for the critic and the reader to be constantly aware that concerns of this sort do not exist in Milosz's poetry in isolation. On the one hand, they form an extension of a much more general, all-encompassing, superbly rich and consistent system of thoughts and ideas; on the other, they cannot be assessed properly without taking into account other—aesthetic—extensions of this system, revealed in Milosz's constant quest for "a more spacious form," a more flexible and versatile diction, style, poetics, and genre. By gathering at last under one cover a wide, representative, chronologically ordered, and excellently translated selection from all the phases of the poet's career, *The Collected Poems* has the potential to bring Milosz's poetry—and perhaps, as a further consequence, Polish poetry in general as well—much more attention than heretofore. If we consider that the past few months have seen the publication of perhaps the three single most important works of modern Polish literature ever translated into English—Witold Gombrowicz's *Diary*, Aleksander Wat's *My Century*, and Milosz's *Collected Poems*—we have every reason to hope that for the literatures of America and Poland the year 1988 marks, as Humphrey Bogart says at the end of *Casablanca*, "the beginning of a beautiful friendship."

[1986, 1988]

184

The Power of Taste

The title *Report from the Besieged City*[1] could, in fact, stand above each and every poem of Zbigniew Herbert, who at sixty-one is undoubtedly the most admired and respected poet now living in Poland. The image of a city under siege, one of several symbols that constantly recur in his work, has a historical poignancy that makes it much more than just a figure of speech. In September 1939, as a fifteen-year-old, Herbert experienced the annexation of his hometown, the ancient city of Lvov, by the Soviet Union. After the Molotov-Ribbentrop pact turned sour, the city was seized by the Nazis; then, at the end of the war, it was recaptured by the Soviets and retained within the new borders of their empire. Young Herbert had to move to central Poland, but for him the state of siege continued. Now the entire country was under siege by "barbarians," the supporters of the new totalitarian order.

The final, unequivocal formulation of this crucial symbol came during the months of martial law, in the poem that lent its title to Herbert's latest collection. In retrospect, his entire work to date appears as a continuous "report from the besieged city." The poet identifies himself as a chronicler of the defense carried out against barbarians' everpresent threat:

Too old to carry arms and fight like the others—
they graciously gave me the inferior role of chronicler
I record—I don't know for whom—the history of the siege
I am supposed to be exact but I don't know when the invasion began
two hundred years ago in December in September perhaps yesterday at
   dawn
everyone here suffers from a loss of the sense of time

But speaking of the symbolic role of titles, it is very fortunate that almost simultaneously with *Report* another book by Herbert came out in English translation—his collection of essays titled *Barbarian in the Garden*.[2] At first sight, there seems to be a contradiction here: the chronicler of the defense against barbarians now portrays himself as one of them. It is, in fact, this deliberate contradiction that makes Herbert's poetic voice unique and meaningful. The fundamental paradox of his work is that his literary persona is both "the chronicler of the siege" and "the barbarian," someone who sticks, against all odds, to the traditional values and someone who has been forcibly disinherited of them. Like other defenders of the symbolic city, he doesn't want to be forced out. But sometimes he would welcome a little vacation abroad—with a reentry visa, to be sure. The trouble is, once he finally enters the quiet and manicured garden of the outer world, he is not able to identify himself with it. Combating the barbarians has had such an effect on him that he now seems to be a barbarian himself.

Like everything else in Herbert, this sense of incurable duality has its roots in a personal experience. *Barbarian in the Garden* appeared in Poland in 1962, after Herbert had made his first trip to the West. Instead of "trip," one should rather say "pilgrimage." The poet had behind him several years of misery under Stalinism, when he was one of very few intransigent intellectuals who rejected the temptation to join the new order; as a consequence, he was reduced to poverty and isolation. A brilliant mind, thoroughly educated in art history and philosophy, he had to take a variety of bizarre and pitifully paid jobs—such as a designer of protective wear in something called the Bureau of Research and Projects of the Peat Industry—in order to make ends meet.

Absent by his own choice from official literary life, he wrote "for his desk drawer." The breakthrough came in 1956 when, in the wake of political and cultural thaw, his first book of poems was published, followed by the next two in 1957 and 1961. The Western translations and literary awards that ensued provided Herbert with a chance to meet face to face with the world of culture he had known only from books and reproductions. Some of the effects of that confrontation are presented in his famous poem "Mona Lisa," in which the Eastern European visitor finally, after many years of separation by "mountain frontiers" and "barbed wire of rivers," stands before the legendary painting. His initial

186

sense of triumph (he repeats: "so I'm here / you see I'm here / I hadn't a hope / but I'm here") soon evaporates. He realizes that another frontier, a psychological one, still sets apart his twentieth-century Eastern European experience and the world of the Western cultural past:

between the blackness of her back
and the first tree of my life

lies a sword
a melted precipice[3]

The notion of frontier or separation also accounts for the peculiar perspective of Herbert's essays. I don't mean by this that he has to relate his impressions of Italy and France to the not very well-traveled Polish reader of the early 1960s and thus is forced, for example, to explain in detail what a pizza is. More important, Herbert himself approaches the heritage of Western culture with a persistent sense of inner split: he looks at it with the eye of a legitimate heir and, at the same time, with the eye of someone who has been—illegally, but irrevocably—deprived of his heritage. After visiting the cave paintings at Lascaux, he confesses: "Never before had I felt a stronger or more reassuring conviction: I am a citizen of the earth, an inheritor not only of the Greeks and Romans but of almost the whole of infinity."

But such moments of uninhibited euphoria are rare. More typical are the instances when the perspectives of the "inheritor" and the "barbarian" merge: when, for example, Herbert tells the story of the destruction of the Templar order as if he were describing the atmosphere of the Moscow show trials in the 1930s. In such cases it is evident that he is concerned not merely with "the eternity of Piero della Francesca" and "how stone is laid upon stone in a Gothic cathedral," but also with the question of what all those triumphs of Mediterranean culture mean for a modern "barbarian" who, in his own part of the world, faces a methodical extermination of the basic values of civilization.

What is exceptional about Herbert is not the mere realization of that discrepancy but the fact that he is far from blaming culture and civilization for what has happened to them in our century. On the contrary, his respect for the common "heritage" of the Western cultural past never diminishes. He stubbornly reiterates that even though the "heritage" seems to be irreversibly lost, the "disinherited" must claim their rights to

187

it. This is, in fact, their only chance not to forget the nature of the difference between them and the true barbarians. Twenty years after the first Polish publication of *Barbarian in the Garden,* this particular motif has returned with striking force in Herbert's recent poetry, which, among other meanings, can be read as quite a direct commentary on the nature of totalitarianism and art's relation to it. I have in mind, in particular, the splendid poem "The Power of Taste," which offers a surprisingly simple explanation of Herbert's own steadfastness during the years of Stalinism:

> It didn't require great character at all
> our refusal disagreement and resistance
> we had a shred of necessary courage
> but fundamentally it was a matter of taste
>   Yes taste
> in which there are fibers of souls the cartilage of conscience
>
> Who knows if we had been better and more attractively tempted
> sent rose-skinned women thin as a wafer
> or fantastic creatures from the paintings of Hieronymus Bosch
> but what kind of hell was there at this time
> a wet pit the murderers' alley the barrack called a palace of justice . . .
>
> So aesthetics can be helpful in life
> one should not neglect the study of beauty
>
> Before we declare our consent we must carefully examine
> the shape of architecture the rhythm of the drums and pipes
> official colors the despicable ritual of funerals . . .

All this is said by a defender of the City who is back within its walls: after another prolonged stay in the West, Herbert returned to Poland in the beginning of 1981, eventually to experience both the harsh reality of martial law and the tremendous upsurge of his own popularity among Polish readers. Amazingly, Herbert's lyrical persona, Mr. Cogito—initially just a figure of a troubled modern intellectual—has recently become a model for the spiritual situation of a contemporary Pole: an individual who exists (in a given sociopolitical reality) and therefore, to reverse Descartes, has to think, to defend the self by using his or her conscience or its aesthetic equivalent, taste.

Is there any hope in this kind of defense? Not necessarily. Another of Herbert's features, without which his image as a poet would be dis-

188

torted, is that he promises nothing. The conclusion of "The Power of Taste" is sober and bitter:

> Yes taste
> that commands us to get out to make a wry face draw out a sneer
> even if for this the precious capital of the body the head
> must fall

In other words, the defeat is more probable than the victory. If any notion of hope appears in Herbert's poetry, it is hope without guarantee. No philosophy, no religion, no ideology is going to assure us paradise on earth. The only thing we can count on is that, as one earlier poem put it, by not bowing to sheer force, by "maintaining an upright attitude," we will at least avoid "suffocation in sleep." Or, in the words of "Report from the Besieged City":

> . . . if the City falls but a single man escapes
> he will carry the City within himself on the roads of exile
> he will be the City.

Whoever wishes to understand the spirit within the walls of the embattled fortress of today's Central European culture may well begin by memorizing these sentences.

[1985]

189

Solitary Solidarity

The death of Miron Bialoszewski in 1983 has deprived contemporary Polish literature of an irreplaceable figure. Loathed and ridiculed by some, he was extolled by many others as Poland's most innovative, independent, and inimitable poet. Characteristically, over the last decade of his career and after his death, the small squad of his admirers has grown into a veritable army; more important, the perception of his work has dramatically changed. Once considered, at best, a marginal example of avant-garde experimentation and even attacked for its alleged incomprehensibility, today his output is often viewed as, ironically, the most accurate literary record of the everyday experience of an average Polish citizen—experience bracketed by the Second World War and General Jaruzelski's "state of war."

From his very beginnings as a writer, Bialoszewski occupied the paradoxical position of both outsider and fellow sufferer in his society's ordeal. Born in 1922 in Warsaw, he spent virtually all his life within this city's limits. In 1942 he graduated from a clandestine high school in Nazi-occupied Warsaw and began to study Polish literature at the underground university. This was, however, interrupted by the Warsaw Uprising in 1944; after its defeat, Bialoszewski, along with thousands of other civilian survivors, was deported by the Germans to the Western territories. He spent the rest of the war in the city of Opole, where he worked as a bricklayer's apprentice. After the war, he returned to Warsaw; here for a time he tried to continue his study of literature and journalism but finally gave it up in 1947. For the next several years—the years of Stalinist rule in postwar Poland—he made his living by doing various odd jobs: he was a letter sorter in a post office, a newspaper reporter, an author of children's verse. In the first postwar years he managed to publish several poems in the literary press, but beginning in 1949, temperamentally incapable of conforming with the forcibly imposed norms of Socialist Realism, he wrote only "for his desk drawer." Unemployed from 1952, he spent the last years of Stalinism in extremely straitened circumstances, not unlike another excellent poet of his generation, Zbigniew Herbert. During this time of political oppression and personal destitution, Bialoszewski adopted that way of life for which he was to become famous: he transformed himself into a modern-day hermit confined by choice to his shabby Warsaw apartment and aloof from any official public activity.

The year 1955, however, marks the beginning of Bialoszewski's public reappearance as a poet. Together with his two friends Ludwik Hering and Lech Stefanski, he established a one-of-a-kind private theater in Stefanski's apartment, the so-called Theater at Tarczynska Street. Shortly afterward, the theater moved to Bialoszewski's own apartment and changed its name to the Separate Theater. Prior to 1963 the troupe, consisting of Bialoszewski, Hering, and Ludmila Murawska, managed to stage five premieres, four of which were based on Bialoszewski's own poems and mini-plays (collected, years later, in the volume *The Separate Theater, 1955–1963*, published in Polish in 1971). Despite its purely unofficial nature—or, rather, because of it—the Separate Theater quickly became the talk of the town and one of the most widely discussed signs of the coming thaw in Polish culture.

Bialoszewski's "second debut" in the literary press proved to be an even more significant indication of the thaw. His poems, along with those of Zbigniew Herbert, appeared as part of a famous presentation of five "new" poets in one of the December 1955 issues of the weekly *Zycie Literackie*. The year 1956—which saw a whole wave of debuts by young and not-so-young (but previously suppressed) poets—also heralded Bialoszewski's first book of poems, *The Revolution of Things*. The collection provoked a wide range of critical responses, from insightful analyses to indignant attacks. Critical reaction grew even more polarized after the publication of the poet's subsequent collections, *Calculus of Whims* (1959), *Misdirected Sentiments* (1961), and *There Was and There Was* (1965). These books were met with more penetrating studies on Bialoszewski's art but also with increasing hostility on the part of some critics. At this point, Bialoszewski was generally considered a sort of lyrical solipsist, shut tight within the four walls of his bizarre linguistic laboratory.

Thus, the publication of *Memoir of the Warsaw Uprising* (1970) came as a total surprise to everybody, including Bialoszewski's critical supporters. In this book, his first major work in prose, he dealt with a clearly recognizable fragment of the Polish people's shared historical past: the shattering experience of the 1944 Warsaw Uprising. He did it, however, in his own highly unconventional way, looking at the military upheaval from the antiheroic perspective of a civilian and freely combining elements of memoir, intimate diary, lyric, reportage, and oral tale. Thanks to both its politically sensitive subject matter and original perspective and style, the book was an instant success. Since its publication, the circle of Bialoszewski's readers has been constantly growing. The *Memoir* also marked the beginning of a new period in the poet's generic preferences: from that point on, he published more and more books consisting of prose or combining prose, verse, and dramatic presentation. More strictly speaking, his subsequent books, such as *Reality's Denunciations* (1973), *Noises, Clumps, Flows* (1976), *Heart Attack* (1977), *To Cut Loose* (1978), *Pulverization* (1980), and *Oho* (1985), contain fragments that, regardless of their narrative, lyrical, or dramatic aspects, are all generically posed between diary and reportage and thematically focused on the immediate circle of Bialoszewski's everyday experiences.

The name of Bialoszewski's legendary Separate Theater aptly illustrates his position in postwar Polish literature. Indeed, his was, in many ways, a separate poetry. Bialoszewski has neither distinct predecessors nor direct disciples. He refused the convenient shelter of literary groups and fashionable trends. Stubbornly insisting upon his personal independence and hermitlike way of life, he avoided participating in any official institution or collective initiative. And yet the impact he has made on contemporary Polish literature is enormous. His significance lies perhaps mostly in the fact that he has boldly overstepped the limits of what is usually recognized as literature, thus making his readers, critics, and fellow writers realize the restrictive conventionality involved in most literary production.

From this point of view, one can speak of several consecutive breakthroughs made by Bialoszewski in the course of his career. To be sure, his strikingly consistent creative path can hardly be divided into phases or stages: it would be more exact to say that at certain points different features of his work attracted the critics' attention. In the beginning, for instance, Bialoszewski's poetry from *The Revolution of Things* struck critics mostly as a rediscovery of the material object. After the years of Socialist Realism, which had suffocated its readers with its idealized, beautified, or plainly falsified images of reality, Bialoszewski offered a lyricism of concrete, tangible, everyday, down-to-earth objects—pieces of furniture, kitchen utensils, dusty floors, trashy artifacts of popular culture— with all their banality, shabbiness, and defectiveness. The critic Artur Sandauer's term "poetry of junk" remains an accurate description of that first phase of Bialoszewski's work, especially if we consider that the category of "junk" encompasses not merely material objects but also the peripheries of culture, substandard ways of life, bad neighborhoods, lower social strata—everything that had usually been considered "lower," "inferior," "less worthy" of literary portrayal. Bialoszewski's early poems are, in fact, more than just such portrayals of "lower" objects or phenomena; whatever is lower or inferior becomes elevated and even sanctified here, as though the objects' concreteness provided the speaker with the only reliable transcendence and the only kind of experience he is able to share with others.

With the publication of *Misdirected Sentiments,* another aspect of Bialoszewski's art began to overshadow his emphasis on the material object. At this stage, he appeared in the eyes of many critics as, first and foremost, a poet of language and linguistic experimentation. To all intents and purposes, the focus in his poetry shifted then from material to verbal junk: read superficially, his new poems could indeed seem, as one unsympathetic critic put it, "a salad of broken syntax and degenerate grammar." Only some of the more careful and detailed critical analyses proved later that, in fact, Bialoszewski did not really "break" or violate anything: whatever seemed unusual in those poems could be traced back to forms of speech known from everyday experience. In other words, Bialoszewski's poetic language is based on the kinds of speech that, while substandard, are nonetheless definitely common and widespread. His alleged "experimentation" is nothing more than a faithful recording of peculiarities of the oral (as opposed to written) and lower-class (as opposed to educated-class) style, with an admixture of characteristic erroneous forms that can be found, for instance, in the language of children. These "lower" or "inferior" kinds of speech are used by Bialoszewski not merely because they correspond with the "lower" or "inferior" nature of his objects, but also because their spontaneity and flexibility makes them better instruments for naming elusive and changing reality—and reality remains the chief point of reference even in the most "linguistic" of Bialoszewski's poems.

The reaction to the *Memoir of the Warsaw Uprising*—where Bialoszewski first established his image as a scrupulous portraitist of social reality rather than a narrowly specialized poet of material objects or linguistic experimentation—marked the third stage of the poet's critical reception. Since that time, critical opinion has incorporated all the peculiarities of Bialoszewski's work into a specific aesthetic system. This aesthetic system stems from a basic dichotomy permeating Bialoszewski's poetic world: the opposition between the value of the individual self and the value inherent in external reality. Extreme individualism and inclination toward a solitary way of living, perceiving, and thinking coexist here quite amazingly with an almost humble attitude toward everything that surrounds the "I," from material objects to social relations. Hence, in Bialoszewski's inimitable aesthetics, we see how a highly individualized manner of perception and speech combines with an intense obligation to render faithfully the minutest details of surrounding reality.

In spite of the obvious difficulties in translating Bialoszewski into any language, a small but representative part of his work has already been made available to the English-speaking audience. *The Revolution of Things: Selected Poems by Miron Bialoszewski*[1] includes about thirty poems, mostly from his first two volumes. The entire *Memoir of the Warsaw Uprising* has been translated by Madeline G. Levine.[2] Anthologies, such as Czeslaw Milosz's *Postwar Polish Poetry*, usually confine themselves to presenting Bialoszewski's earlier (and more translatable) poems; the most notable exception consists of several poems from the collection *To Cut Loose*, translated by Tadeusz Slawek, which can be found in the anthology *Contemporary East European Poetry*.[3]

Bialoszewski's posthumous publications, however, remain largely unknown in the West. During the years that have passed since the poet's death, much of his previously unpublished work has been made available, but so far only to Polish readers. In these poems, mini-plays, and

194

prose fragments, Bialoszewski appears, to an even greater extent than before, as an ironic individualist who simultaneously pays close attention to the concrete particulars of society's life. At times, the very concreteness of his essentially apolitical observations still offends the censor of People's Poland: in the collection *Oho,* for instance, a few poems, supposedly too straightforward in their treatment of the subject of martial law, have been deleted. In other instances, the author's death as well as the "light," humorous form he employed seems to have defused the censor's potential objections. This is the case with a sequence of poems-songs and quasi-dramatic scenes entitled "The Cabaret of Kitty Katty" and included in the same officially published collection *Oho,* which was a major sensation in the aboveground literary life of 1985. Here, for example, is how the title character (Bialoszewski's older and more practically minded female alter ego) solves the problem of food lines in downtown Warsaw:

KITTY KATTY *passing triple lines in front of stores*
   Queuers' strike!
Keeps walking down Marszalkowska Street, turns onto Swietokrzyska
Addresses the lines
   Queuers' strike!
   Queuers' strike!
An ever-growing column of people who've left the lines marches behind Kitty
   Katty in single file
KITTY KATTY *turns onto Nowy Swiat Street*
   Queuers' strike!
They reach the King Sigismund Column like this
KITTY KATTY
   Stop!
   Homage!
   From a column to a column.
   And now let them pass out everything to all of us.
   Only take turns and no ration cards.[4]

And this is how Kitty Katty and her friends react to the imposition of martial law:

BLESSED GRANDMAYA FROM VISHNUVILLE
   state of war!

KITTY KATTY
   what state is that?
STRESSA
   in Poland, we've always had three states: prewar, state-of-war, and
   postwar
SIBYL OF GROCHOW
   now we've got that middle one
KITTY KATTY
   I see[5]

Astonishingly, this pure-nonsensical "cabaret" (in which the action takes place in the streets and apartments of Warsaw and the main roles are played by four old ladies with hilariously fanciful names and esoteric interests) has captured the grim atmosphere of martial law in Poland much better than most of the patriotic and martyrological poetry from this period. Thus, Bialoszewski the individualist and realist has won his final—posthumous—victory.

[1986]

Shades of Gray

If we asked any group of Polish critics today to compose their individual lists of the five most important volumes of poetry published in Polish in the 1980s, we could be sure that each of these lists would include a book or two by Czeslaw Milosz, Zbigniew Herbert's *Report from the Besieged City*, and Wislawa Szymborska's *The People on the Bridge*. The late Miron Bialoszewski's *Oho* is also widely considered one of the major literary sensations of recent years, but Bialoszewski, though already a classic for some, is still viewed by many as too unorthodox and antipoetic to be treated as anything more than a literary experimenter. In contrast, Szymborska's equally well-deserved fame seems to rest upon an exceptionally solid foundation of popular acceptance. With the exception of Herbert, there is probably no other major poet based in Poland who enjoys such universal respect. And among the many highly accomplished woman poets who have contributed to contemporary Polish literature, Szymborska is definitely the best.

Her career, spanning the entire postwar period, seems far from dramatic, even more so as Szymborska deliberately shuns public life and very seldom comments directly on her own life and work. Instead, her biography is punctuated by the rare appearances of her collections of poems, each of them slimmer and better than the previous one. She was born July 2, 1923, in the small town of Bnin in the Poznan area. Since 1931 her life has been closely tied to the city of Krakow, where from 1945 to 1948 she majored in Polish literature and sociology at the Jagellonian University, and where she worked after 1953 as the poetry editor of the local literary weekly. She made her debut in the literary press in 1945, but the planned publication of her first collection in 1948 hit a political snag: the book was not ideologically orthodox enough for the Stalinist times. Szymborska's first volume, entitled *That's What We Live For*, came out only in 1952, followed by *Questions Put to Myself* (1954).

The semantic difference between these titles is telling: from the programmatic certainty implied in the statement that forms the first title, her poetry shifted in the next two years to intellectual anxiety and moral anguish. Indeed, all her later poems could be defined as lyrical "questions put to herself." This is increasingly true of her subsequent volumes, each of which was met with even greater critical acclaim: *Calling Out to Yeti* (1957), *Salt* (1962), *A Million Laughs* (1967), *There But for the Grace* (1972), *A Great Number* (1976), and finally *The People on the Bridge* (1986). She has also published a number of translations of French poetry and a collection of brief humorous essays on various nonliterary books titled *Nonobligatory Reading* (1973). An exceptionally private figure among Polish writers, Szymborska nonetheless takes a political stance when necessary: in 1977 she was among the intellectuals who founded the Flying University, and since the imposition of martial law she has made a point of steadfastly refusing to accept awards from the State. Her work has been widely translated into many languages; for several years now, she has also been read and appreciated in this country, mostly thanks to the appearance in 1981 of *Sounds, Feelings, Thoughts*, a bilingual selection of seventy of her poems.[1]

The People on the Bridge is, at first glance, nothing out of the ordinary in the context of Szymborska's work: it consistently follows the thematic, philosophical, and stylistic lines initiated and developed in her previous volumes. In many ways, however, it is also Szymborska's crowning achievement, the highest point of her already high-flying career. Containing a mere twenty-two poems and appearing after a ten-year hiatus, the collection ultimately refines Szymborska's characteristic creative method: building a poem as a highly complex ironic conceit that evolves from a deceptively simple observation.

To be more exact, one could describe the logical construction of a typical Szymborska poem as a tripartite process. The first step is an ordinary observation of this or another fact. The second is a sudden, willful objection, a sort of "all right, but . . ."—as if the mind accepted the fact but at the same time realized its unexpected logical consequences. The third step consists in finding a stylistic device that will lay bare the mutual opposition between the initial observation and its logical-but-unexpected continuation, and thus convey the irony inherent in their clash. The important thing is that both the first and the second step form an elementary mental process which fits into the scope of everyday thinking of an average individual. Only the third step is the poet's unique input. In other words, Szymborska discovers ironies that could be discovered by virtually anybody. It is the way in which she intensifies these ironies and brings them to the reader's attention that reveals her unique inventiveness and mastery.

The best example of this mechanism is the poem "In Broad Daylight." The observation that ignites the logical chain reaction here (and that remains only indirectly implied throughout the poem) borders on the obvious: the poet Krzysztof Kamil Baczynski was only twenty-three years old when he died a hero's death in the Warsaw Uprising of 1944. An "all right, but . . ." follows: All right, but what would have happened to him had he survived? What kind of man would he have become in postwar Poland? Would he still be a hero?

Here the actual poem starts. It portrays an older writer (his name, Baczynski, is revealed only in the poem's later part) who is nothing but an ordinary aged man, sitting in the dining room of the state-funded writers' retreat in Zakopane and attracting nobody's attention. The poetic discovery lies not only in the striking physical and social concreteness of this portrayal but also in what Roman Jakobson once called the "poetry of grammar": throughout the poem, conditional forms—given further emphasis thanks to their placement in verse clauses—grow more and more frequent, eventually to dominate the poem's ending. The answer to the question "What would Baczynski have become had he survived?" can be given only in the conditional—but, ironically, it is precisely the drumbeat of this conditional that gives the answer the weight of an irrevocable verdict:

> While waiting to be served his noodle soup, he would
> read a paper with the current date,
> giant headlines, tiny print of ads,
> or drum his fingers on the white tablecloth, and his hands would
> have been used a long time now,
> with their chapped skin and swollen veins.
>
> Sometimes someone would
> yell from the doorway: "Mr. Baczynski, phone call for you"—

199

and there'd be nothing strange about that
being him, about him standing up, straightening his sweater,
and slowly moving toward the door.

At this sight no one would
stop talking, no one would
freeze in mid-gesture, mid-breath
because this commonplace event would
be treated—such a pity—
as a commonplace event.[2]

Despite the discreet political undertones of such poems as "In Broad
Daylight" and despite the universal perspective of many others in this
collection, *The People on the Bridge* shows Szymborska as, distinctly and
unmistakably, a poet of the individual. But since it so happens that one
of the most nagging universal problems of our epoch is the terror of the
collective, Szymborska's defense of the right to an individual perspective
becomes a political act in itself. Each of her poems undertakes in its own
way the task of defending individual uniqueness from imposed uniformity, randomness from determinism, concreteness of existence from abstractness of time, the exception from the rule, the right to doubt from
the blind self-assurance of utopia. In one of the poems, she assumes the
role of a contemporary Noah; by the same token, her work becomes
Noah's Ark whereby at least samples of these individual values may be
saved from the deluge of uniformity:

An endless rain is just beginning.
Into the ark, for where else can you go:
you poems for a single voice,
private exultations,
unnecessary talents,
surplus curiosity,
short-range sorrows and fears,
eagerness to take things in from all six sides.

Rivers are swelling and bursting their banks.
Into the ark: all you chiaroscuros and halftones,
you details, ornaments, and whims,
silly exceptions,
forgotten signs,
countless shades of the color gray . . .

If this ark moves on, it is because its sail is poetic irony. Many critics have already pointed out that Szymborska's irony comes in many shades, "countless shades of the color gray." It is significant, though, that ironic distance, whatever its specific forms and degrees of intensity, always serves here as a weapon to defend the individual's rights to uniqueness, doubt, and dissent. This is especially noticeable in those of her poems which seemingly condemn these attitudes—whereas in fact they employ a dramatic speaker whose outlook is directly opposed to the author's, and their aim is to make the speaker discredit himself (and the beliefs he represents) in the course of his monologue. This is the case with the poem "An Opinion on the Question of Pornography," in which the cement-headed speaker maintains with dead seriousness that "there's nothing more debauched than thinking":

There's nothing more debauched than thinking.
This sort of wantonness runs wild like a wind-born weed
on a plot laid out for daisies.

Nothing's sacred for those who think.
Calling things brazenly by name,
risqué analyses, salacious syntheses,
frenzied, rakish chases after the bare facts,
the filthy fingering of touchy subjects,
discussion in heat—it's music to their ears.

In broad daylight or under cover of the night
they form circles, triangles or pairs.
The partners' age and sex are unimportant.
Their eyes glitter, their cheeks are flushed.
Friend leads friend astray.
Degenerate daughters defile their fathers.
A brother panders for his little sister.

They favor the fruits
from the forbidden tree of knowledge
over the pink buttocks found in glossy magazines—
all that ultimately simplehearted smut.
The books they savor have no pictures.
What variety they have lies in certain phrases
marked with a thumbnail or a crayon.

It's shocking, the positions,
the unchecked simplicity with which
one mind contrives to fertilize another!
Such positions the Kamasutra itself doesn't know.

During these trysts of theirs the only thing that's steamy is the tea.
People sit on their chairs and move their lips.
Everyone crosses only his own legs
so that one foot is resting on the floor,
while the other dangles freely in midair.
Only now and then does somebody get up,
go to the window
and through a crack in the curtains
take a peep out at the street.

In the last lines of this monologue, the self-righteous speaker unwittingly unmasks the true nature of the kind of "law and order" he supports: it is the reality of a totalitarian country where the very act of thinking entails fear of police persecution. The same narrative device opens even broader perspectives in the collection's title poem, "The People on the Bridge." This is a monologue by an enemy of art, concerning art's treacherous subversion of the world's order by trying to "stop time":

This picture is by no means innocent.
Time has been stopped here.
Its laws are no longer consulted.
It's been relieved of its influence over the course of events.
It's been ignored and insulted.

On account of a rebel,
one Hiroshige Utagawa
(a being who, by the way,
passed on long ago and in due course),
time has tripped and fallen down.

In a reverse reflection of irony, such poems reveal Szymborska's own convictions about the role of the artist in society. The artist's task does not consist in showing the only right way, spreading universal truths, or building utopias. It consists merely in "stopping time"—and thus manifesting humanity's helpless but unending resistance against the dark forces of nothingness.

[1987]

The Ethics of Language

Time is far greater than space.

—*Brodsky, "Lullaby of Cape Cod"*

It was almost exactly twenty-two years ago that an unknown young man by the name of Joseph Brodsky was summoned before the Leningrad court on the charge of "social parasitism"—that is, writing poems while neither belonging to the Soviet Writers' Union nor holding a steady job. "But who determined that you're a poet? Who accepted you into the ranks of poets?" went the judge's cross-examination. The defendant's answer: "I guess it's . . . from God . . ."

This timid response, which would have been considered glaringly obvious by a Dante, George Herbert, or Rilke, sounded, under these circumstances of history and geography, like a provocation. Brodsky was immediately punished with exile to a collective farm near the Arctic Circle. At the same time, he was rewarded with international publicity, which to all intents and purposes saved his skin. Eight years later he "switched Empires" (as he puts it in one of his American poems). The globe made a half-turn and the exiled poet found the Western Hemisphere under his feet. This other Empire, to be sure, is far more propitious to poets; at least it does not require police registration or certification of employment stamped on an identity card.

Yet Brodsky's response, if repeated on American soil, would sound provocative here, too. In the Soviet Union you are a poet because you have been granted permission to be one by the appropriate authorities. In the United States you are a poet because no authority can prohibit you from being one (more exactly, from enrolling in a course in creative writing, publishing two poems in *Chattanooga Review*, and winning a grant from the National Endowment for the Arts). In either case, God (who in this context is just shorthand for "poetic calling") seems to have nothing to do with writing poems.

Which perhaps accounts for the fact that Brodsky, with his intense convictions about poetry and poets, is a unique figure in the world of letters. He is distinguished not merely by his talent, or by his one-of-a-kind success story. (He is, to my knowledge, the only example of a Russian poet who succeeded in achieving bilingual status in the West; there was Nabokov, but he had been fluent in English since his early childhood, and Brodsky is far more of a poet than he was.) What also sets Brodsky apart is his overtly expressed belief that a poet has a special mission to accomplish in contemporary society. Not just in a totalitarian society of the Soviet sort; there, the poet's mission, his role as a spokesman for the voiceless community, is something traditional and, unnatural as the entire situation is, natural. He also has a mission in an open, democratic society that seems to be doing just fine without poets. A citizen of both hemispheres, Brodsky is concerned with nothing less than the place of the poet in the global system of civilization.

Less Than One,[1] a hefty volume of Brodsky's essayistic output during his stay in the West, reflects the sweep of his interests in what appears to be a whimsical diversity of subject matter. The protagonists here are, first of all, poets—Russian giants of poetry or prose such as Akhmatova, Mandelstam, Tsvetaeva, Dostoevsky, and Platonov, but also Western poets like Cavafy, Montale, Auden, and Derek Walcott. The "protagonists" are cities as well—Constantinople (in "Flight from Byzantium"), Cavafy's Alexandria, Brodsky's own Leningrad (in three more or less autobiographical essays, "Less Than One," "A Guide to a Renamed City," "In a Room and a Half"). Finally, the "protagonists" are certain apparently extraliterary problems—tyranny (in "On Tyranny") and evil (in "A Commencement Address"). The essays span an equally wide range of genres, from personal reminiscences (the Leningrad essays) and a combination of travel notes with historical reflection (the Byzantine essay), through an obituary (the essay on Nadezhda Mandelstam) and a public address ("A Commencement Address," actually delivered at Williams College), to critical portraits of poets and extensive analyses of single poems (Tsvetaeva's "New Year's Greetings" and Auden's "September 1, 1939").

Yet one detects a peculiar unity in all this thematic and generic hodgepodge. I don't mean the kind of unity that is customarily characterized, in such cases, by the vague label "an intellectual autobiography."

204

True, this is, directly or indirectly, Brodsky's self-portrait. But the more essential unifying theme in the book is its concern with the profession (or better, vocation—or better still, calling) that he represents. In fact, *Less Than One* is a series of variations on a theme. Who is the poet? What is poetry? What is their function within the system of civilization?

As with every work of verbal art, it is possible to read Brodsky's essays in two intersecting ways. We can read them in their linear sequence and at the same time read "crosswise" by spotting recurrent motifs and thematic threads that stretch from one essay to another. The most important thread is the function of poetry. (That function, incidentally, is defined in a rather broad fashion. It may include not only lyricism, but also a kind of prose characterized by heightened self-consciousness of language and represented, in the Russian tradition, by the fiction of Dostoevsky or Platonov and by the nonfictional prose of Tsvetaeva or Mandelstam.) Everything that Brodsky has to say about poetry stems from two basic assumptions. The first seems to be disarmingly obvious: whatever else can be said about a poem, the only sure thing that can be said is, as Mallarmé noted, that a poem is composed of words. Accordingly, "the poet is the one who masters language." Poetry is "the supreme version of language," its "highest form of existence." Such lofty expressions are justified in that poetry is—or at least can be—much more than just a verbal skill: "In purely technical terms, of course, poetry amounts to arranging words with the greatest specific gravity in the most effective and externally inevitable sequence. Ideally, however, it is language negating its own mass and the laws of gravity; it is language striving upward— or sideways—to that beginning where the Word was."

Consequently, "a poem is the result of a certain necessity; it is inevitable, and so is its form." Hence the colossal weight that Brodsky attaches to those determinants of poetic speech that are considered by a superficial reader to be merely decorative fringes. For Brodsky, rhyme, alliteration, meter, stanzaic pattern are by no means irrelevant ornaments. Rather, they are signals of the "inevitability" that separates a poetic utterance from the chaotic randomness of everyday speech. (This conviction lies behind Brodsky's extremely critical attitude toward the prevailing American practice of translating poetry—even poetry so "linguistically oversaturated" as Mandelstam's—into bland prose divided into lines.)

205

In short, "lyricism is the ethics of language." At this juncture, Brodsky's first, "linguistic" assumption dovetails with his second, "ethical" one. Being a moralist of language, the poet comes into unavoidable conflict with nonethical (or even, more often than not, anti-ethical) external reality. His lyrical attitude sentences him to the continuous experience of the "unacceptability of the world," as Brodsky puts it in one of the essays on Tsvetaeva. This encompasses far more than the world in its social or political dimensions: "A poet gets into trouble because of his linguistic and, by implication, his psychological superiority, rather than because of his politics. A song is a form of linguistic disobedience, and its sound casts a doubt on a lot more than a concrete political system: it questions the entire existential order."

The outcome of this clash is a natural companionship between lyricism and individualism. Of course, the poet's individualism, his constant "estrangement," may lead in extreme cases to his isolation, solitude, or even physical annihilation. But it may also, if realized and consciously cultivated, become "the art of estrangement" and thus serve as a driving force for creativity. The motif of "the art of estrangement" is clearest when Brodsky turns to autobiography, particularly when he speaks of his coming of age in Leningrad. In fact, however, it is a common denominator for all of his essayistic portraits of Eastern and Western poets: not only the tragic lives of Mandelstam, Tsvetaeva, and Akhmatova, but also the careers of Cavafy or Walcott are viewed as exemplary here. All of them are marked by the poet's "estrangement," his marginal position within society, his continuous state of conflict with a majority, or at least his being representative of some "provinces" or "outskirts" of civilization (Cavafy's Alexandria, Walcott's West Indies) as opposed to the "metropolis."

Here we hit a paradox, though: the notion of lyricism as "the ethics of language," and more generally the individualistic attitude, condemn the poet to isolation; at the same time, however, they are the most precious gifts that the poet can offer to society. Individualism, as Brodsky points out in "A Commencement Address," can be a curse, but it can also serve as a defensive weapon: "The surest defense against Evil is extreme individualism, originality of thinking, whimsicality, even—if you will— eccentricity. That is, something that can't be feigned, faked, imitated . . .

Evil is a sucker for solidity. It always goes for big numbers, for confident granite, for ideological purity, for drilled armies and balanced sheets."

Individualism is a safeguard not just against the immediate, tangible evil of the surrounding reality, but also against the evil that lurks beneath the surface of every utopia, only to raise its head when the utopia is being transformed into reality. Unlike various utopians, Brodsky spent thirty-two years of his life in a country where such a sobering transformation had taken place; he cannot help being anti-utopian. In his view, every utopia, based on Rousseau's notion of the inherent goodness of human nature, overlooks the "human negative potential." The result of such an oversight is that the "negative potential" is given free rein and, as a rule, ravages souls and continents with impunity, until it finally tramples the very idea of the autonomy of the individual.

In what sense, however, can poetry's "ethics of language" serve as a similar defense against evil? It is at this point in his line of reasoning that Brodski the essayist is most original and revealing. In his view, poetry, while reorganizing language, reorganizes time as well: "Song is, after all, restructured time." Even at its lowest level—at the level of phonetic material—a poem "carves notches" on the time axis by dividing speech into rhythmic units and thus giving the elusive flow of moments some appearance of regularity and sense. Likewise, at the highest level—at the level of the whole of literary history—every poem is a "notch" on the axis of historic time by necessarily relating to both tradition and the future. Inasmuch as this "carving of notches" or restructuring time is "a profoundly solitary activity," it forces the individual "toward an understanding, if not of his uniqueness, then at least of the autonomy of his existence in the world." And the notion of the autonomy of individual existence is, after all, no longer an individualistic trait. Rather, it is "the basis of our civilization."

In his magnificently thought-provoking "Flight from Byzantium," from which I have quoted the above words, Brodsky gathers all the themes and strands of his essayistic work and, helped by the symbolism provided by history and geography, binds them together in a complex knot. What promises to be just a tourist's notebook—a record of impressions from a trip to Istanbul—expands into a series of reflections on the mutual incompatibility of two models of civilization.

The opposition of space and time, an obsessive and sometimes puzzling theme in Brodsky's poetry, here becomes clearer as it is supplemented with a series of other, parallel oppositions. The Eastern model of civilization (the fullest historical embodiment of which was Byzantium) is interpreted as a system based on the "linear principle," on the dominant notion of space, on contempt for the individual. Its fundamental mode of activity is territorial expansion, and its archetypal hero is a conquerer or a tyrant who rules over wide expanses of land. In contradistinction, Western civilization replaces the "linear principle" with the idea of cyclic return. Not space but time—in both its existential and historical dimensions—becomes the dominant category here, which results in a turn toward individualism. In the West, the restructuring of time is the fundamental activity, and the archetypal hero is none other than the poet.

Needless to say, Brodsky never bothers to abide by the rules of neutrality or objectivity. On the contrary, he declares his sympathies and antipathies. A former citizen of the Third Rome and now a visitor to what's left of the Second, he views both as cradles of "human negative potential." This doesn't mean, though, that Brodsky engages in blind pro-Western idolatry, or that he advocates some kind of ostracism of the other civilization. In fact, he goes so far as to blame the First Rome and its spiritual heritage for the modern world's failure to stop the tide of evil. "By divorcing Byzantium, Western Christianity consigned the East to nonexistence, and thus reduced its own notion of human negative potential to a considerable, perhaps even a perilous, degree."

Whether or not the reader agrees with all of Brodsky's statements (he is the first to admit that he deals more with ideal models than with detailed images of historical reality), "Flight from Byzantium" is a pivotal piece in the collection. In light of this essay, Brodsky's idea of what poetry should be emerges as a direct consequence of his idea of what the world should not be. Presumptuous as it might sound, poetry is for him the exact opposite of—indeed, a counterbalance to—tyranny in its Byzantine version, and even more in its countless modern versions. The poet's individualism is the obverse of his respect for the autonomy of all other individuals. His mastery of language is a form of respect for the rhythms of existence and history that language contains and preserves. His watchful awareness of the borderline between good and evil opposes the relativistic imprecision of these notions, which is both a precondition and a product of every tyranny.

It seems that Brodsky—a poet whose life and work bridge the banks of the Neva and the Hudson, a poet of two hemispheres and two languages—is one of the very few authors in the West who can risk such a maximalist formulation of poetry's tasks without sounding preposterous or irresponsible. But then Brodsky has always been an author who sets improbable tasks for himself. In his essay on Auden, he describes his decision to start writing in English as a wish "to please the shadow" of the admired poet. After the publication of *Less Than One*, the shadow of the author of *The Dyer's Hand* can be nothing but pleased.

* * *

Stockholm's limelight has dimmed and now Joseph Brodsky faces the usual tribulation of a freshly crowned Nobel laureate: the critical reception of his first new book published after the prize. After death and taxes, the third most certain thing in life is the ritual Nobelist-bashing. You can bet your life's savings that more than one critic will approach Brodsky's new book with a single intent in mind: to prove by its example that something's wrong with the Nobel Prize. Some others, who might have sympathized with the poet's striving for greatness before, will now look upon him with the kind of automatic suspicion that rises in us whenever someone's greatness has been officially certified. Still, being bashed may be less upsetting than being smothered with mass-media praise, all those endlessly repeated clichés about a Russian boy who made good in America—stereotypes heaped upon stereotypes and derived for the most part not from studying Brodsky's books but from reading other newspapers' stories about him. I am sure that Brodsky himself will take all this in stride, but it would not hurt if at least some critics approached his new books without anti-Nobel or pro-Nobel bias and appreciated the fact that, apart from all the laurels and dinners with the Swedish king, he is that rare gift: a poet who tells us important things in a way only he can.

Brodsky's originality stems in large part from his art of exploiting the unique background of crisscrossing traditions that lie behind him. A poet who now belongs to both Russian and American literatures and who, in his Leningrad years, grew up on a mixed diet of the Russian nineteenth- and twentieth-century classics, the English tradition from Donne to Auden, and modern Polish poetry, could not but make generative comparisons, choices, and combinations throughout his career. A prominent thread in this fabric of traditions—one about which Brodsky has not written explicitly very much thus far—is now brought to light in *An Age Ago,* a slim anthology of nineteenth-century Russian poetry from Zhukovsky and Batyushkov to Tyutchev and Fet, translated by Alan Myers but provided by Brodsky with an illuminating foreword and equally enlightening biographical notes.[2] Myers' elegant and technically dexterous translations (he is at his best when he is dealing with what seems to be the least translatable, that is, with compact and semantically dense lyrical miniatures such as Vyazemsky's "Tears" or Fet's "Butterfly") make the anthology a highly enjoyable little album of lyrics, many of which are as arresting as they are charmingly old-fashioned. (The only exception is, not surprisingly, the three poems by Nekrasov, whose pounding rhythms combined with heavy-handed didacticism do not fare well in the English version at all.)

At the same time, however, a Brodsky fan may profit from reading this book as one more of the poet's indirect comments on the nature of his own work. In trying to explain what makes the nineteenth century interesting for people of the twentieth-century, Brodsky offers a couple of thought-provoking clues. His view on the relationship between the two epochs is paradoxical. On the one hand, nineteenth-century culture appears to the modern age as a sort of "grammatical *déjà vu*"; it already contains "nearly every insight or concept which our century claims as its own achievement." On the other hand, a world of spiritual difference seems to separate our times from the nineteenth century, "perhaps the last period in the history of our species when its scale of reality was quantitatively human," and when "much less stood between man and his thoughts about himself than today."

Accordingly, in what he writes about specific authors in his biographical notes (each expanding into a mini-essay pregnant with salient observations on everything from a poet's position in society to his style), Brodsky is equally interested in what is historically dead and gone and what is aesthetically or philosophically still alive and kicking. The former is, roughly speaking, the traditional version of Romanticism conceived as a clash between lofty ideals and disappointing reality, and leading inevitably toward the shallow sentimentalism of self-pity characteristic of "a cultural tradition whose main tenor is consolation." The latter is the best Russian poets' "incessant quest . . . for the unique through the thick of the ordinary," which results in intellectual tension and dramatic conflict—in, for instance, Vyazemsky's poems that "describe, inform, argue, suggest rather than sing," Pushkin's "disquieting . . . ability to combine a light touch with breathtaking profundity," Baratynsky's "analytical" lyricism, or Lermontov's "thoroughly corrosive, bilious self-knowledge."

In fact, all these qualities taken together might well serve as components of a critical portrayal of Brodsky himself. Searching for his genealogical roots in the nineteenth century, he makes, for a Russian poet, very fastidious choices: he rejects the overwhelming Russian tradition of sentimental "consolation" clothed in conventional imagery and songlike mellifluousness, and instead prefers anything that has to do with the restless intellect's metaphysical, cognitive, and ethical dramas. In his own poetry, this preference is reflected mainly in the semantic ambiguity and tension that result from the constant clash between the spontaneity of colloquial speech and the discipline of highly complex and conspicuous formal restraints. In that sense, Brodsky owes a great deal to nineteenth-century poetry, but only to its specific and, in Russia, rather atypical undercurrent. He is indebted a great deal more to the much earlier school of seventeenth-century metaphysical poetry, which never made its mark on his native literature and which he appropriated on Russia's behalf from the English tradition. Ironically, his own strikingly modern lyricism, compared to which all the Yevtushenkos and Voznesenskys seem not to have gone very far away from Nekrasov, could not have been born without the twentieth-century experience; but it also owes its existence to the seventeenth-century art of conceit, "felt thought," paradoxical contrast, and dialogic imagination. Thus, his work appears a high-wire act of balancing between two seemingly incompatible tasks: it singlehandedly propels Russian poetry into the late twentieth century and also substitutes for an entire bloc of tradition absent in the Russian cultural past. While he might be called the T. S. Eliot or perhaps the W. H. Auden of Eastern Europe, Brodsky is also the John Donne Russian poetry never had.

This obvious truth is repeatedly confirmed by the poems included in *To Urania,* Brodsky's fourth collection in English but only the second in which he is responsible for both the selection and most of the translations.[3] Just like the earlier *A Part of Speech,* the present selection is representative of the entire course of Brodsky's career, from works written in Russia in the 1960s to new poems composed on Western soil and (with the exception of those written originally in English) collected in his most recent Russian volume, *Urania*. This broad chronological and geographic frame contains a rich variety of genres, modes, and approaches—from a mock funeral elegy ("To a Friend: In Memoriam") and love lyrics ("Polonaise: A Variation," "Seven Strophes") to political philippic ("The Berlin Wall Tune," "Lines on the Winter Campaign"), a fantastic parable with satirical overtones ("The New Jules Verne"), and a metaphysical treatise ("The Fly").

Yet it also presents an amazingly consistent vision and style. The formal key to the implicit philosophy of Brodsky's poetry seems to be the ever-present tension between his spontaneous, fluid, utterly conversational syntax and nonrestrictive vocabulary on the one hand, and, on the other, his highly regular and complicated patterns of rhyme, meter, and stanza, whose level of technical difficulty reaches the point of ostentatious exaggeration and makes them a sort of deliberate semantic statement in their own right. "Gorbunov and Gorchakov," for instance, a forty-page-long poem in thirteen cantos, written in 1968 (and translated now into English, evidently as a labor of love, by Harry Thomas), is based almost entirely on colloquial dialogue: it includes lengthy conversations between two patients in a Soviet psychiatric prison (one of them apparently squealing on another) as well as between each of them separately and the interrogating doctors; the topics range from the taste of the cabbage served for supper to Russia's destiny and the meaning of life. Yet all this raw stuff of spontaneous speech and chaotic reality is squeezed into the rigorous cubes of ten-line stanzas based on two alternating sets of quintuple (!) rhymes. Similarly, "The Fifth Anniversary," a poem that looks back at Soviet reality from the perspective of five years of exile, employs a couple of dozen regular sets of triple rhymes; as if this were not enough, the rhymes are paroxytonic and selected with an eye toward their punlike quality ("terror / there or / error," and so on). In virtually every poem in this collection, the art of juggling rhymes and other formal constraints verges on the impossible and thus attracts the reader's attention, as if the poet wanted the reader not to overlook the fact that his devices serve as a means to tame and overcome reality's threatening pressure rather than merely describe it.

212

This is exactly Brodsky's point, and this also explains his stubbornness in translating his own poetry with such an emphasis on strict subservience to the demands of the original rhymes, meters, and stanzaic patterns. In his case, these supposedly external, detachable props are an intrinsic and irremovable part of the poetic statement as a whole. For the statement he keeps making is precisely about poetry's power to question the natural order of the universe. In his poetry, rhyme opposes time; more exactly, both space and time, both Urania and Klio, both cosmology and history. A poem's inevitably individualistic focus is a challenge to the anonymous tyranny of general laws governing the intergalactic void as well as the biological processes of the flesh and institutions of society; the mutual cohesion and heightened semantic potential instilled by the poet into the words of the ordinary language are an attempt to overcome the destructive forces of isolation and inertia lurking in the world's spatial magnitude and temporal transitoriness. As befits a truly profound metaphysical poetry, Brodsky's work is both a testimony and a prayer. It roams various realms and dimensions of reality, never losing touch with the human experience and always aware of the potential of evil and error inherent in it. Yet for all the thematic variety of its earthly concerns, Brodsky's poetry is also an uninterrupted dialogue with the Maker—the actual addressee of both the poet's diatribe against the world's injustice and his praise of the world's very existence.

What should I say about life? That it's long and abhors transparence.
Broken eggs make me grieve; the omelette, though, makes me vomit.
Yet until brown clay has been crammed down my larynx,
only gratitude will be gushing from it.

[1986, 1988]

Alone but Not Lonely

The first of many things that make Adam Zagajewski's poetry worthy of note is the author's birthdate: 1945. Thus far, America's acquaintance with the most recent Polish poetry (if we take only book-length selections of specific authors into account) has been limited to a few aging giants, now in their sixties or seventies, such as Czeslaw Milosz, Zbigniew Herbert, Tadeusz Rozewicz, or Wislawa Szymborska. *Tremor*[1] is the first book of poems issued by a major American publisher that presents one of the "children of People's Poland," the generation whose birthdates coincide with the establishment of the Communist order and whose youth was spent rebelling against it.

Of course, the multidimensional meaning of Zagajewski's poetry can by no means be reduced to that of "a poetry of protest" of a generational manifesto. The book can (and should) be read also outside the framework of Poland's recent history, and it will not lose much this way. After all, it has something important to say about life, death, love, loneliness, and other rather universal matters. And yet the keen sense of history that pervades and distorts contemporary existence seems to be something that cannot really be subtracted from Zagajewski's poems. Although his work contains a wealth of sensuous imagination and philosophical perspicacity, the reader here is unable to forget that he is dealing with a poet born and raised in our age and in a certain corner of Eastern Europe.

In fact, Zagajewski's literary beginnings were marked by his and his generation's demand that Polish literature be concerned with the *hic et nunc* rather than with universal issues and ahistorical settings. The poetic group he cofounded in the late 1960s in Krakow was called Teraz,

"Now." His early poems owed a great deal to the experience of student protest in March 1968—a protest directed, on the surface, against the abuses of state censorship but also, in its deeper sense, against the omnipresent ideological lie of the system—and its having been crushed in due course by the police and slandered by the official media. In 1974 he stirred up one of the greatest controversies in postwar Polish culture by coauthoring, with Julian Kornhauser, a book of criticism titled *The World Not Represented*—a sweeping assault on the noncommittal literature of the previous decades, with its thematic evasiveness and moral irresolution.

Under the circumstances of Communism, even in its relatively mild Polish version of the early 1970s, voices such as Zagajewski's must, as a rule, be silenced sooner or later. The "1968 generation" of rebels and truth seekers had initially been allowed to speak out, but by mid-decade all its leading representatives found themselves blacklisted. This generation responded by creating an underground publishing network; Zagajewski, among others, served as coeditor of the first uncensored literary periodical, the quarterly *Zapis* ("The Record"). After a few years spent in Western Europe, he returned to Poland at the end of the fateful year 1981, only to witness the imposition of martial law. It took him more than a year to obtain another exit visa and leave for Paris, where he has lived for the past three years and written his best poems to date. Most of these are included in *Tremor*.

From such a biography, one might expect typically dissident poetry—vociferous protest, moralistic instruction, and historical generalization, all dutifully put in the first person plural. Nothing like that takes place in Zagajewski's poems. By his personal inclination, but also by a deliberate choice, his is a poetry of the first person singular, the voice of an individual. It only so happens that this individual's life coincides with that phase of history when everything—from political systems and ideologies on the one hand to the dictates of one's conscience on the other—forces him to be social and makes the very notion of individuality suspect. In other words, if Zagajewski's poetry is a portrayal of an individual mind, it is a mind torn asunder by opposing tendencies—by a moral obligation to speak on behalf of others and by a sense of the need to remain one's unique self. In the poem "Fire," he says:

215

I remember
the blazing appeal of that fire which parches
the lips of the thirsty crowd and burns
books and chars the skin of cities. I used to sing
those songs and I know how great it is
to run with others; later, by myself,
with the taste of ashes in my mouth, I heard
the lie's ironic voice and the choir screaming
and when I touched my head I could feel
the arched skull of my country, its hard edge.

The true "country," the authentic homeland of the individualist, is confined to the circumference of his skull. Whatever remains outside it is either uncertain or inauthentic, marred by banalities and dangerous collective illusions of unity. "The lie's ironic voice" is, actually, the voice of the poet's own ironic consciousness which unmasks lies; which, moreover, never allows him to accept anything that is abstract, general, collectivist:

Who has once met
irony will burst into laughter
during the prophet's lecture.   ("Ode to Plurality")

Irony, the device so characteristic of modern Polish poetry, serves a special purpose in the case of Zagajewski: it is used as a defensive weapon against a leveling abstractness of ideologies and systems. In this capacity, ironic distance is necessary to take in the whole breathtaking *plurality* (the key philosophical concept in Zagajewski's recent poetry) of the concrete, tangible world. As a consequence, one could consider as ironic (in a positive sense of the word) such otherwise ecstatic hymns, compared by Milosz in his preface to Gobelin tapestries, as the above-quoted "Ode to Plurality," "A View of Cracow," or the brilliant poem "To Go to Lvov."

But irony can also reveal its cutting edge—and it does so whenever Zagajewski writes of any attempt to supersede plurality with a false or shallow unity. "A Polish Dictionary" (the title of a poem), a dictionary of the common parlance of the collective imagination, must unavoidably consist of stereotypes: "Lances, banners, sabers, horses . . ." "A Warsaw Gathering," even though it is a gathering of citizens sincerely concerned about their country's freedom (the poem thus titled was written in November 1981), cannot help being a caricature of a group of people who fall prey to the tyranny of grand words and magnificent designs, whereas "In the last row . . . / The author of this little poem is sitting and dreaming of / music, music." The hero of Zagajewski's poems always sits "in the last row." He is a born dissident who (in the etymological sense of the Latin *dissidere*) always "sits apart"—apart not merely from the servants of the despotic system but, more generally, from any collectivity (even the collectivity of dissidents) that threatens his uniqueness and independence.

If Zagajewski stopped at this point, he would be nothing more than a post-Romantic individualist, a eulogist of self-imposed loneliness. His idea of "sitting apart" is, however, much more complicated. If I were to pinpoint the crucial sentence in *Tremor*, I would single out an almost casual statement that appears in the poem "A Wanderer": "I am alone but not lonely." The stance of the ironic individualist finds its counterbalance here in the idea of human solidarity: "Only others save us, / even though solitude tastes like / opium" (from another poem, "In the Beauty Created by Others"). If there is any discrepancy in this, it is the natural discrepancy between ontology and ethics. Reality makes us admire its existential plurality; at the same time, however, this plurality also encompasses evil and injustice, things to which we cannot reconcile ourselves because they affect or may affect, more or less directly, our own lives. This becomes particularly evident when we encounter evil masquerading as History. Zagajewski's poems about the reality of martial law in Poland are, naturally enough, no longer passionate hymns to the beauty of the visible world. Instead, they ask desperately

Why it has to be December.
The dark doves of snow fly,
falling on the slabs of the sidewalk. What is
talent against iron, what is
thought against a uniform, what is music
against a truncheon, what is joy against
fear . . .   ("Iron")

Yet in Zagajewski's world, even despair can be tempered by the ironic craft of poetry. True, those who "sit apart" are engulfed by the omnivorous jaws of History just like everyone else; but the individualist's distance at least gives him the chance to see everything more clearly and soberly. "On a hard dry substance / you have to engrave the truth"—this is the obligation that the poet faces. What truth? Which truth? Of course not the self-assured "truth" of an ideological dogma or a collective stereotype. "My masters are not infallible," says Zagajewski in yet another poem. In his vocabulary, "truth" is associated with probing the surrounding darkness rather than achieving any final clarity:

Clear moments are so short.
There is much more darkness. More
ocean than firm land. More
shadow than form.   ("Moment")

The poet's truth lies in his very search for the truth.

[1985]

Distance and Dialogue

The Confusion of Tongues

Emigration, exile, expatriation—there may be additional synonyms for these in *Roget's Thesaurus,* most of them probably beginning with an "e-" or "ex-," those sad prefixes of exclusion. But the excluding "e-" has its antonymous companion in "in-," as in inclusion or immigration. I suppose just about anybody who has ever crossed the frontier between "e-" and "in-" has at least once experienced a profound sensation of semantic incongruity invading his existence. For the sake of brevity, let us call this sensation "the Babel syndrome." This writer had his first touch of the Babel syndrome a couple of weeks after his arrival in the United States, at a crowded wine-and-cheese reception. Nursing a plastic glass of wine and a cheddar cube, and straining my vocal chords to outshout those who were straining their vocal chords to outshout me (this seems to be the purpose of crowded wine-and-cheese receptions), I was trying to enlighten my American interlocutor on the subject of cooperative housing in Poland. He had just inquired whether it was as difficult to rent an inexpensive apartment in my hometown as it was in the Boston area.

I took a deep breath. "Well," I shouted, "first of all, you rather seldom *rent* an apartment in Poland, since as a nation with a centrally planned economy, we naturally have fewer apartments than families, so there are no spare apartments to rent in the first place. Normally, you pay a housing cooperative plenty of cash up front, and some twelve to fifteen years later you get a place to live. The only thing is, you don't own the apartment you've paid for; the cooperative does. But then again, you have the option to pay a lot more, also up front, and then, also twelve to fifteen years later, you not only get a place to live but become the proud owner of it as well. That is, if they don't change the regulations in the meantime. Anyway, I guess the whole trick is roughly what you call condominium conversion," I concluded, showing off one of my newly acquired Americanisms.

At that very same moment, I was struck by the sudden realization that what I had been saying, perfectly logical as it would have been in Polish, made no sense in English. I had been using the right words and expressions but each of them had somehow missed the point. The coercive state-owned institution whose Polish name I had translated—formally speaking, quite accurately—as "housing cooperative" had nothing to do with whatever a "housing cooperative" might mean in America. The posh associations and immediate availability of the American "condominium" had nothing to do with the drab cubicle of concrete that a Pole is lucky to obtain keys to in his middle age, years after he paid hard-earned money for it. Even the verb "to own," though again a formal equivalent of its Polish counterpart, referred to two distinctly different notions in the American and the Polish contexts. Inadvertently, indeed with the best of intentions, instead of communicating some truth I had created a false image of reality. Instead of trapping things in fitting words, I let myself fall into language's trap.

It is at moments like this that it dawns on you what emigration is all about.

Obviously enough, after moving one's pursuit of happiness abroad, one of the major operating costs of the enterprise is that in most cases the immigrant faces an uphill struggle with the language he has to learn. What is not so easy to understand is that the struggle does not end once he has attained some basic proficiency, or even fluency, in the language of his adopted country. A million subtle ways in which this language diverges from his innate ways of naming the world or expressing himself, and thus constantly remodels his already shaped mentality, continue to keep him in a state of anguish.

If only he could become perfectly bilingual for the price of this anguish! But such a transaction happens very rarely. There is an old saw about having as many existences as the languages you speak. This truth, however, has a slightly ominous underside: a genuinely equal fluency in more languages than one would make you the victim of a multiple personality disorder. The immigrant's brain usually staves off this threat by maintaining a steady difference of rank between his two languages: either the adopted language never fully develops, or the native language gradually shrinks. Sometimes the worst-case scenario takes place: the immigrant irretrievably loses his grip on the first language while never managing to get one on the second.

Be that as it may, transplanting yourself into the soil of a foreign language makes you, as a rule, wilt rather than flourish, feel deprived rather than enriched. As in every translation (for what else is the process of assimilation of an immigrant, if not his attempt to translate his expressible self into another language and culture?), the net result of your labors is a nagging feeling of incompleteness. In our human Tower of Babel not only poetry, according to Frost, but also identity may ultimately come down to what is lost in translation.

Multiply this loss by the millions of today's variously displaced persons, and you face a problem of global proportions. It is the problem of incomplete semantic adjustment, of all that is inevitably "lost in translation" of the self from one language and culture into another. The universal significance and the sheer scope of this kind of formative (or deformative) experience makes one wonder: Where are all the memoiristic accounts and semantic explorations that we might logically expect? Why is it that nobody writes about this problem?

The reason is simple: those who might, can't. The immigrants themselves are obviously those who might have most to say about the losses suffered in this sort of "translation": they serve, after all, both as translators and translated material in the process. The irony is that they also are, naturally enough, the least competent to express the multiple dimensions and subtle degrees of the loss in the language that is appropriated by them rather than owned by birthright. It is extremely rare that a writer emerges among them who is still rooted deeply enough in his native language to realize the problem's significance, while at the same time feeling sufficiently at ease in his adopted language to convey the problem's complexity to those who should realize it: his new countrymen.

Eva Hoffman, the author of *Lost in Translation: A Life in a New Language*,[1] is one of these rare exceptions. Her book, like virtually every immigrant memoir, is an account of great human interest, even more so as her life is a striking exemplar of an immigrant's American career. After all, not every East European newcomer who lands on this continent as a penniless adolescent with no English to speak of winds up with a Harvard graduate degree and a position as an editor at the *New York Times Book Review.* Yet there is more to this book than just the story of a Polish girl who made good in America against all odds. In fact, *Lost in Translation* calls for a new generic category: it should be called a "semiotic memoir." Its focus is on the problem of the immigrant's transition and assimilation viewed from various perspectives at once—cultural, social, mental, and sentimental, to name but a few. Within this general issue, however, the book's most interesting and original theme is that of "a life in a new language," a mind's transition from one language system to another, and its assimilation to the new kind of perception and outlook that the new language entails.

Hoffman's insights into this process are exceptionally illuminating, thanks not only to her keen intelligence and discernment but also to her specific background. She has been the ideal case, as it were, for her own clinical study. To begin with, she left Poland with her family at the age of thirteen—that is to say, at the moment when the immigrant's native language is already developed enough to stay with him for good whereas his mind is still receptive and flexible enough to achieve a full command of the second language. Moreover, as a daughter in a Jewish family that had lived through the Nazi occupation and Poland's turbulent postwar years, she brought along to America a specific kind of sensitivity, one constantly on the lookout for signals of estrangement or maladjustment resulting from ethnic, cultural, and linguistic differences. Finally, as an artistically inclined child and teenager (just before her family's emigration she was on the threshold of a promising career as a pianist), she represented the type of personality that combines rich inner resources with a strong urge to communicate them to others. From this point of view, it is particularly interesting that after just a couple of years spent on this continent she decided, against all logic and despite her initial disappointing experiences with English, to switch from the international language of music to literature, and eventually to try expressing herself as a writer.

She must have achieved full proficiency in her second language relatively early, then. But the book's focus is not so much on the author's success in mastering the second language as on her difficulty in "translating" herself fully from the first into the second. Not only are two languages such as Polish and English incompatible in a strictly linguistic sense (that is, in the sense of all the semantic problems resulting from the obvious fact that any two languages' respective structures never exactly mirror each other); they are also incompatible by virtue of their different built-in associations, connotations, traditions, value systems. This creates a huge number of specific hurdles, pitfalls, and stumbling blocks—from psychological to social—particularly during the period of transition and learning, when the immigrant literally translates his entire mental system from one language to another:

> The problem is that the signifier has become severed from the signified. The words I learn now don't stand for things in the same unquestioned way they did in my native tongue . . . When my friend Penny tells me that she's envious, or happy, or disappointed, I try laboriously to translate not from English to Polish but from the word back to its source, to the feeling from which it springs. Already, in that moment of strain, spontaneity of response is lost. And anyway, the translation doesn't work. I don't know how Penny feels when she talks about envy. The word hangs in a Platonic stratosphere . . . This radical disjoining between word and thing is a desiccating alchemy, draining the world not only of significance but of its colors, striations, nuances—its very existence. It is the loss of a living connection.

The process of linguistic assimilation consists, in fact, precisely in trying to forget the fissure between word and thing, in striving to become, just as the natives are, an unthinking, automatic user of the language with all its semantic and cognitive strings attached. But such liberation from linguistic self-consciousness cannot be easily won. Hoffman's autobiographical story of growing up in Canada and entering academic and then professional life in the United States provides a number of illuminating illustrations of this point. There are social situations requiring linguistic spontaneity, the lack of which makes you immediately an outsider, if only in your own oversensitive perception. There is the psychological self-assurance which you are robbed of, so long as there is the slightest trace of foreignness in your grammar or accent. There is the problem of your inner language: if you think in Polish and communicate in English, the effect this has on your mind may be close to schizophrenic. What about such seemingly simple things as, for instance, writing a diary? Writing it in the English of your outward communication would violate the diary's intimate essence; choosing the Polish of your innermost self would make it impossible for you to record the outer experience of the new world, for this can be adequately named only in its own language. And what about situations that require speech both intimate and outward, such as lovers' entreaties or quarrels? What about the language of your dreams?

Yet even after the process of self-translation has been completed, the native language, though increasingly forced out by the second, nonetheless stays with you for a long time, in most cases forever. If at some point one attains, like Hoffman did in her student years, the precarious state of perfect bilingualism, the ideal equilibrium between two languages, this may indeed result, as I said before, in a literally split personality. Hoffman gives a striking example of the specific moment in her life when, vacillating over her marriage plans, she came to diametrically opposed conclusions depending on whether she was thinking of her future in English or in Polish. The value system programmed imperceptibly into the language in which we speak and think exerts an enormous influence on our behavior; semanticists such as Korzybski and Hayakawa made us aware of that a long time ago. But only a bilingual person can, by way of comparison, realize and give an account of the extent to which our interpretation of the world depends on the dictates of a specific language system. And the extent to which, consequently, not merely individuals but entire nations may differ in their most basic preconceived notions about reality.

"Triangulation" is a word that appears with particular frequency on the pages of this book. It is meant to signify the way in which the immigrant, caught between two languages and their two built-in philosophies, uses these two given angles to find a distant resultant: his own position in life and versus life. As Hoffman points out in the concluding paragraphs of her book, what seems to be the immigrant's deprivation may thus be viewed, at the same time, as a spiritually enriching experience. What from one perspective appears a split personality may turn out to be a profoundly advantageous "multivalent consciousness"; the gap between the two languages may become "a chink, a window through which I can observe the diversity of the world." The immigrant's "Babel syndrome" may be just another name for the ultimate recognition of the human world's maddening yet magnificent plurality.

[1989]

Tongue-Tied Eloquence: Notes on Language, Exile, and Writing

Among many hilarious, outrageous, sublime, crazy, profound, or otherwise memorable scenes that fill the pages of Josef Skvorecky's unparalleled *The Engineer of Human Souls*,[1] one brief episode seems to me particularly pregnant with meaning. One of the novel's minor characters, Milan, a recent Czech defector granted asylum in Canada, is throwing a housewarming party. Except for his Canadian girlfriend, all the guests are, not unexpectedly, Czech émigrés:

> Someone is telling a joke about the Prague policeman who drowned trying to stamp out a cigarette a passer-by had tossed in the river. There is loud laughter.
> Barbara hands Milan his glass.
> "I suppose he's telling jokes?"
> "That's right."
> "Well," says Barbara deliberately, "couldn't you translate them for me?"
> "They're only word games. My English isn't good enough."
> "Then how about making an effort? Your English is good enough for some things."
> But Milan ignores her . . .

. . . and, bad conversationalist though he might seem, he is right to do so. On the list of things that are the hardest to translate into another language, jokes come a close second after rhymed poetry (whereas love entreaties, as Barbara pretends not to realize, are among the easiest, if they require any translation at all). This is particularly true when the jokes are Eastern European, and told anywhere west of the Iron Curtain.

Though no intellectual giant, Skvorecky's Milan understands this instinctively and immediately.

More sophisticated minds sometimes need a dozen years to grasp this simple truth. I have in mind the example of a famous Eastern European wit, the poet Antoni Slonimski, who in pre-1939 Poland had been nearly idolized by the readers of his side-splitting feuilletons published in every issue of the most popular literary weekly. When war broke out, he took refuge in the West and spent the next twelve years in London, but in 1951, of all moments, he decided to come back to Poland for good. Asked many years later why he had chosen to do so, he gave a disarmingly frank answer: in England, he was unable to tell a joke. No, he had no qualms about living under capitalism, especially since Stalinism anno 1951 was hardly a more attractive option. No, he had nothing against the English and their ways either (in fact, he was a declared Anglophile all his life). And no, he did not really feel lonely, or materially underprivileged, or socially degraded. What he could not stand was that whenever he tried to tell a joke to an English friend, he somehow was not funny.

For a while, he was determined to do anything in his power to succeed. He worked doggedly on his English and prepared all his jokes beforehand, endlessly chiseling their fine points and rehearsing for hours on end; once, before meeting some natives he particularly wished to impress, he stooped so low as to jot down a witticism on his cuff. All in vain; every joke of his was a flop. This would have been unbearable enough for a mere mortal. For Slonimski, who had spent twenty years building up his reputation as the wittiest man in Poland, this was sufficient reason to go back to the lion's den. There, hardships or no hardships, censorship or no censorship, he could at least sit down at his regular table in his favorite café, crack a joke, and hear his admirers laugh.

As told by Slonimski, this story of the return of the prodigal joker may well have been a joke in itself—the motives behind his decision were certainly more complex than that—but it says something about the expatriate's experience that usually escapes definition. And it says even more about the experience of the expatriate writer. After all, works of literature, just like jokes, are essentially "word games," as Skvorecky's Milan would have it. Easy for Robert Frost to say that poetry is what's lost in translation! Squarely settled in his homeland, he wrote for an audience that shared both his experience and his language, and it was of secondary concern to him just how much of what he intended to say was lost on some distant Chinese or Chilean reader. A writer who lives in exile has to care much more about what is "lost in translation." His foreign readers are within earshot, since he lives among them: if they don't laugh at his translated "word games," it hurts.

Of course, he may choose to stay forever on the safe side—that is, to lock himself up in the comfortable cell of his native language and write exclusively for the audience formed of his compatriots, either at home, or in the diaspora, or both. (Needless to say, this solution is only relatively safer: literature that deserves its name is always a risky business, and the fact that you share a language, literary tradition, experience, and whatever else with your readers does not necessarily mean that they give a damn.) But once the writer decides to reach beyond his native language and familiar audience, once he lets the very problem of "translation" cross his mind (regardless of whether he is to be translated by someone else, translate his works himself, or write originally in the language of his adopted country), the balance sheet of gains and losses will always loom in his consciousness ominously and inexorably.

What makes things even more bothersome is that the whole process of balancing the necessary losses against the uncertain gains is a two-way street. Trying to adapt his work to a foreign culture, the writer living in exile has no choice but to let this work lose some of its original flavor— that seems an obvious price to pay. Less obvious is the fact that this loss has its reverse side: being, after all, an outsider in the culture he is trying to conquer, the writer sooner or later realizes that some of this culture's qualities are lost on him as well. While attempting to hammer the peg of his work into the hard, resisting log of a foreign culture, he cannot help damaging both pieces of timber—that is, simplifying to some extent both the work and the culture as he sees it.

Again, the telling housewarming-party episode in Skvorecky's novel illustrates this double point in a neatly symmetrical way. Barbara's failure to comprehend an Eastern European joke is paralleled by Milan's failure to appreciate an allusion to American cultural lore. Her playing with a jigsaw puzzle (to which she, left out of the Czech conversation, has resorted) is for him just "a Canadian habit"; for her, it's an echo of a mythical Hollywood shot, one heavy with the symbolism of rejection, loneliness, and disenchanted love: "How could he know it? When *Citizen Kane* last played in Prague, Milan was not yet in this world. 'You never give me anything I really care about,' says Barbara, waiting against hope for Milan to understand."

But the line is lost on Milan, as well as the message that Barbara's quote was supposed to convey. An exiled writer similarly loses a considerable part of the intricate meaning of the culture he attempts to enter. He may try, for instance, to tell a typically absurd Eastern European story; yet in order to believe in the validity of such an undertaking at all, he must block out his awareness of the fact that his American audience has been brought up in a tradition whose pragmatism excludes the very notion of the absurd. Thus, in trying to impose his own vision, his own set of values, his own symbolism upon the foreign culture, he unavoidably distorts it: not only by enriching it but also by ignoring some of its intrinsic laws. And the only difference between him and Milan is that he is more or less aware of his ignorance.

Natural human egotism being a factor, however, it is understandable that what strikes the exiled writer first and foremost is how much of his own message is "lost in translation" or untranslatable altogether. A short poem by my coeval and compatriot, the Polish author Ewa Lipska, expresses it better than any semantic analysis. The poem is entitled "To Marianne Büttrich"; we are not told who Marianne Büttrich is, but it is clear that she lives on the other side of the European Great Divide, presumably in West Germany:

> For a year now I've been trying
> to write you a letter.
> But
> the locusts of my thoughts
> are untranslatable.
>
> Untranslatable are the people on duty
> guarding my words and grammar.
>
> My hours are untranslatable
> into yours.

The black lilacs behind the window.
The unbuttoned gates. The yellowed cigarette end of a day.
The dead eye in the peephole
at six a.m.

Rilke is untranslatable too.
Die Blätter fallen, fallen . . .
Wir alle fallen . . .

I've got so much to tell you
but
a tunnel is approaching
my delayed train.

A long whistle sounds.

I'm tired, Marianne,
I'm leaving for the Bermuda Triangle
to take a rest.[2]

Mind you, Lipska is not an exile (though she has visited the West),
and she wrote this poem from the perspective of someone living in Poland in the 1980s. Still, there is no significant difference between her and
the exiled writer, so far as the notion of the fundamental untranslatability
of Eastern European experience is concerned. If anything, the feeling of
tongue-tied helplessness is stronger in the latter case. It is exacerbated by
an inevitable clash of two facts. On the one hand, any writer who
moves—either voluntarily or under pressure—from behind the Elbe line
to the West is convinced that he has a special mission to carry out. His
task, as he sees it, is to open Westerners' eyes to what is going on "over
there" and what threatens to engulf their free and well-to-do world. But
on the other hand, precisely because he is now in direct touch with his
new audience, he soon finds out, to his utter astonishment and horror,
that Westerners do not exactly desire to have their eyes pried open. Czeslaw Milosz is a writer who should know about this: he came forward
with one of the first such eye-openers when he defected in 1951 and
soon afterward published *The Captive Mind,* to the boos of the largely
pro-Stalinist Western European intellectual community. In his brief essay
"Notes on Exile," written much later in America, he describes this sort
of clash as a classic paradox: in his homeland, the writer's voice was
listened to but he was not allowed to speak; in exile, he is free to say

whatever he wishes but nobody cares to listen (and moreover, Milosz adds, the writer himself may have forgotten what he had to say).

Granted, in real life the stable symmetry of this paradox sometimes wobbles. There are areas and periods of suddenly awakened or slowly growing interest in the part of the world the exiled writer came from, and his voice may come through with unexpected force. But even then his experience is hardly translatable in its entirety. Consider two skimpy lines from Lipska's poem: "The dead eye in the peephole / at six a.m." The Western reader's gaze will slide over this phrase as just another metaphor, perhaps a slightly macabre one: it may remind him of, say, a scene from "The Return of the Living Dead." For the Polish, or Czech, or Russian, or Rumanian reader, the phrase's impact is much more direct and its meaning is much more specific. In the "dead eye" he will recognize the blank stare of a secret policeman he may have seen more than once through the peephole in his own door, and "six a.m.," the typical time for police raids, will refer him unequivocally to the notion of a home search and arrest. If fear is the common semantic denominator of these two readings, it is fear of two distinctly different sorts: the enjoyable and leisurely fear of a horror-movie goer versus the ugly, shabby, completely unalluring yet very genuine fear of a citizen of a police state. The former smells of popcorn; the latter reeks of cold sweat.

"Wer den Dichter will verstehen, muss ins Dichters Lande gehen" (Whoever wants to understand the poet must go to the poet's homeland): old Goethe's noble adage sounded perfectly empirical in his enlightened time, but we, in our posttotalitarian epoch, should know better. Our century has known too many pilgrims who went "to the poet's homeland" only to be given red-carpet treatment, courtesy of Intourist, and a watchful guide, courtesy of the KGB. As the well-known book by Paul Hollander has documented,[3] under certain circumstances there is nothing more false than the so-called eyewitness account. If the eyewitness comes from a nation or system with no experience in matters of all-out deceit and especially if he is willing to be duped, it is enough to hand him a skillfully packaged reality, and *voilà*—in his account all the barbed wire miraculously disappears and citizens' happy faces shine all around. Attempts to penetrate the inscrutable East from outside usually stop at the first banquet table with a generous supply of caviar. It speaks volumes for the futility of such pilgrimages that caviar was indeed the most vivid memory Billy Graham brought home from his preaching tour of the Soviet Union a couple of years ago. During the same tour, the sharp-eyed evangelist did not notice a ten-foot-long banner with precise data about the scope of religious persecution, nearly thrust into his face by some naïve dissident.

Would the West, then, ironically be better off if it believed so-called literary fiction rather than the sort of facts that the conveniently myopic eyewitnesses provide? Have things perhaps gone so far that the Westerner thirsting for first-hand knowledge of the Eastern bloc is much less likely to obtain it by visiting one of the bloc's countries than by reading a poem by Czeslaw Milosz, a novel by Josef Skvorecky, or an essay by Joseph Brodsky?

What I am saying amounts to praise of the cognitive potential of literature, which here, in this hemisphere swarming with deconstructionists, is a rather contemptible opinion to hold. Yet at the risk of sounding hopelessly backward, I hereby admit that I indeed believe in literature's power in naming reality—or, to put it differently, in letting us hear and comprehend reality's many-voiced hubbub more subtly and fully than any other kind of account. In this sense, the testimony supplied by the literary imagination may carry more weight on the witness stand than the evidence of our senses, especially when the evidence has been fabricated in order to fool us; and the imagination may be a more efficient interpretive tool than abstract reasoning, especially when we face a reality whose absurdity transcends rationalistic thinking. As witnesses go, literary fiction nearly always beats both being on the safe ground of supposedly hard facts and being in the clouds of ideological dogmas.

This also—perhaps above all—applies to the works of exiled writers. Their evidence has a special value despite the fact that their precarious balancing between two worlds, two cultures, two value systems, and two languages puts them, in more ways than one, at special risk. For one thing, there is the aforementioned barrier of different experiences: the audience in the exiled writer's adopted country, even if not entirely indifferent, is often unable to understand not merely his interpretation of reality but simply what he is speaking about. And quite naturally so, since neither the material of the readers' own experiences nor their inherited way of viewing reality has prepared them to accept this sort of a literary world. A world in which, for instance (to draw once again on Skvorecky's *The Engineer of Human Souls*), it is perfectly possible that one day workers in a factory are called to a meeting, aligned in single file, and ordered to sign, one by one and with no exception, a petition demanding the execution of the nation's political leader, whom they were told to worship only yesterday. For an American reader, this is an Orwellian fantasy; for a Czech writer, this is what in fact happened in his country and what he could have seen with his own eyes.

Yet different experiences, heterogeneous though they may be, can be forcibly brought together by the writer to reveal some common human denominator; they can be juxtaposed and compared, and their mutual differences can be defined, explained, and reflected upon. The annoying thing about literature is that all this has to be done in this or that ethnic language, which naturally limits the defining, explaining, and reflecting to the writer's native audience. (Classical dancers are, obviously, better off in this respect: the language of their art is international. But then, I somehow cannot picture myself pirouetting in public. Toiling at my untranslatable manuscripts poses, I should think, a relatively smaller risk of making a fool of myself.)

The problem of translation rears its ugly head once again. Once someone has tried to translate a literary text, his own or someone else's, he knows well that the chief difficulty of this endeavor lies not in the mere tedium of rummaging through dictionaries and laboriously substituting one word for another. The chief difficulty is that two different languages are never a mirror reflection of each other; their seemingly corresponding parts never exactly match. The semantic ranges of supposedly equivalent words in fact only partially overlap; or a meaning may be expressed by three different synonyms in one language and five in the other; or a word may have no counterpart in the other language at all; or the emotional tinge of a word may disappear in its foreign equivalent . . . And we are still on the level of separate words. What about phrases, sentences, verse lines, stanzas, paragraphs? What about the nation's accumulated historical experience, which is reflected in words' and expressions' elusive connotations, not to be found in any dictionary? What about complications of a literary and poetic nature that raise the elementary incompatibility of two language systems to the second and third power? There is no end to the translator's woe, and his most brilliant effort may result at best in an approximation that is more ingenious than other approximations.

But the author—particularly the author who lives in exile and harbors the ambition to conquer the minds of his foreign-tongued hosts—is not interested in approximations. He wants his one-of-a-kind message to come across in unaltered and unbent shape, just as he intended it to look and sound. In this situation, the translator is the author's adversary rather than his ally, a spoiler rather than helper, a necessary evil. Even if the translator is the author himself.

A glance at the contemporary literary scene makes one realize that the panorama of ways of dealing with this problem stretches between two extremes. One extreme solution, represented, I believe, by Milan Kundera, consists in minimizing the translator's potential interference. The author is to make his original work as translatable as possible—in fact, he makes himself write in a deliberately translatable, clear, and unequivocal style, so that the translator will not be prodded into too many deviations from the intended meaning.

The other extreme, best illustrated by Kundera's opponent in other matters, Joseph Brodsky, consists in skipping translation altogether. Brodsky's literary evolution in exile—as an essayist but also a poet—has aimed at achieving linguistic self-sufficiency, becoming capable of writing the most artistically complex works directly in the language of his adopted country, so that a translator's services would no longer be called for.

Both extreme solutions may be admired for their radical boldness, and in fact it is very rare that a writer dares adopt either of them in their pure form. The more common solutions can be located somewhere in between: these are the fairly usual cases of authors who, for instance, are capable of writing a decent essay or article in their second language but wisely refrain from writing poems or novels in it, and instead rely on translators (at best trying to keep the translators' arbitrariness in check by cooperating with them). Even though the Kundera and Brodsky solutions have their respective advantages, the risk involved in either is indeed great. In the first case, the writer constantly faces the danger of losing his unique voice, slipping into some bland, abstract, international

236

style, sounding like translationese even before the translation as such has been undertaken. In the other, the writer is constantly engaged in a high-wire act of imposture, usurping a language that will never be genuinely his own; and the more breathtaking the heights of stylistic bravado he manages to reach, the more painful may be the fall. Of course, both Kundera and Brodsky are artists masterful enough to dodge these dangers. Yet even they are not shielded from criticisms by those whose opinions matter the most—the readers for whom the French or English of these authors' works is a native language.

This is also true of anybody who attempts to bypass the translation problem on a more limited scale, for instance by trying to write—like the author of these words—some relatively plain essayistic prose directly in his second language. Perfect bilingualism is not a very common ability, even when it comes to you naturally (for instance, by virtue of having been raised by an ethnically mixed pair of parents), much less when you try to attain it by learning. As a practical consequence, the exiled author who writes in his adopted language can do pretty well without a translator but, as a rule, he cannot do without an editor. No matter how hard he tries, and no matter how linguistically proficient he is, there will always be some wrongly used the's or a's, some misshaped syntactic patterns, some ill-fitting idioms that will expose his hopeless position as an eternal outsider. After all, even in Joseph Conrad's English, some Polish turns of phrase occasionally occur. Or so I'm told by native speakers of English.

This, obviously, teaches you humility. The chief reason the exiled writer tries to write in the language of his adopted country is his desire to accomplish his mission—that is, to get his message across to a broader audience. But, ironically, exactly by accomplishing his mission in this way he fails to accomplish it in another, arguably more important sense. For his mission as a writer is not merely to get his message across but also to leave his individual imprint on this message; literature's essence is not so much the message itself as the endless spectrum of "word games" (to quote Skvorecky's Milan once more) in which the writer's uniqueness may be revealed. This is extremely hard, in fact almost impossible to achieve if you write in a language that is not yours by birth.

True, even though the absolutely perfect command of a language is something an outsider cannot really acquire, he can, through a lot of effort, finally attain a fluency and glibness that make him sound almost like a native writer. But literature is something more than glib writing. It also includes the right—and necessity—to violate glibness, to make light of rules, to speak in a novel way without bothering to be correct. In literature, a new thought cannot emerge except from a new way of speaking: in order to say anything relevant, you must break a norm. And this is precisely what an outsider cannot afford, since if breaking is to make any sense at all, you may break only the norms that bind you, not those that bind someone else. If a native writer purposely violates language, it's called progress; if an outsider does it, it's called malapropism.

The exiled writer is someone who has left the cage of an oppressive political system; but if he is to remain a writer at all, he must never really leave another cage—that of his native language. There, he was gagged; here, he is tongue-tied. The ultimate irony: those who are the most tongue-tied may have the most to say.

[1989]

"The Revenge of a Mortal Hand"

It was in the late fall of 1982 that I first heard the news about the death of Grazyna Kuron. She was the wife of my friend Jacek Kuron, one of the most charismatic leaders of the human rights movement in Poland. I had been close to them during my years in Poland, particularly in the late seventies, when the Kurons (along with hundreds of their "dissident" friends) were working to make the regime's ways a little less inhuman. But in the fall of 1982 I was living peacefully in Cambridge, Massachusetts, where I had moved a year and a half before, while in Poland the first year of martial law (or "the state of war," as it was officially named there) was just coming to a close.

With a rather morbid sort of pride, the military regime claimed in those days that its imposition of martial law had actually been bloodless: several dozen people shot by the police in street demonstrations, nothing to speak about. Grazyna was one of the indirect victims of the "state of war." Jailed in an internment camp, she developed a lung disease. She was released only when her situation was already hopeless: despite intensive treatment, she died in a hospital. Jacek, jailed too, was granted permission to leave the prison for a few days to attend the funeral.

The funeral elegy was one genre I had never tried before, but this time I felt that I simply could not help writing a poem on Grazyna's death. What happened to her was a stupefying blow not only to me but to everyone who had known her: it seemed unbelievable that this brave, strong-willed, good-natured woman who had so cheerfully coped with so much adversity in her life was suddenly gone, had ceased to exist. Why her? Why now and not later? Every death of a friend makes us ask such silly questions, but this particular death was the hardest to accept and understand. Still, even though I sincerely wanted to bid farewell to Grazyna, I wasn't able to write a single word for quite a long time. I lived in agony for several weeks, immobilized, on the one hand, by the sense of the absurdity of that loss, and, on the other, by the sense of the exasperating conventionality of all the words, metaphors, rhetorical devices that the genre of the funeral elegy would have inevitably entailed.

In our illiterate times the classical "Eureka!" would be Greek to virtually everyone, so it is habitually replaced by an icon: a lightbulb flashing above the head of a comic strip hero. Something like this flashed in my head one November evening, when I suddenly found a solution. I realized that the only way to commemorate the death of someone like Grazyna—a death that was so blatantly undeserved, unjustified, unacceptable—was to write a poem which would be a total reversal of all the norms of the traditional funeral elegy; a poem which, instead of accepting the loss, would remain defiantly unreconciled to it; a poem which, instead of shedding tears over Grazyna's grave, would *talk to her* as if she were alive; a poem which, instead of bidding her good-bye forever, would try to fix and preserve her remembered presence.

To Grazyna

To remember about the cigarettes. So that they're always at hand,
ready to be slipped into his pocket, when they take him away once again.

To know by heart all the prison regulations about parcels and visits.
And how to force facial muscles into a smile.

To be able to extinguish a cop's threatening yell with one cold glance,
calmly making tea while they eviscerate the desk drawers.

To write letters from a cell or a clinic, saying that everything's O.K.

So many abilities, such perfection. No, I mean it.
If only in order not to waste those gifts,
you should have been rewarded with immortality
or at least with its defective version, life.

Death. No, this can't be serious, I can't accept this.
There were many more difficult things that never brought you down.
If I ever admired anybody, it was you.

240

If anything was ever permanent, it was that admiration.
How many times did I want to tell you. No way. I was too abashed
by the gaps in my vocabulary and the microphone in your wall.
Now I hear it's too late. No, I don't believe it.

It's only nothingness, isn't it. How could a nothing like that
possibly stand between us. I'll write down, word for word and forever,
that small streak in the iris of your eye, that wrinkle at the corner of your
    mouth.
All right, I know, you won't respond to the latest postcard I sent you.
But if I'm to blame anything for that, it will be something real,
the mail office, an air crash, the postal censor.
Not nonexistence, something that doesn't exist, does it.[1]

I'm reminded of this poem whenever someone asks me if I find pleasure in writing. In this particular case, perhaps more than in any other, I'm unable to give a straight answer. The experience that led to my writing this poem was, needless to say, anything but pleasure. The several weeks of conceiving the poem were one long wave of mental anguish. And yet I'll never forget the feeling which, in this mournful context, I'm a little ashamed to admit: the feeling of intense joy that flared up in me when, still in despair over the insoluble problem of Grazyna's death, I finally found a solution at least to my literary conundrum. It would seem that mourning and joy are two mutually exclusive states of mind. What, then, is there in literature (or maybe especially in poetry) that makes us simultaneously feel the deepest and sincerest pain and equally deep and sincere joy flowing from the very writing out of that pain? Isn't this joy—let's put it a bit cynically—a *Schadenfreude* of revenge? Don't we find pleasure in writing because writing as such, even though it doesn't make the pain actually disappear, is nonetheless a way of retaliating against what causes the pain?

The simplest definition of a graphomaniac holds that he is a person who likes to write. Should, then, the definition of a good poet hold that he is a person who doesn't like to write poems? If so, I would qualify for inclusion among the greatest. In the more than twenty years of my career, I have written perhaps two hundred poems; I like some of them, but I didn't like *writing* any of them.

Am I, however, completely sincere in saying this? True, the process of writing, especially in its initial stages of groping in the dark in search of a convincing concept, can be real torture; and true, the chief difference between a good poet and a graphomaniac is that writing is easier for the latter, since he lets himself be carried away, unabashed, on the plucked wings of literary conventions. Still, when after much aggravation the lightbulb finally flashes in your head (sometimes accompanied by a huge exclamation point), when you finally realize that a good poem has just been conceived, it is a feeling that can be compared with only a few other pleasures of life—perhaps with only one.

In other words, an outside observer has every right to treat the poets' complaints with utter suspicion. Logically speaking, if writing is really such a pain in the neck, it must be recompensed with some kind of pleasure—otherwise, who would bother to write poems at all? And, since there are apparently thousands of contemporary poets and none of them can seriously count today on any of the more tangible rewards (such as making money or winning a Maecenas' favor), the very joy of writing is most probably the only compensation for the pain of writing.

But wait a minute. Mixing pain with pleasure . . . Aren't we talking about masochism? Would writing poems amount to some kind of perversity?

Why, yes, of course, writing poems is a kind of perversity. And the joy of writing is, in fact, a very perverse kind of pleasure. Just as with every perversity, it results mainly from the deliberate breaking of a taboo, from defiant resistance against a powerful rule or law, from rebellion against the commonly accepted foundations of existence. It's enough to put a verse line down on paper to scoff, in effect, at all the basic laws on which the world rests. For the very act of writing creates another world in which all those laws can be suspended—more, held in suspension interminably by the enduring power of conceit, rhyme, pun, metaphor, meter. No one, I think, has expressed it better than the contemporary Polish poet Wislawa Szymborska in the conclusion of her poem "The Joy of Writing":

> Is there then such a world
> over whose fate I am an absolute ruler?
> A time I can bind with chains of signs?
> An existence made perpetual at my command?

The joy of writing.
The power of preserving.
The revenge of a mortal hand.[2]

"The revenge of a mortal hand" that holds a pen is perhaps the only retaliation against the laws of Nature accessible to a human being. Since in the real, extratextual world I am unable to change or nullify any of the omnipresent laws of transience, decay, suffering, or death—in other words, since I can do nothing about the lurking presence of Nothingness in every atom of this world—the only solution is to create a separate world "bound with chains of signs," closed within lines and stanzas, subject to the absolute rule of my imagination. In such a world the flow of time can be magically stopped, suffering can be avoided, death can be rendered invalid, Nothingness can be scared away.

More important, this artificial world can seem more convincing than reality. After all, what makes poetry different from any other verbal description of the world is that a poem (only a very good poem, to be sure) strikes us with its determinateness, inner necessity, essential existence; to an even greater extent than "each mortal thing" in Hopkins' sonnet, it cries to us, "What I do is me: for that I came." To put it differently, a truly good poem, colloquial and seemingly spontaneous as it might be, differs from any form of extrapoetic speech in that it couldn't possibly be changed: even a single word replacement, even a slight shift of stress would disturb the balance. As a consequence, such a poem appears to be endowed with a certain special force of argument: it proves by itself not only the necessity of its own existence but also the necessity of its own form. And this is an additional source of perverse pleasure for both the poet and his reader: an encounter with such a poem breaks another rule of our everyday experience, a rule according to which the world is based on randomness and chaotic unpredictability.

The joy of writing (and reading) poems, then, lies in the fact that poetry willfully spoils Nature's game; while fully realizing the power of Nothingness in the outside world, it questions and nullifies it within the inner world of a poem. But what is especially challenging for the twentieth-century poet is, I think, his awareness that the same can be done about the power of Nothingness revealed in modern History. Today's world is dominated by the seemingly inflexible laws of History

243

even more than by the laws of Nature (some of which have been at least ameliorated by science). All the historical dimensions of this world conspire to overwhelm the individual with a sense of his insignificance and expendability; what counts is only the great numbers, statistical probabilities, historical processes.

And here again every good poem, by its sheer emergence and existence, appears to be, on its own miniature scale, History's spoilsport. History may compel us to think that the individual and his personal world view do not count in the general picture; and yet poetry stubbornly employs and gives credence to the individual voice (moreover, as if to contradict the law of mimicry underlying modern society, the more inimitable and unique a poem is, the longer it survives in the memories of its readers). History may teach us abstract thinking; and yet poetry insists on seeing things in their specificity and concreteness, on viewing the world as an assemblage of Blake's "minute particulars." And finally, History may demonstrate by millions of examples the continuous triumph of Newspeak, a deliberate and systematic falsification of words' meanings; and yet a single good poem is enough to counter all this tampering with language by making the reader aware of the word's hidden semantic possibilities. A poet who is offended by the course of modern History doesn't even have to write political poetry to find an appropriate response to it. It's enough that he write his poems well.

All this may sound awfully optimistic and self-congratulatory. In fact, I am no exception among contemporary poets: just like the majority of them, I feel much more often helpless and desperate than victorious and elated in my private campaign against Nothingness. I do not stand on a sufficiently firm ground of positive belief to say with Donne, "And death shall be no more; Death thou shalt die," or even with Dylan Thomas, "And death shall have no dominion." Not even a poet (a representative of an otherwise rather presumptuous breed) can be as cocksure as to claim that his word can *really* stop the flow of time, invalidate suffering and death, put a stick in the spokes of History's wheel, make the earthly powers shrink and earthly injustices disappear.

In that sense, to return to my poem, I obviously have not managed to keep Grazyna among the living nor have I wrestled her back from the dead. I have done only what I could, and that is to challenge the power of Nothingness by flinging my poem in its featureless face, by showing it that even though it engulfed Grazyna's life I am still there to remember how much her life meant to me—just as someone may be there after my death, just as something will always be there to exist in spite of Nonexistence (which, as its own name indicates, is "something that doesn't exist, does it"). To spite Nothingness—this is perhaps the essence of the perverse "joy of writing," "the revenge of a mortal hand."

[1987]

Notes

Breathing under Water

1. The text of this speech appeared in *Partisan Review* 4 (1983).

From Russia with Love

1. Alexander Zinoviev, *Homo Sovieticus,* trans. Charles Janson (Boston: Atlantic Monthly Press, 1985).

The New Alrightniks

1. Vassily Aksyonov, *In Search of Melancholy Baby,* trans. Michael Henry Heim and Antonina W. Bouis (New York: Random House, 1987).

The Cardinal and Communism

1. Andrzej Micewski, *Cardinal Wyszynski: A Biography,* trans. William R. Brand and Katarzyna Mroczkowska-Brand (San Diego: Harcourt Brace Jovanovich, 1984).

Praying and Playing

1. Karol Wojtyla, *The Collected Plays and Writings on Theater,* trans. Boleslaw Taborski (Berkeley: University of California Press, 1987).

Walesa: The Uncommon Common Man

1. Lech Walesa, *A Way of Hope* (New York: Holt, 1987).

The Absolute Horizon

1. Václav Havel, *Letters to Olga: June 1979–September 1982,* trans. Paul Wilson (New York: Knopf, 1988).

2. The essay is available, along with other essays by and on Havel, in English translation in the collection *Václav Havel, or Living in Truth,* ed. Jan Vladislav (Amsterdam: Meulenhoff/Faber & Faber, 1986).

Big Brother's Red Pencil

1. *The Black Book of Polish Censorship,* trans. and ed. Jane Leftwich Curry (New York: Random House, 1984).

Renouncing the Contract

1. Translated by John and Bogdana Carpenter, in Zbigniew Herbert, *Selected Poems* (Oxford: Oxford University Press, 1977), pp. 60–61.
2. Update: At this point (late August 1989) it is still not clear what will happen to independent culture—or, rather, to the division between "official" and "independent" cultures—in the wake of the recent momentous events in Poland. So far, the admittedly significant relaxation of censorship over the past few years has not rendered the existence of independent cultural institutions superfluous. Even though, for example, the state-owned publishing houses have recently been issuing many previously blacklisted authors and books, the underground presses have still been able to compete with them successfully, thanks to their greater efficiency and lower production costs. It seems very likely that in the near future, censorship will grow less and less oppressive, if not disappear completely, whereas at least some of the independent cultural institutions will come out into the open and continue their activities on a more professional basis.

The Godfather, Part III, Polish Subtitles

1. Jan Jozef Szczepanski, *Kadencja* (Warsaw: Oficyna Literacka, 1986).
2. Update: In June 1989 the Association of Polish Writers (Stowarzyszenie Pisarzy Polskich) came into existence, with Szczepanski as its elected chairman. This association does not replace the Union of Polish Writers; rather, it serves as a separate organization, open to any Polish writer who wishes to join it, including writers residing abroad.

The State Artist

1. Miklós Haraszti, *The Velvet Prison: Artists under State Socialism,* trans. Katalin and Stephen Landesmann, with Steve Wasserman (New York: Basic Books, 1987).

Gombrowicz: Culture and Chaos

1. Witold Gombrowicz, *Diary: Volume One,* trans. Lillian Vallee (Evanston, Ill.: Northwestern University Press, 1988).
2. In presenting Gombrowicz's System, I am indebted to the substantial body of Polish criticism dealing with this subject, particularly to the works of Jerzy Jarzebski.

The Face of Bruno Schulz

1. *Letters and Drawings of Bruno Schulz, with Selected Prose,* ed. Jerzy Ficowski, trans. Walter Arendt with Victoria Nelson (New York: Harper & Row, 1988).
2. Bruno Schulz, *Listy, fragmenty: Wspomnienia o pisarzu,* ed. Ficowski (Krakow: Wydawnictwo Literackie, 1984).

A Masterpiece of Memory

1. Aleksander Wat, *My Century: The Odyssey of a Polish Intellectual,* ed. and trans. Richard Lourie (Berkeley: University of California Press, 1988).

The Ecstatic Pessimist

1. Czeslaw Milosz, *The Land of Ulro,* trans. Louis Iribarne (New York: Farrar, Straus & Giroux, 1984).
2. Czeslaw Milosz, *The Witness of Poetry: The Charles Eliot Norton Lectures, 1981–1982* (Cambridge, Mass.: Harvard University Press, 1983).

A Russian Roulette

1. Anatolii Kuznetsov, *The Journey,* trans. William E. Butler (New York: New Horizon Press, 1984).
2. Vasily Grossman, *Forever Flowing,* trans. Thomas P. Whitney (New York: Harper & Row, 1986).
3. Yuri Trifonov, *The Old Man,* trans. Jacqueline Edwards and Mitchell Schneider (New York: Simon and Schuster, 1984).
4. Sergei Dovlatov, *The Zone: A Prison Camp Guard's Story,* trans. Anne Frydman (New York: Knopf, 1985).
5. Vassily Aksyonov, *The Burn: A Novel in Three Books (Late Sixties–Early Seventies),* trans. Michael Glenny (New York/Boston: Random House/Houghton Mifflin, 1984).
6. Yuz Aleshkovsky, *Kangaroo,* trans. Tamara Glenny (New York: Farrar, Straus & Giroux, 1986).

Science Friction

1. Stanislaw Lem, *Hospital of the Transfiguration,* trans. William Brand (San Diego/New York: Harcourt Brace Jovanovich, 1988).

Wake Up to Unreality

1. Kazimierz Brandys, *Rondo,* trans. Jaroslaw Anders (New York: Farrar, Straus & Giroux, 1989).

The Polish Complex

1. Tadeusz Konwicki, *Kompleks polski* (Warsaw: Zapis, 1977). Quotations are from Konwicki, *The Polish Complex,* trans. Richard Lourie (Harmondsworth: Penguin Books, 1984).
2. Translated from the Polish by Jaroslaw Anders and Lynne Shapiro.

Searching for the Real

1. Czeslaw Milosz, *Unattainable Earth,* trans. Czeslaw Milosz and Robert Hass (New York: Ecco Press, 1986).
2. Czeslaw Milosz, *The Collected Poems, 1931–1987* (New York: Ecco Press, 1988).

The Power of Taste

1. Zbigniew Herbert, *Report from the Besieged City and Other Poems,* trans. John Carpenter and Bogdana Carpenter (New York: Ecco Press, 1985).
2. Zbigniew Herbert, *Barbarian in the Garden,* trans. Michael March and Jaroslaw Anders (Manchester: Carcanet, 1985).
3. "Mona Lisa," trans. Peter Dale Scott, in Zbigniew Herbert, *Selected Poems* (Harmondsworth: Penguin Books, 1968).

Solitary Solidarity

1. *The Revolution of Things: Selected Poems by Miron Bialoszewski,* trans. Andrzej Busza and Bogdan Czaykowski (Washington, D.C.: Charioteer Press, 1974).
2. Miron Bialoszewski, *Memoir of the Warsaw Uprising,* trans. Madeline G. Levine (Ann Arbor: Ardis, 1977).
3. Emery George, ed., *Contemporary East European Poetry* (Ann Arbor: Ardis, 1983).

4. Translated by Stanislaw Baranczak and Clare Cavanagh.
5. Translated by Stanislaw Baranczak and Clare Cavanagh.

Shades of Gray

1. Wislawa Szymborska, *Sounds, Feelings, Thoughts,* trans. Magnus J. Krynski and Robert A. Maguire (Princeton: Princeton University Press, 1981).
2. This and all subsequent extracts in this chapter have been translated by Stanislaw Baranczak and Clare Cavanagh.

The Ethics of Language

1. Joseph Brodsky, *Less Than One: Selected Essays* (New York: Farrar, Straus & Giroux, 1986).
2. Joseph Brodsky, ed., *An Age Ago: A Selection of Nineteenth-Century Russian Poetry,* trans. Alan Myers (New York: Farrar, Straus & Giroux, 1988).
3. Joseph Brodsky, *To Urania: Selected Poems* (New York: Farrar, Straus & Giroux, 1988).

Alone but Not Lonely

1. Adam Zagajewski, *Tremor: Selected Poems,* trans. Renata Gorczynski (New York: Farrar, Straus & Giroux, 1985).

The Confusion of Tongues

1. Eva Hoffman, *Lost in Translation: A Life in a New Language* (New York: Dutton, 1989).

Tongue-Tied Eloquence

1. Josef Skvorecky, *The Engineer of Human Souls,* trans. Paul Wilson (New York: Washington Square Press, 1985).
2. Translated from the Polish by Stanislaw Baranczak.
3. Paul Hollander, *Political Pilgrims: Travels of Western Intellectuals to the Soviet Union, China, and Cuba* (New York: Harper & Row, 1983).

"The Revenge of a Mortal Hand"

1. Translated from the Polish by Stanislaw Baranczak, with Reginald Gibbons.
2. Translated from the Polish by Stanislaw Baranczak. The entire text of this poem in a different translation can be found in *Sounds, Feelings, Thoughts: Seventy Poems by Wislawa Szymborska,* trans. Magnus J. Krynski and Robert A. Maguire (Princeton, N.J.: Princeton University Press, 1981).

Acknowledgments

With the exception of "The Polish Complex," an essay written in Poland in 1978 and originally published in the underground quarterly *Zapis,* all the essays and reviews collected in this book have been written with the English-speaking audience specifically in mind, since I settled in this country in 1981. Most of them would not have come into being, had it not been for the encouragement I received from the editors of several journals and magazines who either commissioned these pieces or accepted my unsolicited submissions. I am especially grateful to Martin Peretz, Leon Wieseltier, and Ann Hulbert, editors of the *New Republic;* to William Phillips, editor of *Partisan Review;* and to Robert Boyers, editor of *Salmagundi.* In additon to these periodicals, to which my contributions over the past eight years have been particularly frequent, some of the essays and reviews included here have also appeared in *Antaeus,* the *Boston Globe, Cross Currents: A Yearbook of Central European Culture,* the *New Criterion,* the *New Leader,* the *New York Times Book Review,* the *Threepenny Review,* and the *University of Toronto Quarterly.*

In working on almost all of these essays, I have been greatly aided by my consecutive editorial assistants, Clare Cavanagh, Beth Holmgren, and Alexandra Barcus, who have spent many hours polishing (or, if I may allow myself a bad pun, un-Polishing) my immigrant's English. The final touches have been added with remarkable skill and sensitivity by the book's editor, Maria Ascher.

As is the case with every book I have written thus far, this one owes its existence largely to numerous people whose spiritual kinship and emotional support I have enjoyed over the years, among whom my wife Anna has always been the most indispensable presence.

* * *

With the exception of "Renouncing the Contract," "On Adam Michnik," and parts 1 and 3 of "Breathing under Water," all of which are here published for the first time, the essays in this book have been previously published as follows:
Antaeus: "The Revenge of a Mortal Hand."
Boston Globe: "Walesa: The Uncommon Common Man."

Acknowledgments

Cross Currents: "Solitary Solidarity" (as "Miron Bialoszewski, 1922–1983"), "Shades of Gray" (as "'Countless Shades of the Color Gray': The Recent Poetry of Wislawa Szymborska").

New Criterion: "The Ecstatic Pessimist" (part 2, as "Hope against Hope").

New Leader: "The Confusion of Tongues." Reprinted with permission of *The New Leader,* February 6, 1989. Copyright © the American Labor Conference on International Affairs, Inc.

New Republic: "E.E.: The Extraterritorial," "From Russia with Love," "The New Alrightniks," "The Cardinal and Communism," "Praying and Playing," "Big Brother's Red Pencil," "The Face of Bruno Schulz" (as "The Faces of Mastery"), "A Masterpiece of Memory," "Science Friction," "Wake Up to Unreality," "The Power of Taste," "The Ethics of Language" (part 1, as "Time's Lines"), "Alone but Not Lonely."

New York Times Book Review: "Searching for the Real" (part 1, as "Garden of Amazing Delights"). Copyright © 1986 by The New York Times Company. Reprinted by permission.

Partisan Review: "Breathing under Water" (part 2), "Gombrowicz: Culture and Chaos," "A Russian Roulette," "The Polish Complex," "The Ethics of Language" (part 2), "The Ecstatic Pessimist" (part 1, as "In Defense of the Imagination").

Salmagundi: "The Absolute Horizon," "*The Godfather,* Part III, Polish Subtitles," "The State Artist."

Threepenny Review: "Searching for the Real" (part 2, as "Between Repulsion and Rapture").

University of Toronto Quarterly: "Tongue-Tied Eloquence: Notes on Language, Exile, and Writing."

Excerpt from "Mona Lisa" translation copyright © Czeslaw Milosz and Peter Dale Scott, 1968; copyright © 1968 by Zbigniew Herbert; from *Selected Poems,* published in the United Kingdom by Penguin Books in 1968, and first published by The Ecco Press in 1986. Excerpts from "Report from the Besieged City" and "The Power of Taste" copyright © 1985 by Zbigniew Herbert; from *Report from the Besieged City,* first published by The Ecco Press in 1985, and published in the United Kingdom by Oxford University Press in 1987. Excerpts from "After Paradise" and "Consciousness" copyright © 1986 by Czeslaw Milosz; from *Unattainable Earth,* first published by The Ecco Press in 1986. All excerpts reprinted by permission.

Excerpt from "May 24, 1980" from *To Urania,* by Joseph Brodsky. Copyright © 1981 by Joseph Brodsky. Reprinted by permission of Farrar, Straus and Giroux, Inc. Excerpts from "Fire," "Ode to Plurality," "Iron," and "Moment" from *Tremor,* by Adam Zagajewski. Copyright © 1985 by Adam Zagajewski. Reprinted by permission of Farrar, Straus and Giroux, Inc.

Index

Index

Index